Collins
English for Exams

D1470628

SKILLS FOR THE TOEIC® TEST

Listening and Reading

Wiltshire College

94054

Collins

HarperCollins Publishers
77-85 Fulham Palace Road
Hammersmith
London W6 8JB

First edition 2012

Reprint 10 9 8 7 6 5 4 3 2 1 0

© HarperCollins Publishers 2012

ISBN 978-0-00-746057-1

Collins® is a registered trademark of HarperCollins Publishers Limited.

www.collinselt.com

A catalogue record for this book is available from the British Library.

Editorial Services: Content*Ed Publishing Solutions, LLC

Writing Services: Content*Ed Publishing Solutions, LLC and Creative Content, LLC

Typeset in India by Aptara

Printed in China by South China Printing Co.

All rights reserved. No part of this book may be reproduced, stored in a retrieval system, or transmitted in any form or by any means, electronic, mechanical, photocopying, recording or otherwise, without the prior permission in writing of the Publisher. This book is sold subject to the conditions that it shall not, by way of trade or otherwise, be lent, re-sold, hired out or otherwise circulated without the Publisher's prior consent in any form of binding or cover other than that in which it is published and without a similar condition including this condition being imposed on the subsequent purchaser.

HarperCollins does not warrant that www.collinselt.com or any other website mentioned in this title will be provided uninterrupted, that any website will be error free, that defects will be corrected, or that the website or the server that makes it available are free of viruses or bugs. For full terms and conditions please refer to the site terms provided on the website.

Contents

How to Use This Book   v

Overview of the TOEIC® Test   vi

Guide to the Listening Section   x
Overview
Challenges and Solutions

Part 1   Photos   6
Walk Through
Get It Right: Tips and Tasks for Answering Correctly
Progressive Practice: Get Ready
Progressive Practice: Get Set
Progressive Practice: Go for the TOEIC Test

Part 2   Question-Response   28
Walk Through
Get It Right: Tips and Tasks for Answering Correctly
Progressive Practice: Get Ready
Progressive Practice: Get Set
Progressive Practice: Go for the TOEIC Test

Part 3   Conversations   43
Walk Through
Get It Right: Tips and Tasks for Answering Correctly
Progressive Practice: Get Ready
Progressive Practice: Get Set
Progressive Practice: Go for the TOEIC Test

Part 4   Talks   66
Walk Through
Get It Right: Tips and Tasks for Answering Correctly
Progressive Practice: Get Ready
Progressive Practice: Get Set
Progressive Practice: Go for the TOEIC Test

Listening Practice Test   84

Guide to the Reading Section

98

Overview
Challenges and Solutions

Part 5 Incomplete Sentences 104
Walk Through
Get It Right: Tips and Tasks for Answering Correctly
Progressive Practice: Get Ready
Progressive Practice: Get Set
Progressive Practice: Go for the TOEIC Test

Part 6 Text Completion 136
Walk Through
Get It Right: Tips and Tasks for Answering Correctly
Progressive Practice: Get Ready
Progressive Practice: Get Set
Progressive Practice: Go for the TOEIC Test

Part 7 Reading Comprehension 152
Walk Through
Get It Right: Tips and Tasks for Answering Correctly
Progressive Practice: Get Ready
Progressive Practice: Get Set
Progressive Practice: Go for the TOEIC Test

Reading Practice Test 186

Answer Key 212
Audio Scripts 221

How to Use This Book

Collins Skills for the TOEIC® Test: Listening and Reading and its companion edition, *Speaking and Writing*, offer a comprehensive guide to the TOEIC (Test of English for International Communication). If you use this series to prepare for the test, you will be able to improve your score on the TOEIC test and demonstrate your skills in using English in a business setting.

No matter the level of your English, *Collins Skills for the TOEIC® Test* provides you with all the tools you need to succeed on the test. Here's a glimpse of the learning tools included in this book.

» Skill-specific *Challenges and Solutions* sections. These sections offer strategies and suggestions to help you learn how to overcome the most common challenges in each section of the test.

» *Quick Guide* question overviews. Each lesson provides a brief summary of a specific part of the test in an easy-to-read chart. This allows you to quickly understand what is important to know in order to answer the questions correctly.

» *Walk Through* samples. Clear, visual and/or audio examples show you the types of questions, passages, and answer options you can expect to find on the test. Knowing what to expect is an important part of preparing for the exam.

» *Get It Right* presentations. These presentations give an overview of the most important steps, skills, and language needed for doing well on each part of the test. They include useful vocabulary and expressions that are needed when answering the questions and provide tips and tasks for noticing and understanding the important elements of each question type.

» *Progressive Practice*. For each part of the test, these carefully designed activities gradually prepare you to take the actual TOEIC test. This step-by-step practice builds the knowledge and skills you need for a good score and encourages independent learning while working up to TOEIC testing levels.

  • *Get Ready* activities require you to listen or read for certain pieces of information, practice structured activities, and notice why answers are correct or incorrect.

  • *Get Set* activities allow you to respond to TOEIC-style test questions more independently but still offer additional support and modeling to help you as you go.

  • *Go for the TOEIC Test* activities put you in an authentic test situation and allow you to practice what you have learned in a simulated test environment.

» *Answer Analysis* presentations. Answer analyses offered throughout the book teach you how to eliminate incorrect answer options and select the best answers for various question types.

» Skill-specific *Practice Test* sections. At the end of each section, you'll be able to put your skills for the test to use by taking a timed practice test. These practice tests will help you identify your weaknesses so you can know what areas to focus on before the real test.

» *Quick Tips.* Throughout the book, you'll see *Quick Tips*, which offer best-practice strategies and useful advice on how to approach certain activity types and perform better on the test.

» Dictionary definitions. *Collins COBUILD Advanced Dictionary* definitions are provided throughout the book to help you understand words and build your knowledge of vocabulary that may be found on the TOEIC test and in business settings where English is the language of communication.

» Answer Key and Audio Scripts. Found at the back of this book, these tools will help you check your answers and improve your listening comprehension as you prepare for the TOEIC test.

Tips for Success

Start getting ready to take the TOEIC test by following these tips.

» **Find out where you can take the test.** Begin by asking the organization requiring the test information if the TOEIC test can be administered on its premises. There are also test sites around the world with specific test dates available. Finally, if neither of these options is available in your country, you or your organization can contact ETS to find out how the test can be made available.

» **Find out the score requirements for your organization.** Your organization will decide how to use the score you receive on the TOEIC test.

» **Start to study early.** The more you practice, the more you will improve your skills. Give yourself at least one or two months to review the materials and complete all of the practice activities in this book. Try to spend at least one hour a day studying. Remember, by using this book, you are on your way to good scores on the TOEIC test!

» **Time yourself.** When you do exercises and *Practice Test* sections in this book, track the time used to match TOEIC test requirements. By practicing in a timed setting, you will feel more comfortable with the time limits of the actual test.

» **Listen to the audio.** For practice activities, you can listen to the audio as many times as you need to in order to understand the concepts taught in this book. As you listen, or after you listen, read along in the script. This can help improve your listening comprehension. However, when you do the Listening *Practice Test* section, stay with the audio and listen only once. You cannot go back in the actual test, so this will help you get used to the process.

» **Complete all the exercises in this book.** The practice activities have been designed to develop specific skills that will help you perform better on the test. Also, don't be afraid to make your own notes on the page. For example, writing down the definitions of words you don't know will help you remember them later on.

Overview of the TOEIC® Test

The TOEIC test measures your proficiency in the type of English used in business settings around the world. The test does not evaluate your knowledge of the English language. Rather, it measures your ability to use English in a variety of business settings.

The TOEIC test is divided into two smaller, timed tests: Listening and Reading, and Speaking and Writing. The Listening and Reading Test is a paper and pencil test. The Speaking and Writing Test is administered on a computer. Each test evaluates key skills that you will need in order to use English in a business setting, regardless of where in the world this might be. You can choose to take either test first and the other second. You may also opt to take only the test that is needed to gauge your skills in a specific area, listening and reading or speaking and writing.

Listening and Reading

The TOEIC Listening and Reading Test takes approximately 2.5 hours to complete.

- Listening Section = 45 minutes
- Reading Section = 75 minutes
- Filling out forms = approximately 30 minutes

For the Listening and Reading Test, you will receive an answer sheet and a test booklet. The TOEIC test for Listening and Reading is a multiple-choice test. You will mark each answer by filling in the oval on your answer sheet, not by marking the test booklet. You must fill in the oval completely. Look at the example. This test taker has marked (B) as the answer.

You must use a #2 pencil to mark your answers on the answer sheet. For security reasons, you may not use a mechanical pencil. You may not use a pen, either.

You can erase an answer if you decide a different answer is the correct one. If you change your mind, be sure to erase the answer completely. Never cross out an answer. The machine that scores the test will count that as two answers, and two answers are always wrong.

You may not mark your answers in the test booklet.

Listening Section

The Listening Test is first on the TOEIC paper and pencil test. The Listening Test consists of four parts and 100 questions total. The Listening Test lasts 45 minutes. You cannot go back during any of the four parts and listen again, and you cannot go back between the parts or at the end.

Part 1: Photographs	10 questions
Part 2: Question-Response	30 questions
Part 3: Conversations	30 questions (10 conversations with 3 questions each)
Part 4: Talks	30 questions (10 talks with 3 questions each)

Reading Section

The Reading Test is second on the TOEIC paper and pencil test. The Reading Test consists of three parts and 100 questions total. The Reading Test lasts 75 minutes. Because the reading material is in the test booklet, you can go back to check or adjust your answers during the Reading Test.

Part 5: Incomplete Sentences	40 questions
Part 6: Text Completion	12 questions
Part 7: Reading Comprehension	
Single Passages	28 questions (7–10 passages with 2–5 questions each)
Double Passages	20 questions (4 pairs of passages with 5 questions per pair)

Scoring for the Listening and Reading Test

You will receive a score for each section of the Listening and Reading Test. A raw score—the actual number of correct answers—is converted to a scaled score by the testing center using statistical analysis. The scores for the Listening and Reading Test are all done by computer. The raw score ranges per section are as follows.

Listening	0–100
Reading	0–100

Speaking and Writing

The speaking and writing portion of the TOEIC test takes approximately 2 hours to complete.

- Speaking Section = 20 minutes
- Writing Section = 60 minutes
- Filling out forms = approximately 30 minutes

For the Speaking and Writing Test, you will be tested on a computer. You will complete each task by responding into a microphone or typing your response on-screen. You cannot go back and rerecord or retype most task responses.

Speaking Section

The Speaking Test is first on the TOEIC Speaking and Writing test. The Speaking Test consists of 11 tasks total and lasts about 20 minutes.

Questions 1–2: Read a Text Aloud

Question 3: Describe a Picture

Questions 4–6: Respond to Questions

Questions 7–9: Respond to Questions Using Information Provided

Question 10: Propose a Solution

Question 11: Express an Opinion

You will wear a headset with both earphones and a microphone during the test. You should speak clearly and carefully to be sure your speech is heard correctly by the scorers. You will be given the opportunity before you start to check that your microphone is in the best position and at the best levels to record your responses. Should you have any technical issues before or during the test, you will be able to call an administrator for help.

You will be expected to speak for a specific amount of time on some of the tasks and will be given a specific amount of time to prepare for some of the tasks. The audio program will indicate when preparation and speaking times begin and end. An on-screen timer may also be used to help you gauge how much time you've used and how much time you have left to speak.

Writing Section

The Writing Test is last on the computer-based Speaking and Writing Section of the TOEIC test. The Writing Test consists of 8 tasks total and lasts about one hour.

Questions 1–5: Write a Sentence Based on a Picture

Questions 6–7: Respond to a Written Request

Question 8: Write an Opinion Essay

The test is given on a standard English-language keyboard. You should therefore practice typing and working with this type of keyboard (called a QWERTY keyboard) if possible to ensure that you will be able to perform well on the test day. A QWERTY keyboard is the most common English keyboard layout, and you can check to see if you have this version by looking at the first six letters that are located at the top left edge of the keyboard. The letters should read Q-W-E-R-T-Y. If you do not have a QWERTY keyboard, you may wish to find one on which you can practice before you take the test.

In the Writing Test, you will be expected to complete specific tasks in a certain amount of time. When your time is over, a pop-up window will notify you that your time is finished and that you need to move to the next question. As with the Speaking Section, the on-screen timer may also be used to help you gauge how much time you've used and how much time you have left to write.

If at any given point during the test you are unsure how to do a task, you can click on the "Help" button to get information about how to do the test. You can also call an administrator for help with technical issues.

Scoring for Speaking and Writing

You will receive a score for each section of the Speaking and Writing Test. Each score is based on a scale of 1–200, given in increments of 10. The individual task scores, which are most often referenced in this book, are rated based on performance and range from 0–5 for the task types listed below.

Speaking

Questions 1–2: Score range 0–3

Question 3: Score range 0–3

Questions 4–6: Score range 0–3

Questions 7–9: Score range 0–3

Question 10: Score range 0–5

Question 11: Score range 0–5

Writing

Questions 1–5: Score range 0–3

Questions 6–7: Score range 0–4

Question 8: Score range 0–5

In addition to this scaled score, you will receive an indication of your general skills and abilities in the skills. The Speaking Test has 8 levels of proficiency, and the Writing Test has 9 levels of proficiency. These proficiency levels are based on common general English skills for speaking and are assigned according to the total scaled scores a test taker receives.

General Test Information

On the day of the test, you must present an original, valid photo ID with a signature. The ID must be current, and the photo must be a recent one. Other types of ID may be required as well.

You may not bring any personal items, food, cell phones, or other electronic devices into the testing room. You may not bring in any books or paper, either.

Score Report

All test takers receive a TOEIC Score Report, which lists the test taker's name, birth date, identification number, test date and location, individual scores and total score, score descriptions, abilities measured, and so on. It can also include a photo of the test taker, if requested. If you take the test through an organization or employer, a report will be sent directly to that organization or employer and it will report the score to you.

Certificate of Achievement

Test takers in some parts of the world can request a TOEIC Certificate of Achievement, which lists the test taker's name, test date and location, individual scores and total score, and administering organization. This certificate is suitable for framing.

Guide to the TOEIC® Test Listening Section

The first section of the TOEIC Listening and Reading Test is the Listening Section. It consists of four parts with a total of 100 questions. It is a test of your ability to understand spoken English in a business context. You will listen to audio recordings and answer questions.

QUICK GUIDE: Listening Section

Definition	The Listening Section tests your comprehension of English statements, questions, conversations, and talks. There are four parts to this section. You will choose the best descriptions of photos and the best responses to questions, and you will answer comprehension questions about conversations and talks.
Targeted Skills	In order to do well on the Listening Section, you must be able to: • understand basic vocabulary pertaining to business and everyday activities. • identify objects and activities in photographs of common business and everyday scenes. • respond to common questions and statements in business and everyday conversation. • understand the main ideas and details of conversations and talks. • make inferences about information you hear in conversations and talks. • keep pace with the audio recordings and answer questions within the time given.
The Parts of the Listening Section	**Part 1:** You will see photographs and hear statements about them. **Part 2:** You will hear questions and statements and possible responses to them. **Part 3:** You will hear conversations and answer comprehension questions about them. **Part 4:** You will hear talks and answer comprehension questions about them. (See below for more detailed descriptions of each part of the Listening Section.)
Question Types	Each part of the Listening Section has different types of questions. **Part 1:** Choose the statement that best describes the photo. **Part 2:** Choose the most appropriate response to the question or statement. **Part 3:** Answer main idea, detail, and inference questions about a conversation. **Part 4:** Answer main idea, detail, and inference questions about a talk.
Timing	The Listening Section of the TOEIC test takes a total of 45 minutes. After you hear each question, you will have a short time to choose your answer. Then you will hear the next question. You have five seconds to choose each answer in Part 1 and Part 2 and eight seconds to choose each answer in Part 3 and Part 4. No part of the audio will be repeated. You cannot control the audio, and you must keep pace with the audio.

Parts of the TOEIC® Test Listening Section

Part 1

In Part 1 of the TOEIC test, you will see photos and hear statements about them. There are a total of ten photos. For each photo, you will hear four statements about the photo. One of the statements gives true information about the photo. The other three statements are incorrect in some way. These incorrect answer options are called *distracters*. You must choose the statement that gives the correct information. You will see the photos, but you will only hear the statements. The statements are not written anywhere on the page, so you must listen to them carefully.

The photos show scenes of everyday life in places such as:

- Offices
- Restaurants
- Airports and airplanes
- Train stations and trains

- Hotels
- Stores
- Streets
- Parks

The photos may focus on objects and their location or on people and their activities. Photos of people show them involved in everyday and business activities, such as:

- Meetings and conferences
- Desk work
- Phone conversations
- Eating

- Shopping
- Traveling
- Checking into a hotel
- Playing sports

Part 2

There are a total of 30 items in Part 2 of the TOEIC test. For each item, you will hear a question or statement followed by three possible responses. You must choose the most appropriate response to the question or statement. You will not read the questions or statements or the responses; you will only hear them. They are not written anywhere on the page, so you must listen carefully.

The questions and statements are things you would hear in normal business or everyday situations, such as:

- Requests for information (*Wh-* and *yes-no* questions)
- Requests for help (polite requests)

- Statements of opinion
- Statements about problems

The questions and statements deal with topics such as:

- Personal information
- Office procedures
- Weather
- Everyday objects

- Schedules
- Plans
- Preferences, needs, and wants

Part 3

In Part 3 of the TOEIC test, you will hear conversations and answer questions about them. You will hear a total of ten conversations and will answer three comprehension questions about each one, for a total of 30 questions in this part of the test. Each conversation is between two people and is fairly short, usually with four lines of dialogue. Unlike Parts 1 and 2, in Part 3 you will see the questions and answer options written on the test page. The questions ask about the main ideas and details of the conversations and may require you to make inferences, or logical guesses, about the information you hear.

The conversations are about things you would hear in normal business or everyday contexts in places such as:

- Offices
- Stores
- Hotels
- Restaurants

- Theaters
- Banks
- Post offices

The conversations are about normal business and everyday topics, such as:

- Office issues
- Travel plans
- Making purchases
- Ordering in a restaurant
- Planning events

- Ordering supplies
- Giving directions to a place
- Giving instructions
- Making appointments
- Leaving messages

Part 4

In Part 4 of the TOEIC test, you will hear short talks and answer questions about them. You will hear a total of ten talks and will answer three comprehension questions about each one, for a total of 30 questions in this part of the test. Each talk is fairly short, lasting approximately 30 seconds. As in Part 3, in Part 4 you will see the questions and answer options written on the test page. The questions ask about the main ideas and details of the talks and may require you to make inferences about the information you hear.

The talks are about things you would hear in normal business or everyday situations, such as:

- Announcements
- Speeches
- Tours
- Advertisements

- Reports
- Voicemail messages
- Lectures
- Introductions

The talks deal with topics such as:

- Travel information
- Tourism
- Weather
- News
- Business advice

- Store information
- Appointments and schedules
- Meeting agendas
- Office procedures

Listening Section Challenges and Solutions

» **CHALLENGE 1: "Some of the words I hear on the test are completely unfamiliar to me."**

SOLUTION: Listen to English as much as possible—including in advertisements, notices, and instructions—to get used to the language. TV and radio programs are good places to hear English. Internet sites, such as video hosting sites and various news sites, are also good places to find listening material. Watching movies in English will also help you improve your general listening vocabulary. When you are watching by yourself, replay parts you don't understand.

SOLUTION: Learn vocabulary related to common topics found on the TOEIC test, including words associated with specific business tasks, occupations, travel and transportation, banking, sports and entertainment, dining out, hotels, and so on. Make a list of these common topics and words often associated with them to help you study. Here is an example.

Topics	Associated Words
Business tasks	*submit, review, evaluate, supervise, duplicate, organize, project*
Occupations	*accountant, lawyer, dentist, engineer, physician, event planner*
Travel and transportation	*reservation, transfer, luggage, fare, passenger, gate, boarding pass*
Banking	*deposit, withdraw, account, teller, loan, mortgage, interest rate, percentage, balance*
Sports and entertainment	*player, tickets, performance, program, applaud, musician, entertainer*
Dining out	*waiter, server, appetizer, beverage, menu, course, chef, check, tip*
Hotels	*check in, check out, front desk, room service, bellhop, concierge*

SOLUTION: Remember that you don't have to understand every word to understand the audio or to answer all the questions. Focus on what you *do* understand and on getting the overall meaning.

SOLUTION: Recognizing homonyms (words that are spelled differently but sound alike) is key to finding correct answers in the TOEIC Listening Test. Look for lists of common homonyms and learn to distinguish among them. Here are a few examples.

Homonyms	
Words	**Examples**
by	*She is waiting **by** the car.*
buy	*Where did you **buy** that computer?*
billed	*Have you **billed** the client?*
build	*The company plans to **build** a new mall.*
blew	*The wind **blew** the roof off the building.*
blue	*A room painted in **blue** can be calming.*
read	*The assistant **read** the report yesterday.*
red	*The light on the machine is flashing **red**.*
know	*Do you **know** what time it is?*
no	*I have **no** idea.*
knew	*He **knew** the answer.*
new	*Several **new** employees were hired.*
hear	*The workers didn't **hear** the alarm.*
here	*When did they get **here**?*

» **CHALLENGE 2: "I sometimes have no idea what answer option to choose!"**

SOLUTION: Answer options are often paraphrased, or reworded, versions of words and phrases from the audio. Study the paraphrasing skills on pages 47–53.

SOLUTION: Quickly eliminate answer options you know aren't correct. Each section in this book helps you become familiar with the types of questions found in each part of the test and ways to identify correct and incorrect answers. Every answer option you can eliminate improves your chances.

SOLUTION: If you really don't know what the answer is—guess! On the TOEIC test, incorrect answers are simply not totaled with your score. You do NOT *lose* points for wrong answers.

» **CHALLENGE 3: "Listening is really difficult for me. I just can't understand everything that the speakers say."**

SOLUTION: Understanding varieties of native-speaker pronunciation is often part of the problem. You can use the scripts at the end of this book as you listen to the audio. This will help you connect sound and meaning. Get used to native-speaker English by listening to news reports from different English-speaking countries. Watch movies and TV programs from different English-speaking countries while you're at home or online. Have conversations with native speakers as much as possible.

SOLUTION: As you read the scripts and listen to the audio, mark words with unusual pronunciation. Look up words you don't know and keep a vocabulary log—it will increase your vocabulary.

SOLUTION: Listen to the audio from the practice activities and repeat what you hear. This will help your pronunciation and help you get used to native-speaker pronunciation.

SOLUTION: Try to listen selectively, and don't panic! Remember, it's also a matter of knowing what to listen for. You don't have to understand every word; you just need to be able to understand the most important information in order to answer the questions.

SOLUTION: Watching English-language movies and TV shows is especially good for improving listening comprehension because you can also see what is happening. Seeing gives you extra clues about the context. You can find many of these listening opportunities on the Internet. Practice watching and listening to English as much as you can to improve your listening skills.

» **CHALLENGE 4: "Sometimes I have no problem answering the first questions, but then I have trouble answering the last ones."**

SOLUTION: As you take the test, you'll discover that the questions generally get harder as you progress through each section. Be sure to move quickly through test questions that you consider easy, saving time for the more difficult ones that follow.

SOLUTION: DON'T spend a lot of time on any one question if you can't think of the answer. It's much more important to keep up with the audio recordings. First, answer the questions that you can. Then, if you have time, go back and try to answer the questions you couldn't do while listening.

SOLUTION: DON'T leave any questions unanswered. Guess or just fill in an answer if you are really stuck.

» **CHALLENGE 5: "I forget what the people said when it's time to answer the questions!"**

SOLUTION: You'll need to boost your short-term memory skills to overcome this problem. One way to do this is to listen to the audio in this book and try to remember as much as you can. After you listen, quickly write down everything you remember. Include the main idea and details. Then check the audio scripts at the back of the book how well did you do? Did you remember the facts correctly?

SOLUTION: For some people, answering the questions while listening can be distracting. If this doesn't work for you, focus on listening. What's happening? What are the people saying? Why are they saying it? Then answer the questions.

SOLUTION: Focus on the context. Every conversation and every talk tells a little story. Ask yourself the following questions: Who is talking? What are they talking about and why? Where are they? What do they want or need? Keeping the context in mind will help you remember what was said.

» **CHALLENGE 6: "I forget what the answer options are when they're on the recordings!"**

SOLUTION: In Part 1, you'll hear <u>four</u> answer options, which do not appear on the page. In Part 2, you'll hear a question followed by <u>three</u> answer options, which also do not appear on the page. Some students have a hard time remembering all this information. A good technique is to make a mental note of only the possible answer options when you hear them. If something does not make sense or seems completely irrelevant, it's probably not the correct option. Select the best option from the possible ones and wait for the next question to begin.

SOLUTION: Anticipate the answer. When you see a photo in Part 1, think of some phrases or words that describe it. When you hear a statement or question in Part 2, think of how someone might respond to it. This will help you be ready to recognize the correct response when you hear it. The correct response is the only one you have to remember.

» **CHALLENGE 7: "I do well in class and when I take practice tests, but when it comes to taking the real test, I feel so nervous that I have difficulty answering the questions."**

SOLUTION: Learn stress-reducing techniques, such as deep breathing and visualizing. Before you enter the exam room, take a few deep breaths. Do this again before you begin each section of the test and whenever you start feeling nervous. This will help you relax and focus.

SOLUTION: When you take practice tests, simulate the conditions of the real test as much as you can. You should be in a quiet room without a phone or other distractions. Don't replay any part of the audio; you will not be able to do this in the real test. Keep going and complete the entire Listening Section before taking a break. The more you practice under realistic conditions, the more confidence you will have when you take the real test.

SOLUTION: Get plenty of sleep the night before you take the test, and then eat a good breakfast, including orange juice and some protein. You will be in top condition to take the exam.

» **CHALLENGE 8: "I miss questions sometimes because I'm still thinking about my answer to the last question."**

SOLUTION: Stay with the audio. <u>No part of it is ever repeated</u>. If you miss a question or part of a conversation because you were thinking about something else, you won't have a chance to hear it again. If you spend too much time trying to decide on an answer, you may miss part of the audio. That hurts your chances of answering the next question. When you're unsure of an answer, try to narrow down the options or guess. Then mark an answer and move on with the audio. Remember, you won't lose points wrong answers.

More Tips for Doing Well on the Listening Section of the TOEIC Test

1. Become familiar with the format of the test.

If you know what to expect in each part of the TOEIC test, you won't have to worry about not understanding what you are supposed to do. You'll be able to focus your energy on answering the questions. This book will help you become familiar with the format of the test. As you work through the sections, you will learn what the TOEIC test contains. You'll become familiar with the directions for each part of the test, and you'll learn about the types of questions you'll encounter in each part.

2. Develop a regular study plan.

It's best to schedule time to study every day, but if you can't do that, try to make time at least every other day, and try to make it at the same time. You're more likely to follow a study plan if you make it into a regular habit. It's a good idea to write out your study schedule on a piece of paper or on your computer. This will help you commit to the plan. If you study every day or every other day, this will help you stay focused on practicing for the TOEIC test and keep your mind prepared for the test.

3. Do exercises and take practice tests.

Practice answering TOEIC test questions as much as possible. This will improve your test-taking skills. It will also help you identify your areas of weakness by showing which questions you get incorrect. Then you can concentrate on improving in these areas.

4. Develop your vocabulary.

You need both everyday and business vocabulary for the TOEIC test, so build your vocabulary in these areas. You can do this by reading and listening to English. Choose articles and programs with content related to the topics that appear on the TOEIC test, such as:

- Personal finances
- Business advice
- Restaurant reviews

- Vacation information
- Weather information
- Shopping

Make a vocabulary log and divide it into categories such as the ones above. You can add to the log and your categories as you practice and build your vocabulary.

TOEIC® Test Part 1: Photos

On Part 1 of the TOEIC Listening test, you will see ten photos. They may be photos of indoor or outdoor scenes, with or without people. For each photo, you will hear four statements about that photo. The statements may be about people, objects, activities, or locations. You will need to identify which one of the four statements correctly describes the photo.

Photo scenes for Part 1 may include:

» *Restaurants or cafés*

» *Airports, train stations, or subway stations*

» *Hotels*

» *Stores*

» *Offices*

» *Factories*

» *Streets, sidewalks, or parking lots*

QUICK GUIDE: Photos

Definition	Part 1 is a test of your listening comprehension. It requires you to identify details about photos and listen for the statements that correctly describe those details.
Targeted Skills	In order to correctly choose descriptions for Part 1 photos, you must be able to: • identify people, objects, activities, and locations in photos. • understand descriptive statements using present continuous, simple present and past tenses, *There is/There are* statements and other expressions. • distinguish between correct and incorrect descriptions of photos according to word meanings and sounds.
Statement Types	You will hear four statements. You must listen for the statement that correctly describes the photo. Statements like the following will be used: • **Activities:** *They're drinking coffee.* • **Conditions:** *There's a package on the desk.* • **Location:** *The car is next to the tree.*
Things to Watch For	Distracters, or incorrect answer options, which may include the following: • **Incorrect Information:** Statements may correctly identify people or objects in the photo but give incorrect information about them. • **Similar-Sounding Words:** Some statements may confuse you by using words that sound similar to words that correctly describe the photo but that are incorrect. • **Incorrect Meaning:** Some statements may include similar words with incorrect meanings based on the context of the photo.

WALK THROUGH: Photos

A What You'll See

In Part 1, you will see the directions and a sample photo on the first page and only the photo thereafter. Read the sample directions below. Look at the photo and identify what you see. Who are the people? What are they doing? What objects do you see? What is the location?

Part 1: Photos

Directions: Look at the photo. You will hear four statements about the photo. The statements are not in your book. Mark the letter of the statement that best describes the photo. You will hear each statement only once.

QUICK TIP

You have only five seconds between each set of statements! You must make your decision and be ready to listen for the next answer options at this time. Also remember that the words *photograph* or *picture* can also be used for a photo.

B What You'll Hear

You will hear four statements about each photo. Look at the sample script. Then listen to the audio as you read along in the sample script. Underline people, objects, or activities that you see in the photo above. 🎧 Track 1-01

SAMPLE SCRIPT ▶ Narrator: Look at the photo marked number 1 in your test book.
(script not available in test)

(A) They're looking for seating.

(B) They're having a meeting.

(C) They're reading newspapers.

(D) They're eating a meal.

Glossary:

⊜ POWERED BY COBUILD

seating: the seats in a place

meeting: an event in which a group of people come together to discuss things or make decisions

C What You'll Do

In the test, you will choose the letter of the statement that best describes the photo. Look at the photo above and listen to the statements again. Choose the statement that best describes the photo. Use the information you underlined in Part B if needed. 🎧 Track 1-01

GET IT RIGHT: Tips and Tasks for Answering Correctly

STATEMENT TYPES

In Part 1 of the Listening test, you will hear several different statement types that describe the photos you see, including statements about activities, condition, or location.

Statements About Activities

Some statements in Part 1 describe an activity in the photo. These statements often use the present continuous tense: *be* + verb + *-ing*.

Sample statements about activities:

» *They're shaking hands.*
» *He's reading the menu.*

» *The doctor is talking with the patient.*
» *She's buying a train ticket.*

QUICK TIP

Look through a magazine and practice using English to identify people, things, and actions in the photos you see. This will help you get used to identifying the content of photos quickly.

» **TIP Identify verbs that might describe activities in the photo.** When you first look at the photo, quickly identify any activities you see. Then when you hear the statements, listen carefully for present continuous forms of the verbs that correctly describe these activities. This will help you find the right answer.

TASK Look at the photos. Think of verbs that describe the activity you see. Then choose a verb from the box to complete each statement so that it correctly describes the photo. There are three extra verbs.

| checking | climbing | dialing | opening | pulling | pushing | talking |

1. She's _____ on the phone.

2. They're _____ their luggage behind them.

3. He's _____ a cart loaded with boxes.

4. They're _____ the stairs.

Statements About Condition

Some statements in Part 1 describe the condition of objects in the scene—what they are, where they are, or what they are like. These statements may use the expression *there is/are* or the verbs *is/are* or *has/have.*

Sample statements about condition:

» *There are books on the shelf.*
» *The door is open.*

» *The house has two windows.*

QUICK TIP

: There may be types of
: statements on the test
: other than the ones
: you see in this book,
: but the examples given
: here are the types of
: statements you will
: most likely hear.

» **TIP Identify objects and their condition as soon as you see the photo.** When you first look at the photo, quickly identify any objects you see. Think of sentences that could describe the objects' condition. Then when you hear the audio statements, listen carefully for the names of the objects. This can help you identify the correct statement.

TASK Look at each photo and the list of words next to it. Circle the words for the objects that you see in the photo. Then listen to two statements. Mark the letter of the statement that correctly describes the photo.   🎧 Track 1-02

1. clipboard   boxes   glasses

       newspapers   pens   clocks

       Statement (A)   Statement (B)

2. menus   tablecloths   trays

      trees   plates   chairs

      tables

      Statement (A)   Statement (B)

3. vase   printer   phone

clock   chair   drawers

stapler

Statement (A)   Statement (B)

Statements About Location

Some statements in Part 1 describe the location of objects or people in the photograph. These statements use prepositions of place, such as *in*, *on*, *under*, *over*, *above*, *next to*, *beside*, *between*, *behind*, and *in front of*.

Sample statements about location:

» *The computer is on the desk.*
» *The glass is next to the man's hand.*

» *The car is in front of the building.*

Prepositions of location describe where things are. Here are some common prepositions.

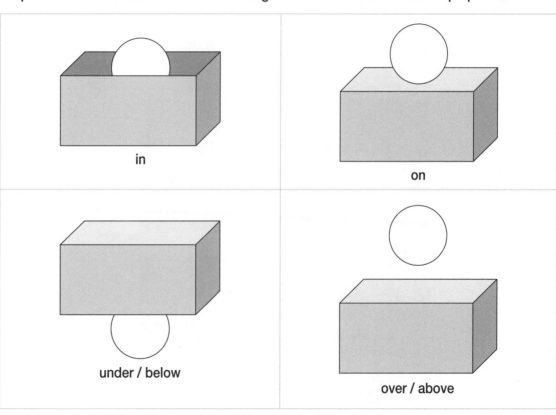

QUICK TIP

Remember! Answer options may include different types of statements. You could hear statements about activities, conditions, and locations for the same photo. Practice checking what you are hearing with what you see in the photo. You may need to check for several different things for one image.

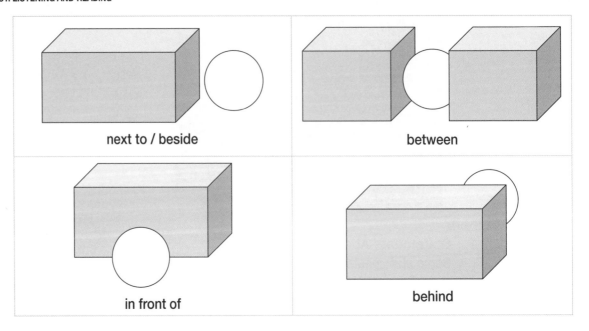

next to / beside

between

in front of

behind

» **TIP Identify objects and people and their locations in the photo.** When you first look at the photo, quickly identify where any objects or people are located. Then you can listen for prepositions that correctly describe the location. This will help you choose the correct answer.

TASK Complete each sentence with a preposition that correctly describes the photo. The preposition may be a phrase, and there may be more than one correct answer.

1. The lamp is _____ the beds.

2. The pictures are _____ the beds.

3. The pillows are _____ the beds.

4. The car is parked _____ the building.

5. The trees are _____ the building.

6. The flowers are _____ the vase.

7. The pen is _____ the book.

8. The computer monitor is _____ the desk.

COMMON DISTRACTER TYPES

In Part 1 of the Listening test, only one of the statements you will hear correctly describes the photo. You must learn to listen for the most common types of distracters, or incorrect answers.

Incorrect Information

Incorrect statements often contain information that seems correct but is not. Statements with incorrect information are common distracter types in Part 1.

» **TIP Watch out for "partly" correct information.** One type of distracter has <u>some</u> false information in the statement. A statement may correctly identify a person or an object in the photo, but the statement does not match the details in the photo. Here are some examples.

QUICK TIP

- Statements with some
- correct information
- along with some
- incorrect information
- are among the most
- common distracter
- types in Part 1.

Distracters with Incorrect Information		
Problems	**Explanations**	**Examples**
Wrong preposition or location	The statement misidentifies the location of a person or an object.	Incorrect: *The book is on the desk.* Correct: *The book is on the floor.*
Wrong condition	The statement incorrectly describes the condition of a person or an object.	Incorrect: *The glass is empty.* Correct: *The glass is full.*
Wrong activity	The statement misidentifies an activity.	Incorrect: *She's carrying the box.* Correct: *She's opening the box.*
Wrong person	The statement correctly identifies an activity, location, or condition but attributes it to the wrong person.	Incorrect: *The man has a clipboard.* Correct: *The woman has a clipboard.*
Wrong description	The statement incorrectly describes the appearance of a person or an object.	Incorrect: *The man has a mustache.* Correct: *The man has a beard.*

TASK Read the incorrect statements about each photo. Change the underlined words to make each statement correct.

1. The <u>woman</u> is holding a book.

   _____

2. The <u>man</u> has glasses. _____

3. The computer is <u>closed</u>. _____

4. The woman is <u>writing</u> the book.

   _____

5. The book is <u>under</u> the computer.

   _____

6. The woman has <u>dark</u> hair. _____

7. The man's hat is <u>in his hand</u>. _____

8. They're <u>waiters</u>. _____

9. They're in the <u>dining room</u>. _____

10. One man is pouring water from a <u>pot</u>.

    _____

11. They're <u>eating</u> a meal. _____

12. The plates are <u>full</u>. _____

Try a TOEIC Test Question

Listen to the audio and circle the people and things in the photo that you hear. Next, read the answer options and mark the statement that best describes the photo. Then write what the problem is for each of the three incorrect options. (Look at the chart on page 13 if needed.) 🎧 Track 1-03

ANSWER OPTIONS ▶

(script not available in test)

(A) He's pointing at the screen. _____

(B) The computer is closed. _____

(C) She's looking at the screen. _____

(D) He's buying a computer. _____

Similar-Sounding Words

In Part 1 of the Listening test, a distractor may use a word that sounds like, but is not exactly the same as, a word that would correctly describe the photo. These distracters are often words that rhyme or contain some similar sounds. Look at the example in the *Walk Through* exercise on page 7. Notice that the three incorrect statements all include a word that sounds similar to *meeting*, including *seating*, *reading*, and *eating*.

» **TIP Watch out for words that sound like the things you've identified in the picture.** Here are some examples of common similar-sounding words that you may hear in Part 1.

Similar-Sounding Words	
meeting, greeting, seating, eating, reading	*called, cold, told*
rain, train, plane, cane, chain	*marry, merry, ferry*
hair, chair, fare, pear, stair	*tell, hotel, bell*
look, cook, book, hook, notebook	*baggage, package*
shake, make, take, cake	*lift, left, gift*
drink, think	*coffee, coughing*
coat, boat, note	*warm, warn, form*
smile, file, pile, aisle	*white, wait, way*

QUICK TIP

You can often recognize distracters with similar-sounding words because the answer option may not make sense in relation to the photo, or it may talk about something that is not in the photo at all. If you hear something that seems really off topic, it is probably wrong!

TASK 1 Look at the photo and read the four statements. Underline the words in the statements that sound similar to things that are in the picture. Then mark the statement that best describes the photo.

(A) He has a stomachache.

(B) He's eating a steak.

(C) He's cutting a piece of cake.

(D) He's sitting by the lake.

TASK 2 Listen to each statement. Circle the word that you hear. 🎧 Track 1-04

1. thinking		drinking
2. pile		aisle
3. train		plane
4. warning		warming
5. meeting		eating
6. package		baggage
7. coffee		coughing
8. coat		boat

Try a TOEIC Test Question

Listen and circle things in the photo that you hear mentioned in the four statements. Next, mark the statement that best describes the photo. Then underline the incorrect similar-sounding words in the three incorrect options. 🎧 Track 1-05

ANSWER OPTIONS ▶

(script not available in test)

(A) She has a big smile.

(B) The aisle drawer is empty.

(C) She's looking at the files.

(D) The pile is very high.

Similar-Sounding Words with Incorrect Meanings

English has many words that are pronounced the same but spelled differently, words with the same spelling but different pronunciations, and words that are spelled and pronounced the same but with completely different meanings. Incorrect statements about the Listening test Part 1 photos may use any of these types of words.

» **TIP Watch out for words that have the wrong meaning but sound similar.** Here are a few of the many examples in English.

Words with Similar Sounds but Different Meanings			
Words	**Definitions**	**Words**	**Definitions**
right	correct	*wave*	move the hand
right	opposite of *left*	*wave*	movement of water
write	make marks on paper		
left	past tense of *leave*	*bat*	a type of animal
left	opposite of *right*	*bat*	a large stick of wood
glasses	items used to correct vision	*ring*	jewelry for the finger
glasses	items used for drinking	*ring*	a circle
		ring	a sound made by a bell
		wring	twist
close	shut	*pain*	hurt
clothes	things to wear	*pane*	a piece of glass in a window
cross	a shape like an *X*	*weigh*	measure how heavy something is
cross	go from one side to the other	*way*	method
cross	in a bad mood	*way*	path or direction
change	make different	*weight*	measurement of heaviness
change	coins	*wait*	expect or hope for something
ate	past tense of *eat*	*rose*	past tense of *rise*
eight	the number after seven	*rose*	a kind of flower
		rows	lines
record	the best of something	*read*	present tense of *read*
record	set down in permanent form	*read*	past tense of *read*

QUICK TIP

Distracters can be tricky! Be sure to look carefully at the distracters in the Part 1 Progressive Practice and the Practice Test. Try identifying distracters with incorrect meanings, similar-sounding words, and words with similar sounds but different meanings.

TASK Look at the photo and listen to the two statements. Mark the letter of the statement that best describes the photo. 🎧 Track 1-06

1. (A)

    (B)

2. (A)

   (B)

3. (A)

   (B)

4. (A)

   (B)

Try a TOEIC Test Question

Listen and circle things in the photo that you hear mentioned in the four statements. Next, mark the statement that best describes the photo. Then underline the incorrect similar-sounding words in the three incorrect options. Track 1-07

ANSWER OPTIONS ▶

(script not available in test)

(A) He's watching the plane.

(B) He's looking at his watch.

(C) He's handing the man his bag.

(D) He's wearing a plain jacket.

PROGRESSIVE PRACTICE: Get Ready

A Look at each photo. Quickly identify the people and objects, and think about their actions, location and condition. Then read and listen to the four statements. Mark the letter of the statement that best describes the photo. Remember, you will not be able to read the statements on the test. 🎧 Track 1-08

1.

(A) The lamps are over the bed.

(B) The curtain is open.

(C) The phone is next to the lamp.

(D) The pillows are on the floor.

2.

(A) They're looking at a book.

(B) They're trying to cook.

(C) They're reading a newspaper.

(D) They're greeting each other.

3.

(A) There's a clock on the wall.

(B) The book is open.

(C) There are words on the monitor.

(D) Someone is sitting in the chair.

4.

(A) The men are taking cans.

(B) The men are waving at each other.

(C) The men are wearing glasses.

(D) The men are shaking hands.

B Now check your answers. Read the explanations in the *Answer Analysis* box and examine the answer options in Part A again. Note why each statement is correct or incorrect. This will help you learn to identify incorrect answer options.

1.

ANSWER ANALYSIS ▶

✗ (A) The lamps are next to, not over, the bed.

✗ (B) The curtain is closed, not open.

✓ **(C) On the bedside table, there is a phone next to the lamp.**

✗ (D) The pillows are on the bed, not on the floor.

2.

ANSWER ANALYSIS ▶

✓ **(A) A man and a woman are looking at a book together.**

✗ (B) They have a book, and the word "cook" sounds similar to this.

✗ (C) They're reading a book, not a newspaper.

✗ (D) They're reading, and the word "greeting" sounds similar to this.

3.

ANSWER ANALYSIS ▶

✗ (A) There is a clock on the desk, not on the wall.

✓ **(B) There is a book on the desk, and it is open.**

✗ (C) There are no words on the monitor; it is blank.

✗ (D) The chair is empty; no one is sitting in it.

4.

ANSWER ANALYSIS ▶

✗ (A) The phrase "taking cans" sounds similar to the correct answer, "shaking hands."

✗ (B) This is an incorrect activity; the men are shaking hands, not waving them.

✗ (C) A woman is wearing glasses, but the men aren't.

✓ **(D) Two businessmen are shaking hands with each other.**

PROGRESSIVE PRACTICE: Get Set

A Look at each photo. Quickly identify the people and objects and think about their actions, location and condition. Then listen to the four statements. Mark the letter of the statement that best describes the photo. 🎧 Track 1-09

1. (A)
   (B)
   (C)
   (D)

2. (A)
   (B)
   (C)
   (D)

3. (A)
   (B)
   (C)
   (D)

4. (A)

(B)

(C)

(D)

5. (A)

(B)

(C)

(D)

6. (A)

(B)

(C)

(D)

B Now check your answers. Look at the statements for each question in the scripts at the back of this book. Then look at the explanations in the *Answer Analysis* box. Write the letter of each answer option from Part A next to the reason why it is correct or incorrect. This will help you learn to identify incorrect answer options.

1.

> ANSWER ANALYSIS ▶
>
> _____ ✗ The tray is empty because the man has removed the plate and is putting it on the table.
> _____ ✓ **A waiter is putting a plate of dessert on the table in front of the woman.**
> _____ ✗ There are several items on the table that are associated with having a meal, but none of them is a cup.
> _____ ✗ The word "water" sounds similar to "waiter." There is a waiter in the picture, but there is no water.

2.

> ANSWER ANALYSIS ▶
>
> _____ ✗ The photo shows a park, but there are no people walking through it.
> _____ ✗ "Dark" sounds similar to "park," but the photo shows a bright day, not a dark night.
> _____ ✗ The bench is empty, so there is plenty of room to sit on it.
> _____ ✓ **The photo shows a scene of a bench in a park.**

3.

> ANSWER ANALYSIS ▶
>
> _____ ✗ "Plane" sounds similar to "train." The photo shows a train.
> _____ ✗ "Rain" sounds like "train." This is an indoor scene, so it is impossible to see rain in it.
> _____ ✓ **The photo shows a subway train in the station.**
> _____ ✗ We can see passengers on the platform but not on the train.

4.

> ANSWER ANALYSIS ▶
>
> _____ ✓ **Two women are crossing the street at a crosswalk.**
> _____ ✗ This confuses the meaning of "cross." The women want to cross the street. They don't look cross, that is, angry.
> _____ ✗ "Steep" sounds like "street." We can see part of a street in the photo, but there is nothing steep.
> _____ ✗ The woman's bag is on her arm, not in a car.

5.

> ANSWER ANALYSIS ▶
>
> _____ ✗ "Farm" sounds similar to "car," but the man is working on a car, not at a farm.
> _____ ✓ **A man is working on a car engine, so he is fixing the car.**
> _____ ✗ "Mixing" sounds similar to "fixing," and "good" sounds similar to "hood." The man is under the hood fixing the car.
> _____ ✗ The man is not opening the hood; the hood is already open.

6.

> ANSWER ANALYSIS ▶
>
> _____ ✗ "Door" sounds similar to "floor." The rug is on the floor, not under the door.
> _____ ✗ "Stairs" sounds similar to "chairs." The chairs, not the stairs, are in front of the sofa.
> _____ ✗ The lamps are on tables, not on the wall.
> _____ ✓ **A picture hangs on the wall over the sofa.**

PROGRESSIVE PRACTICE: Go for the TOEIC® Test

Directions: Look at each photo. You will hear four statements about the photo. The statements are not in your book. Mark the letter of the statement that best describes the photo. You will hear each statement only once. 🎧 Track 1-10

1. (A)
   (B)
   (C)
   (D)

2. (A)
   (B)
   (C)
   (D)

3. (A)
   (B)
   (C)
   (D)

4. (A)

    (B)

    (C)

    (D)

5. (A)

    (B)

    (C)

    (D)

6. (A)

    (B)

    (C)

    (D)

7. (A)

    (B)

    (C)

    (D)

8. (A)

(B)

(C)

(D)

9. (A)

(B)

(C)

(D)

10. (A)

(B)

(C)

(D)

TOEIC® Test Part 2: Question-Response

Part 2 of the TOEIC Listening test consists of 30 questions or statements. Each question or statement is followed by three possible responses. You will choose the most appropriate response. Everything is spoken; there will be nothing for you to read on the page. The questions or statements are things you might hear in a conversation among colleagues, customers, clients, friends, or relatives. Questions might be requests for information or for assistance, and statements might be about needs, plans, or feelings.

Topics for Part 2 questions or statements may include:

» *Work*

» *Shopping*

» *Travel*

» *Transportation*

» *Movies, theater, concerts*

» *Health*

» *Weather*

» *Entertainment*

» *Banking*

QUICK GUIDE: Question-Response

Definition	Part 2 is a test of your listening comprehension. You will listen to a line from a conversation and identify an appropriate response.
Targeted Skills	In order to correctly choose responses to Part 2 questions and statements, you must be able to: • distinguish between a question and a statement. • understand the content of a line of conversation. • distinguish between correct and incorrect conversational responses.
Question and Statement Types	Question or statement types will include the following: • **Information Questions:** *Where is your office?* • ***Yes-No* Questions, Embedded Questions, and Polite Requests:** *Has the meeting started yet?* • **Embedded Questions:** *Can you tell me what time it is?* • **Polite Requests:** *Could you open the door for me?* • **Questions with *or*, Tag Questions, and Statements:** *Did she call last night or this morning?* • **Tag Questions:** *You work in this building, don't you?* • **Statements:** *It's cold in here.*
Things to Watch For	Distracters, or incorrect answer options, may include the following: • **Similar-Sounding Words:** Some responses use words similar to a word in the question, but that are homonyms, or have the wrong meaning. • **Other Distracter Types:** Some distracters use repeated words, or the same word as the question, but in the wrong context. Some distracters use related words, or words associated with something in the question, but in the wrong context. Other distracters may include *yes-no* responses to information questions. There are also distracters that use the wrong verb tense.

WALK THROUGH: Question-Response

A What You'll See

In Part 2, the only things you will see are the directions and instructions to mark your answer sheet. The questions and answer options are not on the page.

Part 2: Question-Response

Directions: Listen to the question or statement and three possible responses. You will hear them only one time, and they are not in your book. Choose the best response, and mark the corresponding letter on your answer sheet.

1. Mark your answer on your answer sheet.

2. Mark your answer on your answer sheet.

3. Mark your answer on your answer sheet.

4. Mark your answer on your answer sheet.

B What You'll Hear

You will hear a question or statement followed by three possible responses. Look at the sample script. Then listen to the sample questions and responses. Underline the question words in the script. Then underline words in the possible responses that could help you answer that question. 🎧 Track 2-01

SAMPLE SCRIPT ▶ **Number 1.**

(script not available in test)

Where should I put this package?

(A) It's from the Tokyo office.

(B) On that table over there.

(C) Ms. Jones sent it.

Number 2.

Who made these photocopies?

(A) Peter made them.

(B) He made ten copies.

(C) The copies are on your desk.

Glossary:

⬤ POWERED BY COBUILD

package: a small parcel

photocopies: copies of a document made using a machine

C What You'll Do

In the test, you will listen to the audio and choose the best response to each question. Now listen to the audio and choose the best response. Use the information you underlined in Part B if needed, but remember that you won't have the scripts on the test! 🎧 Track 2-01

GET IT RIGHT: Tips and Tasks for Answering Correctly

QUESTION AND STATEMENT TYPES

Information Questions

Information questions are also called *wh-* questions. These are the questions that begin with question words (or phrases), such as *Who, Whose, What, When, Where, Which, Why, and How.* Each different question word asks for a different type of information.

Questions	Information requested	Sample Responses
Who put the package on my desk?	Person	*John did.*
Whose car is this?	Owner	*It's Ms. Park's.*
What did you buy?	Thing	*A new computer.*
What did they do last night?	Activity	*They had dinner at a restaurant.*
When/What time did they arrive?	Time	*Late last night.*
Where is your office?	Location	*On the third floor.*
Which desk do you want?	Choice	*I'll take the one by the window.*
Why was he late?	Reason	*His car broke down.*
How do you get to work?	Manner or method	*By bus, usually.*
How many people work here?	Quantity	*Only three.*
How much paper do we need?		*About twenty sheets.*
How often do you get paid?	Frequency	*Every two weeks.*

QUICK TIP

Be careful not to confuse *Whose* and *Who's*. They sound the same but ask for different information. *Whose* is followed by a noun and a verb, often *is* or *are*. The correct answer will usually include a possessive. *Who's means Who is*. The correct answer will usually be a person.

» **TIP 1 Identify any question words you hear.** When you correctly identify the question word, you will know what type of information to listen for when you hear the possible responses.

TASK Listen to each question. Circle the question word(s) that you hear. 🎧 Track 2-02

1. Where	What	When
2. Which	Whose	Who
3. How many	How often	How much
4. Where	Why	How
5. What	When	Who

» **TIP 2 Listen for the correct type of information.** Be sure to listen for the type of information that the question asks for. If you hear *When*, listen for time, if you hear *Where*, listen for a place, and so on.

TASK Read the possible responses in the box. Then listen to the questions. Write the letter of the correct response next to the number of each question. There are two extra responses. 🎧 Track 2-02

a. My boss did.	**d.** Just once a month.	**f.** Usually in August.
b. It's Jim's.	**e.** There are about ten of them.	**g.** There's a cafeteria downstairs.
c. I prefer this one.		

1. ____ **2.** ____ **3.** ____ **4.** ____ **5.** ____

Try a TOEIC Test Question

Pre-read the question and response options. Then listen to the audio as you read along in the script. Underline the question word and think about what it is asking for—a thing, an activity, or a time? Then choose the best response to the question. 🎧 Track 2-03

SAMPLE SCRIPT ▶
(script not available in test)

What time does the train leave?

(A) The rain has stopped.

(B) Buy your ticket here.

(C) At ten o'clock.

Yes-No Questions

In Part 2, some of the questions will be *yes-no* questions. *Yes-no* questions begin with auxiliary verbs, such as *is/are, was/were, do/does, did, have/has,* or *will.* They might also begin with negative forms of auxiliaries, such as *wasn't, didn't,* or *won't.* The correct response usually begins with *yes* or *no,* but watch out! Sometimes the response will be a direct answer to the question, without *yes* or *no.*

Yes-No Questions	Possible Responses	Auxiliary Verbs
Is this your desk?	Yes. I like working by the window. No. Mine's over there.	*Is/Are*
Are you going out for lunch?	Yes, I think so. Not today.	
Weren't you out of town last week?	Yes. I got back yesterday. No. I was in the office all week.	
Was that your new assistant?	Yes. He started last week. No. That's my boss.	*Was/Were*
Do you work here?	I'm the manager. No. I'm a client.	*Do/Does*
Doesn't your wife work here, too?	Yes, she's in the Legal Department. She used to, but she got another job.	
Did you sign the document?	Yes, and then I put it on your desk. I'll sign it right now.	*Did*
Didn't you hear the news?	Yes. It was terrible, wasn't it? No. What happened?	
Have you finished the report?	I finished it last night. Not yet, but I'll finish it soon.	*Have/Has*
Hasn't John left for vacation yet?	He left last night. He's leaving tomorrow.	
Will you be at the staff meeting tomorrow?	I plan to be. No, I have another commitment.	*Will*
Won't you be at the concert tonight?	I'll be sitting in the front row. I wasn't able to get a ticket.	

Embedded Questions

Some *yes-no* questions contain embedded questions—a question within a question. For example: *Can you tell me where the meeting is? Do you know when he arrived?*

This type of question begins with a *yes-no* question but contains an embedded question in **subject-verb** order. Although the first part of the question could be answered with *yes* or *no*, the answer to the *embedded question* is what the speaker really asks for. The correct response must answer *that* part of the question.

QUICK TIP

Simple and embedded *yes-no* questions have rising intonation at the end, but embedded *wh-* questions have falling intonation. Pay attention to whether the speaker's voice rises or falls at the end of the question to help find the correct response.

Embedded Questions	Possible Responses
*Can you tell me **where the bank is?***	*Yes. It's on the next block.* *I'm sorry. I don't know where it is.*
*Do you know **what time the meeting starts?***	*It starts at 9:15.* *I'm not sure, but I think before 10:00.*
*Do you think **it will rain today?***	*It probably will.* *No. There's not a cloud in the sky.*
*Do you remember **how many people were at the meeting?***	*I think about 25.* *No. I don't remember at all.*

Polite Requests

Polite requests are another type of *yes-no* question. Although they are structured like *yes-no* questions, they usually aren't answered with *yes* or *no*. Instead, the responses contain polite phrases, such as *Of course, Certainly, I'd be glad to, I'd be happy to, I'm sorry,* or *I wish I could*. Responses may consist of or include an explanation of when or how the request will be met, or an excuse for not fulfilling the request.

QUICK TIP

Listen for clues to polite requests. Polite requests begin with certain modal auxiliaries—*can, will, could, would*. When you hear one of these verbs, it may signal a polite request.

Polite Requests	Possible Responses
***Can you** copy these documents for me?*	*Of course. I'll do it right away.* *I'm sorry. I'm busy right now.*
***Will you** call me when your meeting is over?*	*I'd be glad to.* *I'm sorry, but I'm not sure if I can.*
***Could you** put these letters in the mail for me?*	*I'd be happy to. I'm going by the post office now.* *I wish I could, but I don't have time.*
***Would you** show me how to use this machine?*	*Yes, certainly. It's very easy to use.* *I'm busy right now, but I can show you later.*

» **TIP 1 Identify the type of *yes-no* question.** This will help you choose the appropriate response.

TASK Listen to each question and circle the question type. Track 2-04

1. simple *yes-no* question	embedded question	polite request
2. simple *yes-no* question	embedded question	polite request
3. simple *yes-no* question	embedded question	polite request
4. simple *yes-no* question	embedded question	polite request
5. simple *yes-no* question	embedded question	polite request

» **TIP 2 Listen for an appropriate response option for the question type.** A response to a *yes-no* question does not necessarily begin with *yes* or *no*. The correct response to a simple *yes-no* question will confirm or deny the information asked about. The response to a *yes-no* question with an embedded question will address the embedded question. A polite request may be answered with a polite response.

TASK Read the possible responses in the box. Then listen to the questions and choose the correct responses. There are two extra responses. 🎧 Track 2-04

---

a. He knows how to do it.

b. Yes. There's one across the street.

c. At 7:30, I think.

d. Not yet. It leaves at 5:15.

e. Of course. I'll put them on your desk.

f. No, she can't tell.

g. Yes. He's in his office.

---

1. ___   2. ___   3. ___   4. ___   5. ___

Try a TOEIC Test Question

Pre-read the question and response options. Then listen to the audio as you read along in the script. Underline the word that tells you what type of question it is, and decide whether the question needs a *yes-no* response, a response to an embedded question, or a polite response. Then choose the best response to the question. 🎧 Track 2-05

SAMPLE SCRIPT ▶
(script not available in test)

Will you be working this weekend?

(A) I'm not sure.

(B) I'll get it.

(C) Yes, it is.

Questions with *Or*

Just like simple *yes-no* questions, questions with *or* begin with auxiliary verbs. However, these questions cannot be answered with *yes* or *no*. A question with *or* is about a choice, and the response must indicate the speaker's choice. Here are some sample questions and responses.

QUICK TIP

Questions with *or* will usually have falling intonation at the end. If you hear falling intonation and *or*, the correct response is likely a choice or an option.

Questions with *Or*	Possible Responses
*Are you traveling by train **or** by bus?*	*We're leaving tonight on the ten o'clock train.*
*Do you prefer coffee **or** tea?*	*Neither. I'll just have some water.*
*Will you make the call **or** shall I?*	*I'll do it.*
*Would you like to sit here **or** by the window?*	*I think by the window is more comfortable.*
*Do you work the day shift **or** the night?*	*I work nights until eleven p.m.*

Tag Questions

Tag questions are like *yes-no* questions, but the *yes or no* option is at the end of the sentence. In a tag question, an auxiliary verb and a pronoun are attached to the end of a statement. If the statement is affirmative, the tag will be negative. If the statement is negative, the tag will be affirmative. The responses for these can be either *yes, no,* or something addressing the statement. Here are some sample tag questions and responses.

Tag Questions	Possible Responses
*You work in this building, **don't you?***	*Yes. My office is on the third floor.*
*John isn't your boss, **is he?***	*No, but we work in the same department.*
*You'll be at the party, **won't you?***	*I will if I don't have to work tonight.*
*Mary wasn't at the office yesterday, **was she?***	*She was at a meeting in London.*
*Jim has worked here quite a long time, **hasn't he?***	*He has, and he knows the company well.*

QUICK TIP

: Keep in mind that a
: statement serves to
: extend a conversation.
: The best response
: is usually one that
: will continue the
: conversation.

Statements

In addition to questions, you will hear some statements in Part 2 of the Listening test. A statement may be about an opinion or a problem. The response may agree or disagree with an opinion or suggest a solution to a problem. Here are some sample statements and responses.

Statements	Possible Responses
That movie was really funny.	*I know. I couldn't stop laughing.*
Sam is a very hard worker.	*He is. He deserves a raise.*
I don't understand how to use the fax machine.	*I'd be happy to explain it to you.*
The printer has run out of paper.	*There's more paper in the supply closet.*

» **TIP 1 Identify the type of question or statement.** This will help you choose the appropriate response.

TASK Listen to each question and circle the question type. 🎧 Track 2-06

1. *or* question   tag question   statement

2. *or* question   tag question   statement

3. *or* question   tag question   statement

4. *or* question   tag question   statement

5. *or* question   tag question   statement

» **TIP 2 Listen for an appropriate response to the question type.** The answer to an *or* question doesn't use *yes* or *no*. The answer to a tag question may or may not use *yes* or *no*. The response to a statement may agree or disagree or suggest a solution.

TASK Read the possible responses in the box. Then listen to the audio again and choose the correct responses. There are two extra responses. 🎧 Track 2-06

a. Neither. I come by subway.	**d.** Yes. It's a beautiful city.	**f.** I'll close the window.
b. Don't worry. I have a key.	**e.** Actually, I prefer fish.	**g.** It was very funny.
c. I'll take the red one.		

1. ____   **2.** ____   **3.** ____   **4.** ____   **5.** ____

Try a TOEIC Test Question

Pre-read the statement and response options. Then listen to the audio as you read along in the script. Think about the kind of response the statement needs. Then choose the best response. 🎧 Track 2-07

SAMPLE SCRIPT ▶   These books are so heavy.

(script not available in test)

     (A) I like to read books.   (B) I can book a hotel room.   (C) I'll carry them for you.

COMMON DISTRACTER TYPES

Similar-Sounding Words

» **TIP 1 Beware of similar-sounding words in incorrect answer options.** Just as in Part 1, an incorrect response in Part 2 may use a word that sounds like, but is not exactly the same as, a word used in the question. Here are some examples of similar-sounding words you may hear in Part 2 of the TOEIC Listening test. (See page 15 for more examples.)

Similar-Sounding Words	
weather, wetter	dinner, thinner
father, farther, feather	send, spend, lend, end, tend, mend, extend, men
department, apartment	fine, time, dine, nine
tall, small, call, fall, ball, hall, mall, recall	white, right, night, light, fight, sight, tight
tell, smell, fell, sell, yell	met, bet, get, set
bought, brought, caught, taught	ten, pen, men, again
phone, home, alone	fire, hire, retire, expire, inspire
done, fun	cloud, crowd, loud, allowed

Be careful about homonyms and multiple-meaning words. Be especially aware of distracters that have homonyms, or words that are spelled differently and have different meanings but that sound the same. A word like *weak* might be used as an adjective in a question or statement and the noun form used as a distracter in a response. Also watch out for distracters with the exact same word as the question but with a different meaning. A word like *room* can mean space, or it can mean a part of a building. Though the two meanings are close, they are not the same, and this is probably a distracter. Here are some examples of homonyms and multiple-meaning words you may hear in Part 2 of the Listening test. (See the chart on page 17 for more examples.)

Homonyms and Multiple-Meaning Words			
Words	**Definitions**	**Words**	**Definitions**
here	in this place	week	seven days
hear	perceive sounds	weak	not strong
blue	a color	meet	come together
blew	past tense of *blow*	meat	beef, chicken, pork, etc.
work	have a job	find	discover
work	function, operate	fined	past tense of *fine*
room	part of a building	choose	select
room	space	chews	grind up with the teeth
suit	a set of clothing	read	past tense of *read*
suit	fit, be appropriate	red	a color
fall	go down	like	be similar
fall	autumn	like	enjoy something
order	organization, arrangement	sent	past tense of *send*
order	instruction	cent	1/100th of a dollar
order	ask for, demand	scent	odor

TASK Listen to the audio as you read each question or statement and the possible responses. Choose the best response. In the incorrect answer options, underline the homonyms, similar-sounding words, and words used with the wrong meanings.   Track 2-08

1. Did you hear the news?

   (A) Yes, he's here.

   (B) Yes. It's very exciting.

   (C) Yes, they're quite near.

2. It's time to order more paper.

   (A) Yes, and we need some pens, too.

   (B) Everything is in order.

   (C) The border is closed.

3. Who's in charge of this department?

   (A) They live in a large apartment.

   (B) There's one in that compartment.

   (C) Ms. Brown is the supervisor.

4. The weather is lovely today.

   (A) It is. We should walk in the park.

   (B) Everything is getting wetter.

   (C) I don't know whether she's here.

5. Choose anything you like from the menu.

   (A) He always chews so loudly.

   (B) It was an offer impossible to refuse.

   (C) Thanks. I'll have the baked fish.

6. Do you prefer blue or red?

   (A) I read that article, too.

   (B) The wind blew very hard.

   (C) I always think blue is nicer.

» **TIP 2 Watch out for other distracter types.** Other distracters in Part 2 may include repeated words, related words, *yes-no* answers to information questions, and answers using the wrong verb tense.

Repeated Words

An incorrect response may repeat a word used in the question or statement but in the wrong context. In the example below, responses A and B repeat the word *lunch* but do not answer the question.

Where did you have lunch?

(A) It was a delicious lunch.

(B) I always have a sandwich for lunch.

(C) At the cafeteria downstairs.

Related Words

An incorrect response may use a word associated with something in the question or statement but in the wrong context. In the example below, responses B and C use words associated with the word *bus*—*fare* and *driver*—but are not appropriate responses.

Do you take the bus to work?

(A) No. I always drive my car.

(B) The fare is two dollars.

(C) Yes. He was a very good driver.

Yes-No Answers to Information Questions

Information questions cannot be answered with *yes* or *no*. In the example below, responses A and B cannot be correct because they begin with *yes* and *no*.

What time does the movie start?

(A) Yes, I like movies.

(B) No. It wasn't early.

(C) At 5:00.

Wrong Verb Tense

An incorrect response may use the wrong verb tense. In the example below, responses A and C use verb tenses that are not logical in this context.

Did you play golf last weekend?

(A) Yes, I'll play golf with you.

(B) Yes, I played at the club.

(C) Yes, I do.

TASK Listen to the audio as you read each question or statement and the possible responses. Write the letter (a-d) of the distracter type next to each incorrect answer. The correct answer will not have a letter for a distracter type. Then mark the correct response. 🎧 Track 2-09

Distracter Types	
a. repeated word	**c.** *yes-no* answer to information question
b. related word	**d.** wrong verb tense

1. Is the food at this restaurant good?

(A) Yes, it's delicious. _____

(B) I enjoy eating at restaurants. _____

(C) No, I haven't seen the waiter. _____

2. When will you take your vacation?

(A) No, it wasn't much fun. _____

(B) I usually go to the beach. _____

(C) At the end of August. _____

3. Who uses this desk?

(A) He sat there yesterday. _____

(B) Mr. Stephens works there. _____

(C) It's a very tidy desk. _____

4. Which hotel did you stay at?

(A) Yes, it was a very nice place. _____

(B) The big one near the train station. _____

(C) We had a room with a view. _____

5. Has the mail been delivered yet?

(A) Yes, I put it on your desk. _____

(B) You can buy stamps downstairs. _____

(C) No, that envelope is too small. _____

Try a TOEIC Test Question

Pre-read the question and answer options. Then listen to the audio as you read along in the script. Underline the word that tells you what type of question it is. Then underline distracters and mark the correct response. 🎧 Track 2-10

SAMPLE SCRIPT ▶ **Is the meeting tomorrow at nine?**

(script not available in test)

(A) That's fine.

(B) Yes, it is.

(C) There's a meeting.

PROGRESSIVE PRACTICE: Get Ready

A Read and listen to the question or statement and three possible responses. Choose the best response, and mark the corresponding letter. Remember, you won't be able to see the questions or responses in the real TOEIC test! 🎧 Track 2-11

1. Whose purse is this?

   (A) She's a nurse.

   (B) This is a purse.

   (C) It's Mary's.

2. Where can I park my car?

   (A) In the garage.

   (B) Let's walk in the park.

   (C) It's not very far.

3. It's a very cold day.

   (A) Yes, he sold it.

   (B) I'll wear a coat.

   (C) The meeting is today.

4. When is the party?

   (A) At Peter's house.

   (B) Tomorrow at five.

   (C) I like a good party.

5. Who took this phone message?

   (A) I took it.

   (B) The phone is ringing.

   (C) It's in the book.

B Now check your answers. Read the explanations in the Answer Analysis box and look at the answer options. Note why each response is correct or incorrect. This will help you learn to identify incorrect responses. 🎧 Track 2-11

1. Whose purse is this?

   (A) She's a nurse.

   (B) This is a purse.

   (C) It's Mary's.

ANSWER ANALYSIS ▶

✗ (A) "Nurse" just sounds similar to "purse."

✗ (B) This only repeats the word "purse" but doesn't answer the question.

✓ **(C) The possessive "Mary's" answers the question "Whose?"**

---

2. Where can I park my car?

    (A) In the garage.

    (B) Let's walk in the park.

    (C) It's not very far.

ANSWER ANALYSIS ▶

✓ **(A) "In the garage" answers the question "Where?"**

✗ (B) This uses "park" with the meaning of "a natural area in a city" rather than "to put your car somewhere."

✗ (C) "Far" just sounds similar to "car."

3. It's a very cold day.

    (A) Yes, he sold it.

    (B) I'll wear a coat.

    (C) The meeting is today.

ANSWER ANALYSIS ▶

✗ (A) "Sold" just sounds similar to "cold."

✓ **(B) "I'll wear a coat" is a logical response on a cold day.**

✗ (C) "Today" just sounds similar to "day."

4. When is the party?

    (A) At Peter's house.

    (B) Tomorrow at five.

    (C) I like a good party.

ANSWER ANALYSIS ▶

✗ (A) This would answer a question about "Where?"

✓ **(B) "Tomorrow at five" answers the question "When?"**

✗ (C) This only repeats the word "party."

5. Who took this phone message?

    (A) I took it.

    (B) The phone is ringing.

    (C) It's in the book.

ANSWER ANALYSIS ▶

✓ **(A) "I" answers the question "Who?"**

✗ (B) This repeats the word "phone" but doesn't answer the question.

✗ (C) "Book" just sounds similar to "took."

PROGRESSIVE PRACTICE: Get Set

A Listen to the question or statement and three possible responses. Choose the best response and mark the corresponding letter. 🎧 Track 2-12

1. (A) (B) (C)

2. (A) (B) (C)

3. (A) (B) (C)

4. (A) (B) (C)

5. (A) (B) (C)

6. (A) (B) (C)

7. (A) (B) (C)

8. (A) (B) (C)

9. (A) (B) (C)

10. (A) (B) (C)

B Now check your answers. Look at the questions and responses in the scripts at the back of this book. Then look at the explanations in the *Answer Analysis* box. Write the letter of each answer option next to the reason why it is correct or incorrect. This will help you learn to identify incorrect responses. 🎧 Track 2-12

1.

ANSWER ANALYSIS ▶

_____ ✗ "Hurry" just sounds similar to "hungry."

_____ ✓ **Telling someone to have lunch is a logical suggestion when that person is hungry.**

_____ ✗ "Angry" just sounds similar to "hungry."

2.

ANSWER ANALYSIS ▶

_____ ✗ "Check out" is only related to "hotel" but doesn't answer the question.

_____ ✗ "Tell" just sounds similar to "hotel."

_____ ✓ **"Very comfortable" answers the question "How?"**

3.

ANSWER ANALYSIS ▶

_____ ✓ **"Office supplies" answers the question "What?"**

_____ ✗ "Closed it" just sounds similar to "closet."

_____ ✗ This repeats the word "closet" and is also a "yes-no" answer to an information question.

4.

ANSWER ANALYSIS ▶

_____ ✓ **"Yes, it was very interesting" answers the question and explains why the speaker liked the museum.**

_____ ✗ This uses "like" with a meaning of "similar to" instead of "enjoy."

_____ ✗ This repeats the word "museum" but doesn't answer the question.

5.

ANSWER ANALYSIS ▶

_____ ✗ The possessive noun "John's" answers the question "Whose?" not "Who's?"

_____ ✓ **"My boss" answers the question "Who?"**

_____ ✗ This just repeats the word "there."

6.

ANSWER ANALYSIS ▶

_____ ✗ This is a "yes-no" answer to an information question.

_____ ✗ "Lost" just sounds similar to "cost."

_____ ✓ **"Ten dollars" answers the question "How much?"**

7.

ANSWER ANALYSIS ▶

_____ ✓ **"Of course" is a polite response to a polite request.**

_____ ✗ "Coughing" just sounds similar to "coffee."

_____ ✗ This only repeats the word "cup" but doesn't answer the question.

8.

ANSWER ANALYSIS ▶

_____ ✗ This only repeats "New York" but doesn't answer the question.

_____ ✓ **"I'm leaving tomorrow" answers the question about going to New York.**

_____ ✗ "Noon" just sounds similar to "soon."

9.

ANSWER ANALYSIS ▶

_____ ✓ **"Yes, I'll see her" correctly answers the future tense question.**

_____ ✗ This only repeats the name "Susan" but doesn't answer the question.

_____ ✗ This past tense answer isn't a logical response to the future tense question.

10.

ANSWER ANALYSIS ▶

_____ ✗ The word "deck" just sounds similar to "check."

_____ ✓ **This answers the "yes-no" question about payment methods.**

_____ ✗ This uses "check" with the meaning of "look at" rather than "payment method."

PROGRESSIVE PRACTICE: Go for the TOEIC® Test

TOEIC® TEST PRACTICE

Directions: Listen to the question or statement and three possible responses. You will hear them only one time, and they are not in your book. Choose the best response, and mark the corresponding letter on your answer sheet. 🎧 Track 2-13

1.	(A)	(B)	(C)		11.	(A)	(B)	(C)
2.	(A)	(B)	(C)		12.	(A)	(B)	(C)
3.	(A)	(B)	(C)		13.	(A)	(B)	(C)
4.	(A)	(B)	(C)		14.	(A)	(B)	(C)
5.	(A)	(B)	(C)		15.	(A)	(B)	(C)
6.	(A)	(B)	(C)		16.	(A)	(B)	(C)
7.	(A)	(B)	(C)		17.	(A)	(B)	(C)
8.	(A)	(B)	(C)		18.	(A)	(B)	(C)
9.	(A)	(B)	(C)		19.	(A)	(B)	(C)
10.	(A)	(B)	(C)		20.	(A)	(B)	(C)

TOEIC® Test Part 3: Conversations

Part 3 of the TOEIC Listening test features ten conversations. Each conversation is followed by three questions that you will hear and see on the page. The conversations are quite short and last only about twenty-five seconds. The subject matter of these conversations can cover a range of topics, from standard business interactions to personal topics.

Conversation topics for Part 3 may include:

» *Deadlines, documents, and equipment*

» *Raises, promotions, and training*

» *Contracts, sales, and expenses*

» *Restaurants, real estate, and retail*

» *Travel, hotels, or free-time activities*

QUICK GUIDE: Conversations

Definition	Part 3 is a test of your listening comprehension. The questions focus on your ability to find central ideas and basic details. They also require that you make informed guesses based on the language used or the situation.
Targeted Skills	In order to correctly answer Part 3 questions, you must be able to: • understand the main idea of a conversation. • identify key facts from a conversation. • make conclusions based on details. • understand paraphrased language in answer options. • pre-read questions to predict important information.
Question Types	• **Topic / Main Idea:** *Where are the speakers?* • **Detail:** *When are they going to meet?* • **Inference:** *What will probably happen next?*
Answer Options	• **Topic / Main Idea Questions:** locations, occupations, activities, topics, etc. • **Detail Questions:** time, reasons, plans, problems, suggestions, opinions, etc. • **Inference Questions:** contexts, feelings, meanings, etc.
Things to Watch For	• **Conversation Distracters:** Sometimes there is information in the conversation that will mislead or confuse you. Don't choose an answer just because it includes a word from the recording! • **Vocabulary Clues:** Some correct answers are not stated directly in the conversation. You must listen for vocabulary clues and for paraphrased or slightly changed information to find the answer.

WALK THROUGH: Conversations

A What You'll See

In Part 3, you will see the directions, the questions, and the answer options on the page. Look at the sample questions below. Think about the types of information the questions are asking for. Is each answer related to an action? A time or date? A topic? Look at the answer options. What kinds of key words might you listen for to choose the answer for each one?

QUICK TIP

Read the questions and answer options before you hear the conversation. This will help you predict the context of the conversation and help you choose the correct answer option!

Part 3: Conversations

Directions: Listen to a conversation between two speakers. Then choose the correct answers to the three questions about that conversation. Fill in the letter (A), (B), (C), or (D). You will hear each conversation only once.

1. What problem are the speakers discussing?

(A) A missing document

(B) Some presentation errors

(C) A broken copier

(D) Rising printing costs

2. When is the speakers' meeting?

(A) This afternoon

(B) Tomorrow

(C) This Friday

(D) Next Monday

3. What will the speakers probably do next?

(A) Call a different technician

(B) Delay the presentation

(C) Pay for a new printer

(D) Go to a professional printer

B What You'll Hear

You will first hear a conversation and then three questions about it. Listen to the audio for the questions in Part A and read along in the script. Underline important information that may help you answer the questions. Circle and look up any words you don't know. 🎧 Track 3-01

SAMPLE SCRIPT ▶
(script not available in test)

Man: Has the copier at the reception desk been fixed yet?

Woman: No. I called the technician, but he can't make it out here until next Monday at the earliest.

Man: We have a meeting on Friday, though. We can't do our presentation unless everyone has copies of our work.

Woman: We'll have to get them done by a professional. I'll run to the copy shop tomorrow. It'll cost a little extra money, but we won't have to delay our presentation.

Glossary:

ℂ POWERED BY COBUILD

technician: a person whose job involves skilled practical work with scientific equipment

professional: a person or group producing work of a very high quality or level

C What You'll Do

In the test, you will listen to the audio and choose the best answer for each question. Listen to the recording again and answer the questions in Part A. Use the information you underlined in Part B if needed. 🎧 Track 3-01

GET IT RIGHT: Tips and Tasks for Answering Correctly

QUESTION TYPES

Topic / Main Idea Questions

Topic / main idea questions require you to look at the details and context of the conversation to find the main theme the speakers are talking about.

Possible topic / main idea questions:

» *What is the problem?*

» *What are the people talking about?*

» *What issue are the speakers discussing?*

» *What does the woman want the man to do?*

» **TIP 1 Pay attention to the beginning of the conversation.** Listen carefully to the information given early in the conversation. These requests or pieces of information often give clues to the main idea. You can then look for answer options that have the same information or requests that match the context of the conversation.

TASK Listen to the start of each conversation. Then choose the main idea of the exchange. 🎧 Track 3-02

1. What are the speakers talking about?

   (A) Checking into a hotel

   (B) Getting a new room key

   (C) Changing hotel rooms

   (D) Looking for lost identification

2. What is the woman teaching the man?

   (A) How to use the copier

   (B) Which printer to connect

   (C) Where the supply room is

   (D) What type of paper to use

3. What problem are the speakers discussing?

   (A) A delayed flight

   (B) An expensive limousine

   (C) A late driver

   (D) A car accident

» **TIP 2 Use vocabulary clues.** Speakers will not directly say the main idea. Instead, they will often use words associated with a specific context to talk about the situation or problem. You must use this information to decide what they are discussing. Listen for vocabulary clues like the ones in the chart to help you determine what the speakers are talking about. Use a dictionary to look up any words you don't know.

Possible Vocabulary Clues for Places, Activities, and Jobs	
warehouse	*shipment, forklift, inventory, stack, delivery, package, load, unload, invoice, drop off, stocker, supervisor, loader, driver*
office	*department, accounting, payroll, sales, budget, paycheck, raise, bonus, interview, hire, fire, let go, project, manager, co-worker, employee, boss, applicant, interviewer, CEO, accountant*
doctor's office	*examination, appointment, medicine, prescription, dose, pill, injury, pain, cold, sick, recover, check-up, doctor, nurse, patient*
laboratory	*lab, test results, microscope, test tubes, lab coat, sample, report, scientist, test subject*
airport	*check in, baggage, luggage, boarding pass, seat assignment, overhead bin, baggage claim, board, depart, pilot, ticket agent, passenger, flight attendant*
hotel	*front desk, room service, room key, room number, check in, check out, concierge, desk clerk, guest, visitor, tourist*
police station	*car accident, crime, victim, stolen, lost, arrest, crash, detain, cell, police officer*

(continued)

Possible Vocabulary Clues for Places, Activities, and Jobs	
taxi	*take me to, headed to, coming from, fare, tip, change, take the, meter, driver, passenger*
theater	*ticket, seats, sold out, refreshments, play, movie, opera, performance, actor, singer, attendant*
train station	*ticket, depart, arrive, catch, track number, destination, conductor*
retail store	*charge, total, pay, credit card, cash, sale, discount, clerk, customer, cashier, return*
bank	*account, checking account, savings account, debit card, credit card, withdraw, deposit, loan, mortgage, teller, account holder, ATM, fees*
post office	*letter, package, ship, send, mail, stamp, by air, overnight, mail carrier, postal worker*
restaurant	*menu, order, appetizer, beverage, party, reservation, dish, bill, check, table, waiter, server, host, hostess, chef*
real estate agency	*apartment, condo, home, lease, move in, move out, close on, deposit, landlord, renter, homeowner*

TASK Listen to the audio as you read along in the script. Circle vocabulary clues that may help you understand the place, job, or activity the people are talking about. Then answer the question. 🎧 Track 3-03

1. Man: Your total comes to ten fifty. Will you be paying with cash or credit?

Woman: Actually, I'd like to pay with a debit card, if I can.

Where are the people?

a. A store   **b.** A bank

2. Woman: Hello, sir. Welcome to the Broadwater Inn. Are you ready to check in?

Man: Uh, yes, but first I need to speak with the concierge about getting some tickets for tonight.

What is the woman's job?

a. Real estate agent   **b.** Front desk clerk

3. Man: You've reached the front desk. This is Paul speaking.

Woman: Yes, this is Ms. Aimes in Room 114. I need a menu for room service.

What is the woman's problem?

a. Her dinner is taking too long to arrive.   **b.** She does not have a room service menu.

Try a TOEIC Test Question

Listen to the audio as you read along in the script. As you listen, underline main information or requests that come early in the conversation. Circle vocabulary clues that might help you identify the main idea. Then answer the question. 🎧 Track 3-04

SAMPLE SCRIPT ▶
(script not available in test)

Man: Good afternoon. I've got a delivery for Shannon Meyers.

Woman: Oh, this is Ms. Meyers's office, but she's out on a business lunch with a client. Can you leave it with me?

Man: That's no problem. I'll need you to sign for it, just so we have proof that someone was here when it was dropped off.

Woman: Of course. If you'll put the box by that office, I'll get a pen.

What are the speakers discussing?

(A) A food delivery   (C) The missing signature

(B) A damaged shipment   (D) The arrival of a package

Detail Questions

Detail questions require you to listen carefully for key items in a conversation. You will need to answer questions about specific—not general—information. Anything discussed in a conversation can be the basis of a detail question, including time, reasons, plans, problems, suggestions, opinions, and other items.

Possible topics for detail questions:

» *Plans, problems, requests, or suggestions*
» *Causes and effects*

» *Times*
» *Identifying people and places*
» *Duration, frequency, or quantity*

Detail Questions About Plans, Problems, Requests, or Suggestions

These types of detail questions test your understanding of basic information that comes out in a conversation. They often ask for information about what a speaker will do in the future, an issue the speakers have, something the speakers want, or something the speakers want others to do.

Possible detail questions about . . .

plans:
» *What does the woman hope to do?*
» *What will the man do tomorrow?*
» *What are the speakers going to do next?*

problems:
» *What is the man's problem?*
» *What are the people looking for?*
» *What won't the woman be able to do?*

requests:
» *What does the woman ask the man to do?*
» *What is the man asking the company to change?*

suggestions:
» *What does the man suggest the woman do?*
» *What does the woman suggest as a solution?*

» **TIP 1 Learn to recognize common expressions and paraphrases for plans, problems, requests, or suggestions.** The correct answers for detail questions will usually be phrased in a different way from the conversation. This is called *paraphrasing*. Listen for common expressions like the ones below. This will help you recognize key information for suggestions, requests, problems, and plans. You can then more easily identify which answer options paraphrase the key related points.

Common Expressions for Requests and Suggestions	
Requests	**Suggestions**
Would you please . . . ?	*Why don't you . . . ?*
Do you think you can . . . ?	*Maybe we can . . .*
Would it be possible for you to . . . ?	*I bet we could . . .*
Can you get . . . ?	*It might work if . . .*
Common Expressions for Problems and Plans	
Problems	**Plans**
The X is broken again.	*I need to . . .*
We don't have enough X to . . .	*I'll just . . .*
We're not going to be able to . . .	*The first thing we should do is . . .*
I can't find my . . .	*I'm going to . . .*

TASK Read a sentence from a conversation. Then read the question and choose the answer that correctly paraphrases the sentence.

1. Woman: Maybe you can borrow a notepad from the secretary.

What does the man suggest the woman should do?

a. Use another person's office supplies.　　b. Write down the instructions.

2. Man: I can't find my car keys anywhere.

What problem does the man have?

a. The man has lost his keys.　　b. The man needs a ride.

3. Man: Can you get that budget done by this Wednesday instead of this Friday?

What is the man requesting?

a. That they complete the financial plans early.　　b. That they start work on a different project.

» **TIP 2 Watch for the correct speaker in the answer options.** Incorrect answer options may include correct information from the conversation but will apply it to the wrong speaker. Determining whether the question is about the man or the woman will help you identify the correct answer.

TASK Listen to the speakers. Check (✓) the correct column to identify which speaker mentions each detail. 🎧 Track 3-05

1.

Detail	Man	Woman
The bank		
The downtown train station		
Being new to the area		
The time it takes to get to the station		

2.

Detail	Man	Woman
Old accounts		
A new file cabinet		
Leaving files on a desk		
Checking for orders		

QUICK TIP

For questions that ask what the speaker will do next, listen carefully to the last part of the conversation to find the answer.

Try a TOEIC Test Question

Listen to the audio as you read along in the script. Then look at the question and answer options. Underline one answer option that paraphrases content from the script. Draw a line through one answer option that applies information to the wrong speaker. Then answer the question. 🎧 Track 3-06

SAMPLE SCRIPT ▶
(script not available in test)

Woman: Hi, I just saw a movie here. But when I got to my car, I realized I didn't have my keys.

Man: I'm sorry. Do you think they fell out during the movie?

Woman: Maybe. But I also bought candy. So they could have fallen out when I pulled my wallet out of my purse.

Man: OK. If you still have your ticket, I can let you in to search the theater. I'll check at the refreshment stand.

What problem does the woman have?

(A) She lost her wallet.　　(C) She misplaced her keys.

(B) She needs a ticket.　　(D) She can't find her car.

Detail Questions About Causes and Effects

Questions about causes and effects require you to identify why something happened or how an event changed a situation. These questions test your understanding of why a speaker is addressing the other person, why a change occurred, or why a request was made.

Possible cause and effect questions:

» *Why does the man ask to leave the office?* » *Why is the woman going to Chicago?*

» *Why was it necessary to increase the budget?*

QUICK TIP

You will have a few
seconds between
each test conversation
Take this time to look
at the questions and
answer options before
the listening and think
about the information
you need.

» **TIP 1 Look for infinitives (*to* + verb) when pre-reading to recognize cause and effect questions.**
As you pre-read the questions, look in the answer options for *to* + verb (e.g., *to leave, to increase*). This may signal that the question is asking for the reason someone did something. When you see *to* + verb, be sure to listen carefully for reasons and explanations.

TASK Listen to each exchange. Then fill in the blank with the correct form of a word from the box to make a correct response. There are two extra words. 🎧 Track 3-07

| call | cut | complete | start | visit | withdraw |

1. Why did the woman miss the conference?

She had _____ her mother.

2. Why was the purchase request denied?

They were forced _____ the budget.

3. Why is the woman in the office on a weekend?

She needs _____ a project.

4. Why was the woman charged ten dollars?

She used her credit card _____ money from an ATM.

» **TIP 2 Listen for words and expressions about causes and effects.** Some words and phrases introduce the effects of an action. Others introduce the causes of something. Listen carefully for expressions like the bold ones below to find the answers to cause and effect questions.

Examples of Cause and Effect Expressions	
As a result of (a cause), *we need to* (an effect).	***In order to*** (an effect), *we're going to* (a cause).
Because (a cause), *we will* (an effect).	***Since*** (a cause) *happened, we have to* (an effect).
For this reason, (an effect) *will happen.*	(A cause) *isn't going well,* ***so*** *we have to* (an effect).

TASK Listen as you read each conversation. Circle the expressions for causes and underline the expressions for effects. Then answer the question. 🎧 Track 3-08

1. Man: Carol, why aren't the June sales figures on my desk? I asked for them yesterday.

   Woman: I'm sorry, Mr. James. I still haven't been able to print them, since the printer is broken.

   Why didn't the man receive the sales figures? _____

2. Woman: It's hot in here. Why don't we turn on the air conditioning?

   Man: We've been asked to open windows instead because the electricity bill was too high.

   Why don't the speakers turn on the air conditioning? _____

Try a TOEIC Test Question

Pre-read the question and circle the infinitives in the answer options. Notice the verbs that follow *to*. Then listen to the audio as you read along in the script. As you listen, underline signal words for a cause or an effect. Then answer the question. 🎧 Track 3-09

SAMPLE SCRIPT ▶

(script not available in test)

Woman: Mr. Anderson, is it OK if I get out of the office a little earlier than usual?

Man: Well, I'm expecting a few important phone calls. And the documents for the Howard presentation aren't prepared. Is it an emergency?

Woman: No, it's not like that. I just have to go to my optometrist because my glasses need to be adjusted.

Man: I see. I guess it's all right. But make sure those documents are prepared tomorrow morning. I don't want us making copies just before Mr. Howard arrives.

Why does the woman ask to leave?

(A) To visit an eye doctor

(B) To place a phone call

(C) To make copies

(D) To pick up a client

Detail Questions About Duration, Frequency, or Quantity

These types of questions ask you to find key details about how long something lasts (duration), how often something happens (frequency), or the amount of something (quantity). These questions usually require that you listen carefully for numbers, times, or details relating to days or dates.

QUICK TIP

Read the answer options for cause and effect questions carefully. The correct choices are often significantly paraphrased. For example, a speaker might say: *We hired a new accountant to fix our payroll problem.* If the question asks: *Why was the accountant hired?*, the correct answer could be paraphrased as: *To address a financial problem.*

Possible duration, frequency, or quantity questions:

» *How long will the woman be in China?*

» *How many times should the woman call the client?*

» *How often should the woman take her medicine?*

» *How much of a discount will the man receive?*

» **TIP 1 Learn to identify conversation distracters about duration, frequency, or quantity.** The incorrect answer options for duration, frequency, or quantity questions can be difficult to determine. For example, if the speakers discuss the length of a store sale, you will likely hear several different time, day, or number references. Notice the bold distracters (irrelevant information) in the sample statement.

*The sale was supposed to go for the **first three weeks** of **August**. <u>However</u>, sales in the **first week** of **the month** were stronger than we expected, and we reached our goal in just **seven days**. So we decided to end it after just **two weeks**.*

To help identify the correct answer, listen for transition words like the underlined word above. Transition words often signal a complete change in what a speaker is talking about or planning, so pay careful attention to the information that follows these words. This will help you identify the key point of the exchange.

Important Transition Words			
however	instead	unfortunately	therefore
nevertheless	of course	conversely	as a result
still	but	consequently	for that reason

TASK Listen to each conversation and choose the correct answer. Be sure to watch out for conversation distracters! 🎧 Track 3-10

1. How much of a discount will the man receive after eight months?

(A) Ten percent　　　　　　　　(B) Five percent

2. How long is the man's trip?

(A) One week　　　　　　　　(B) Two weeks

3. How often should the woman take her medicine?

(A) Once every four hours　　　　(B) Once every six hours

» **TIP 2 Learn to identify paraphrases for questions about duration, frequency, or quantity.**
Paraphrases of duration, frequency, or quantity can be very tricky because they make the words in the answer options different from the words in the conversation. Look at the examples in the chart.

Typical Paraphrases for Duration, Frequency, or Quantity Questions		
What You Might Hear	**What the Question Might Ask**	**What the Correct Answer Option Might Show**
We hold the meeting every other Friday.	*How often is the meeting held?*	*Once every two weeks*
We're up to a dozen employees.	*How many people are in the company?*	*Twelve*
I'm going for a week.	*How long is the man's vacation?*	*Seven days*

TASK Read the phrases used to indicate duration, frequency, or quantity. Match each phrase to the correct paraphrase.

1. _____ once a year　　　　　　**a.** seven days
2. _____ every other day　　　　**b.** Monday, Wednesday, and Friday
3. _____ fifty percent　　　　　**c.** annually
4. _____ weeklong　　　　　　**d.** half
5. _____ twenty-five percent　　**e.** a quarter

Try a TOEIC Test Question

Listen to the audio as you read along in the script. As you listen, circle the transition words in the script. Then answer the question. Review the answer options and underline the part of the script that the correct answer paraphrases. 🎧 Track 3-11

SAMPLE SCRIPT ▶
(script not available in test)

Woman: Michael, are you going to Carl's retirement party? It's on Friday the tenth, two weeks from now.

Man: I wish I could. But I'm meeting new clients in Mexico the day after. I'll be getting ready for that trip.

Woman: Oh, too bad. It would be great if you could come, even if you only stayed for an hour or two.

Man: I wanted to do that. Unfortunately, because it's a weeklong trip, I'll need time to pack. I've been working on this account for a month, and I want everything to go perfectly.

How long will the man stay in Mexico?

(A) A few hours　　　　　　　(C) Two weeks

(B) Seven days　　　　　　　(D) One month

Detail Questions About Time

Questions about time require you to recall when a certain event occurred in the past or when it will occur in the future. The answer options can include specific times of day, as well as longer time periods, such as hours, days, weeks, or months.

Possible time questions:

» *When will the speakers meet?*
» *When did the man visit the office?*

» *When is the woman's meeting?*
» *What time is the man's appointment?*

» **TIP 1 Eliminate answer options that do not relate to the question.** Pre-read the questions to determine what event they are asking about. This is important because the conversation may include times for other events. When you know which event the questions are about, you can eliminate unrelated times.

TASK Read each question and circle the event that the question is asking about. Then listen to the audio as you read along in the script. Cross out the times in the script that do not relate to the subject of the question. Then answer the question. 🎧 Track 3-12

1. What time will the meeting occur?

   (A) 4:00
   (B) 5:00
   (C) 6:00
   (D) 6:30

> **Man:** So is the meeting for 6:00 still on?
>
> **Woman:** No. Mary has dinner plans at 6:30. And Tim has an appointment with his doctor at 5:00.
>
> **Man:** OK. Can everyone make it if we have it earlier?
>
> **Woman:** Yes. We moved it to 4:00.

2. When will the speakers meet?

   (A) Today
   (B) Monday
   (C) Wednesday
   (D) Friday

> **Woman:** Michael, I'm so sorry, but I'll have to cancel our meeting today.
>
> **Man:** Oh, that's no problem. Should we reschedule for tomorrow?
>
> **Woman:** Actually, I think next Wednesday is best. We just had a major deadline moved up to this Friday.
>
> **Man:** I understand. I'll call you on Monday to set up a time.

» **TIP 2 Learn to understand paraphrases for questions about time.** Paraphrases of time can be very tricky because they make the words in the answer options quite different from the words in the conversation. Look at the examples in the chart on page 53.

Typical Paraphrases for Time Questions		
What You Might Hear	**What the Question Might Ask**	**What the Correct Answer Option Might Show**
I'll arrive at the airport at noon.	*When will the man arrive?*	*12:00 p.m.*
I'll finish the report next Monday.	*When will the woman complete the report?*	*Next week*
Let's meet at a quarter to one.	*When will the speakers meet?*	*12:45*
I called her at half past eight.	*What time did the man call?*	*8:30*

TASK Read the time phrases. Match each phrase to the correct paraphrase.

1. _____ noon
2. _____ half past one
3. _____ a quarter to two
4. _____ the following Monday
5. _____ the Friday before

a. 1:45
b. last week
c. next week
d. 1:30
e. 12:00

Try a TOEIC Test Question

Pre-read the question to find out what event it is asking about. Then listen to the audio as you read along in the script. As you listen, cross out times given as distracters in the script. Then answer the question. 🎧 Track 3-13

SAMPLE SCRIPT ▶
(script not available in test)

Man: Grace, has that shipment of lab equipment arrived? It was supposed to arrive this afternoon.

Woman: No, I'm sorry. The manufacturer called this morning and said there was a delay. Didn't you get my e-mail about it?

Man: I must have missed it. So when will it arrive? I need those tests completed by Friday.

Woman: The clerk I spoke with said it was coming tomorrow.

When will the shipment arrive?

(A) This morning

(B) This afternoon

(C) The next day

(D) By Friday

Detail Questions About Identifying People or Places

Questions about identifying people require you to figure out several things. You must sometimes find out which person or group will do a task, caused an event, or is talked about in a conversation. The correct answer can be one of the speakers, or it can be another person or group the speakers talk about. This question type usually begins with *Who*.

Questions about places require you to identify what location a speaker is going to or came from. These questions may also be about the location where an event occurred or will occur in the future. This question type usually begins with *Where*.

Possible questions about identifying people or places:

» *Who will call the supplier?*
» *Where will the party be held?*

» *Who suggested the budget change?*
» *Where did the man lose his phone?*

QUICK TIP

If you know what event
or action is being asked
about, it is easier to
listen for it and identify
related information.

» **TIP 1 Identify the event or action in the question during pre-reading.** After you have done this, listen for information about that event or action in the conversation. You will usually hear the person or group associated with the event or action just before or after it is mentioned. This will help you identify the people involved.

TASK Circle the action as you pre-read each question. Then choose the statement that gives the correct associated information. Remember! Look for words with the same or similar meaning.

1. Who will contact the woman?

   a. Mr. Peters, you need to call Ms. North about the contract right now.

   b. Ms. North will replace Mr. Peters.

   c. Mr. Peters will help Ms. North with the contract.

2. Who wants to speak to the manager?

   a. John, do you know where the manager is?

   b. I'd like to have a word with your manager.

   c. Is this the manager's office?

3. Who will increase the budget?

   a. The COO hasn't approved the budget yet.

   b. The Accounting Department is reviewing the budget.

   c. The Board of Directors agreed to raise the budget.

» **TIP 2 Learn to identify conversational distracters about other people or groups.** Conversations in this part of the test often include several names or group references. This can be confusing when you are trying to identify who did something.

TASK 1 Pre-read the question below. Next, read the sample script. Notice the bold distracters. Then answer the question.

QUICK TIP

Listen carefully to see
if the "who" that the
question asks about is
one of the speakers or
a different person. This
will help you reduce
the number of possible
answers.

Who will receive the finished budget report?

(A) The man

(B) The woman

(C) Susan

(D) Carlos

> **Woman: Susan** will be out today, so I need you to fill in for her. Talk to **Carlos, her supervisor,** to find out where her files are. Then find her copy of the budget report, finish it, and bring it to me by the end of the day.

TASK 2 Pre-read the questions. Then listen to the audio as you read along in the script. Cross out any distracters and circle the correct answers in the script. Then answer the questions. 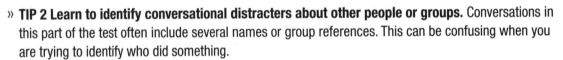 Track 3-14

1. a. Who will meet with a realtor? _____

   b. Who will cancel the conference call? _____

> **Woman:** I have a meeting with my realtor at noon, so I don't think I'll be able to make that conference call with Mr. Jackson at 12:30. I need to cancel it.
>
> **Man:** Yes, Ms. Adams. I'll take care of that for you.

2. a. Who will pick up the pamphlets? _____

   b. Who will work on the presentation? _____

> **Man:** The printer just called, and our pamphlets are ready for pickup. Should I go get them?
> **Woman:** I wouldn't do that. Just send Robert. I need you to work on the presentation for Ms. Anderson.

» **TIP 3 For questions about places using *Where*, carefully pre-read to recognize what the question relates to.** This can help you decide which person or thing the question is asking about. Notice how similar the two questions with *Where* are below. In this case, being certain about the person or thing to listen for will help you identify the correct answer.

Person: *Where is the **woman** going?*

Thing: *Where is the **meeting** going to take place?*

TASK Pre-read each question and circle the person or thing it asks about. Then listen to the exchange as you read along. Underline information about the person or thing in the question. Answer the question.

🎧 Track 3-15

1. Where is the man going?

   a. The bank   **b.** A meeting

> **Woman:** Hi, John, it's Carol Murphy. Can we set up a meeting for later today?
>
> **Man:** Actually, I'm on my way to the bank right now. Can I call you back?

2. Where will the package be delivered?

   a. The manager's office   **b.** The receptionist's desk

> **Man:** Excuse me. I have a delivery for Martin Allen. Do you know where his office is?
>
> **Woman:** Oh, he's the manager. It's upstairs, but I forget the number. Just ask Mary at the receptionist's desk, and she'll let you know.

» **TIP 4 Learn to identify conversational distracters about other places.** Conversations in Part 3 often include several locations. Try to quickly identify where someone is going or where something happened.

TASK 1 Look at the question and script below and notice the bolded distracters. Then answer the question.

Where is the package?

   (A) The Shipping Department

   (B) The office

   (C) The factory

   (D) The warehouse

> **Man:** Where's that package we've been expecting?
>
> **Woman:** Tom in the Shipping Department told me that the package won't get to our **office** on time. I guess **the factory** was running behind schedule. So all deliveries, including ours, are stuck in their warehouse.

TASK 2 Read the question and circle the person or thing it is asking about. Then listen to the conversation and check (✓) the correct answer. Listen again and match the location details to the correct cities. 🎧 Track 3-16

Where is the woman's family?

☐ New York: _____   **a.** the location of the speakers

☐ Boston: _____   **b.** the new location of the meeting

☐ Chicago: _____   **c.** the location of the woman's family

☐ Los Angeles: _____   **d.** the original location of the meeting

Try a TOEIC Test Question

Pre-read the question and circle the name of the person it is asking about. Then listen to the audio as you read along in the script. As you listen, underline any locations you hear. Then answer the question. After you have found the correct answer, cross out the distracter locations in the script. 🎧 Track 3-17

SAMPLE SCRIPT ▶
(script not available in test)

Woman: You've reached the office of Harold Crane. How can I help you?

Man: Hi, Joe Hewett speaking. I'm down in the warehouse, and I have to check with Mr. Crane on an order.

Woman: He's actually on his way to corporate headquarters downtown. Can I take a message?

Man: Sure. We've got a delivery for State Hospital. But it doesn't say which department to send it to.

Where is Mr. Crane going?

(A) To his office

(B) To the warehouse

(C) To the city

(D) To the hospital

Inference Questions

Inference questions require you to gather clues in order to make a conclusion about something. One type of inference question asks you to make inferences about who a person is. A second type asks you to make inferences about where someone is. Some inference questions ask how a person might feel. Remember! The correct answer to an inference question is NOT stated directly. You must decide what the answer is based indirectly on information in the conversation.

QUICK TIP

> In many cases, inference questions include the words *most likely* or *probably*.

Possible inference questions:

» *Who most likely is the man?*

» *Who are the speakers?*

» *Where most likely are the speakers?*

» *Where does this conversation probably take place?*

» **TIP 1 Pay attention to details given about location or speakers.** A place or an occupation may not be stated directly in the conversation, but the speakers will give clues. These clues are found throughout the conversation and are phrases or requests that are common in certain locations or occupations. Listen for these clues to determine where or who the speakers are. Review the chart on pages 45 and 46 for place and occupation words.

TASK Listen to each exchange as you read along. Circle key words in the script that give clues where the conversation takes place or who the speakers are. Then answer the question. 🎧 Track 3-18

1. Man: Are you ready to order, ma'am?

Woman: I'll need another few minutes with the menu, thanks.

Man: Of course. Can I get you something to drink in the meantime?

Woman: Yes, a glass of water, please.

Where are the speakers? _____

2. Woman: OK, here's your room key. You'll be staying in Room 117. It's just past the pool and vending machines.

Man: Great, thanks. Is the kitchen still open? I'm starving.

Woman: It is. Room service is available until 10:00. You can charge it to your room or pay with a credit card.

Man: I'll just put it on the bill for the room, thanks.

Where are the speakers? _____

» **TIP 2 Pre-read questions and answer options to predict key words to listen for.** When you pre-read the question and answer options, think about the kinds of words that you might associate with each answer option. Then listen for those key words in the conversation. For more information about common place and occupation words, go to the chart on pages 45 and 46.

TASK Read the question and answer options. Then write two potential key words from the box next to each answer option. There are two extra words.

copy machine	doctor	firefighter	flight	mail
package	patient	salad	secretary	ticket

Where most likely are the speakers?

Answer Options	Potential Key Words
A post office	
A hospital	
An office	
An airport	

Try a TOEIC Test Question

Read the question and answer options, and think about key words that might guide you to the correct answer. Then listen to the audio as you read along in the script. As you listen, underline the key words that can help you answer the question. Circle key details about location or speaker. Answer the question. 🎧 Track 3-19

SAMPLE SCRIPT ▶
(script not available in test)

Woman: Hello, I'm here to see Principal Henderson.

Man: Do you have an appointment?

Woman: Yes, I'm Amy Reynolds. I'm her 3:00 interview for the chemistry teacher position.

Man: OK. Please take a seat. Ms. Henderson is meeting with the library staff. She'll be out shortly.

Where does the conversation take place?

(A) In a school

(B) In a factory

(C) In a library

(D) In a doctor's office

QUICK TIP

Expanding your vocabulary will help you identify key words for locations and people. Study the chart on pages 45 and 46. Add words to the chart and create your own charts with different categories of words. You can also look for lists of similar words on the Internet.

PROGRESSIVE PRACTICE: Get Ready

Practice Set 1

A Pre-read the questions and answer options below. Think about what type of information you should listen for to answer each question. Circle the correct information type from the options given. Then listen to the conversation and mark the correct answers. 🎧 Track 3-20

1. What are the speakers talking about?　　**Information Type:** Place　　Topic

   (A) Canceling an appointment

   (B) Negotiating a bill

   (C) Leaving a hospital

   (D) Scheduling a meeting

2. Who most likely is the woman?　　**Information Type:** Occupation　　Location

   (A) A doctor

   (B) A patient

   (C) A secretary

   (D) A new client

3. When is the man's meeting with the clients?　　**Information Type:** Reason　　Time

   (A) This morning

   (B) At noon

   (C) In twenty-four hours

   (D) Later this week

B Now check your answers. Read the explanations in the *Answer Analysis* boxes and look at the answer options. Note why each answer option is correct or incorrect. This will help you learn to identify incorrect answer options.

1. What are the speakers talking about?

   (A) Canceling an appointment

   (B) Negotiating a bill

   (C) Leaving a hospital

   (D) Scheduling a meeting

ANSWER ANALYSIS ▶ 　*Information Type: Topic*

　　✓ **(A) The man calls and states that he cannot make it to a morning appointment.**

　　✗ (B) The woman says there will be a cancellation fee but does not discuss the bill. The man does not negotiate.

　　✗ (C) The man states that he will be unable to leave work, not a hospital.

　　✗ (D) The man states that he has a meeting today and mentions calling later to discuss rescheduling.

---

2. Who most likely is the woman?

   (A) A doctor

   (B) A patient

   (C) A secretary

   (D) A new client

ANSWER ANALYSIS ▶ *Information Type:* **Occupation**

   ✗ (A) The doctor is mentioned but is not one of the speakers. The woman works for Healthcare Associates but is probably not a doctor.

   ✗ (B) The woman answers the phone as an employee, so she cannot be one of the doctor's patients.

   ✓ **(C) The woman answers the phone and talks about appointments, fees, and policies, all of which are duties of a secretary.**

   ✗ (D) The man mentions that he must meet with new clients, but the woman is not one of them.

3. When is the man's meeting with the clients?

   (A) This morning

   (B) At noon

   (C) In twenty-four hours

   (D) Later this week

ANSWER ANALYSIS ▶ *Information Type:* **Time**

   ✗ (A) The man states that his appointment with the doctor, not his meeting with the clients, is in the morning.

   ✓ **(B) The man says that he is meeting new clients at 12:00, which can be paraphrased as "noon."**

   ✗ (C) The woman says there is a fee if appointments are canceled with fewer than twenty-four hours' notice, not that a meeting will occur.

   ✗ (D) The man says he will call back later this week to talk about rescheduling.

Practice Set 2

A Pre-read the questions and answer options below. Think about what type of information you should listen for to answer each question. Circle the correct information type from the options given. Then listen to the conversation and mark the correct answers. 🎧 Track 3-21

1. Where most likely are the speakers?　　　**Information Type:**　Person　　　　Place

   (A) An optometrist's office

   (B) A print shop

   (C) A pharmacy

   (D) A repair shop

2. How often should the man come in?　　　**Information Type:**　Frequency　　　Topic

   (A) Every other day

   (B) Once a month

   (C) Every year

   (D) Every two years

3. What did the man have trouble with?　　　**Information Type:**　Location　　　Problem

   (A) Reading a document

   (B) Finding the office

   (C) Fixing his computer

   (D) Completing the chart

B Now check your answers. Read the explanations in the Answer Analysis boxes and look at the answer options. Note why each answer option is correct or incorrect. This will help you learn to identify incorrect answers.

1. Where most likely are the speakers?

(A) An optometrist's office

(B) A print shop

(C) A pharmacy

(D) A repair shop

> ANSWER ANALYSIS ▶ *Information Type:* **Place**
>
> ✓ **(A) The woman is a doctor, and the man describes glasses and vision problems. An optometrist is an eye doctor.**
>
> ✗ (B) The man discusses small print, but neither speaker talks about printing.
>
> ✗ (C) The man refers to his prescription, but it is for glasses, not medication.
>
> ✗ (D) The man says he is having trouble reading print on his computer, but that is due to his vision, not a screen problem.

2. How often should the man come in?

(A) Every other day

(B) Once a month

(C) Every year

(D) Every two years

> ANSWER ANALYSIS ▶ *Information Type:* **Frequency**
>
> ✗ (A) The man talks about "day-to-day" tasks, but it's not in reference to his appointments.
>
> ✗ (B) The man noticed the problem about a month ago, so this is not relative to the question.
>
> ✓ **(C) The woman recommends coming in annually, which is the same as every year.**
>
> ✗ (D) The man says he has not been in to see Dr. Grant for two years, it's not that he should come every two years.

3. What did the man have trouble with?

(A) Reading a document

(B) Finding the office

(C) Fixing his computer

(D) Completing the chart

> ANSWER ANALYSIS ▶ *Information Type:* **Problem**
>
> ✓ **(A) The man states that he had trouble reading a report he typed at home.**
>
> ✗ (B) The woman states that the man has not been in for a long time. She doesn't say that he couldn't find the office.
>
> ✗ (C) The man had trouble reading the print on the screen but not because of a computer problem.
>
> ✗ (D) The woman mentions the man's chart, but there is no mention of completing anything.

PROGRESSIVE PRACTICE: Get Set

Practice Set 1

A Pre-read the questions and answer options below. Think about the type of information needed to answer each question. Then listen to the conversation and mark the correct answers. 🎧 Track 3-22

1. Where most likely are the speakers?

(A) On a boat

(B) In a post office

(C) In an airplane

(D) At a birthday party

3. Why does the man ask for the box?

(A) To check it for damages

(B) To mark the delivery method

(C) To attach the correct postage

(D) To see how much it weighs

2. How long will it take for the gift to arrive by express delivery?

(A) Two days

(B) Four days

(C) Seven days

(D) More than a week

B Now check your answers. Look at the conversation in the scripts at the back of this book. Then look at the explanations in the *Answer Analysis* box. Write the letter of each answer option from Part A next to the reason why it is correct or incorrect. This will help you learn to identify incorrect answer options.

1.

ANSWER ANALYSIS ▶

_____ ✗ The man mentions items traveling by air, but this isn't enough information to infer that they are flying.

_____ ✗ The woman talks about her friend's birthday, but she and the man are not at a party during the conversation.

_____ ✓ **The woman and man talk about mail and postage, which leads to the inference that they are in a post office.**

_____ ✗ The woman mentions sending a gift overseas, but this isn't enough information to infer that the speakers are on a boat.

2.

ANSWER ANALYSIS ▶

_____ ✓ **The man says express delivery takes two days, and the woman selects express delivery.**

_____ ✗ The man says standard delivery takes more than a week, but the woman does not select that option.

_____ ✗ The man says priority delivery takes four days, but the woman does not select that option.

_____ ✗ The woman says her friend's birthday is in a week, but no delivery method mentioned takes seven days.

3.

ANSWER ANALYSIS ▶

_____ ✗ The man says he will determine the postage but never talks about putting it on the box.

_____ ✗ Neither of the speakers mentions the box being harmed in any way.

_____ ✗ The man discusses delivery methods, but he never talks about writing on the box in any way.

_____ ✓ **The man says that in order to determine the correct postage, he must find out how much the box weighs.**

Practice Set 2

A Pre-read the questions and answers below. Think about the types of information needed to answer each question. Then listen to the conversation and mark the correct answers. 🎧 Track 3-23

1. What is the woman concerned about?

(A) Replacing lost medicine

(B) Getting sick on a trip

(C) Refilling a prescription

(D) Correcting a prescription error

2. Where is the woman going next week?

(A) To her doctor's office

(B) On a family vacation

(C) To the pharmacy

(D) On a business trip

3. Who will the man talk to?

(A) A doctor

(B) A secretary

(C) A pharmacist

(D) A business partner

B Now check your answers. Look at the conversation in the scripts at the back of this book. Then look at the explanations in the *Answer Analysis* box. Write the letter of each answer option from Part A next to the reason why it is correct or incorrect. This will help you learn to identify incorrect answer options.

1.

ANSWER ANALYSIS ▶

_____ ✗ The man says a secretary made an error, but the error did not involve the prescription, nor does the woman bring up any error.

_____ ✗ The woman does talk about taking a trip in the future. However, she doesn't mention feeling or becoming ill.

_____ ✓ **The woman says she wants to refill her prescription early because she won't be able to refill it next week.**

_____ ✗ The woman wants to refill a prescription but not because her medicine was misplaced.

2.

ANSWER ANALYSIS ▶

_____ ✓ **The woman says that she will be taking a trip with her children the following week.**

_____ ✗ The woman states that she was directed to a pharmacy by a secretary, but she is already there and makes no statements about returning.

_____ ✗ The woman does mention that she is taking a trip, although she says it will be with her children. She talks about business only when talking about a phone call.

_____ ✗ The woman talks about her doctor's office but never states at any point that she is going there.

3.

ANSWER ANALYSIS ▶

_____ ✗ The woman explains that she was told by this person that she could fill her prescription early, but the man says this was incorrect. He does not say he will contact her.

_____ ✗ The woman, not the man, talks about making a business phone call.

_____ ✗ The man is a pharmacist and cannot change prescriptions. Otherwise, he would have done so himself.

_____ ✓ **The man says that only the primary physician can change the prescription, so that is the person he must call.**

Practice Set 3

A Pre-read the questions and answer options below. Think about the types of information needed to answer each question. Then listen to the conversation and mark the correct answers. 🎧 Track 3-24

1. What are the speakers discussing?

(A) A late assignment

(B) A weekend meeting

(C) A budget increase

(D) A missed e-mail

3. Who was supposed to complete the report?

(A) The man

(B) The woman

(C) Mr. Jenson

(D) The CEO

2. How did the woman deliver her message?

(A) She sent an e-mail.

(B) She called his phone.

(C) She left him a note.

(D) She mailed him a report.

B Now check your answers. Look at the conversation in the scripts at the back of this book. Then look at the explanations in the *Answer Analysis* box. Write the letter of each answer option from Part A next to the reason why it is correct or incorrect. This will help you learn to identify incorrect answer options.

1.

ANSWER ANALYSIS ▶

_____ ✓ **The woman asks why the budget proposal was not turned in on time.**

_____ ✗ The man missed a voicemail message, not an e-mail.

_____ ✗ The CEO has a meeting during the week, and the man talks about the weekend, but no weekend meetings are mentioned.

_____ ✗ The woman talks about a budget proposal, but there is no discussion of increasing a budget.

2.

ANSWER ANALYSIS ▶

_____ ✗ The woman mentions voicemail and a proposal but never a report or mail.

_____ ✗ The woman mentions a voicemail, not an e-mail.

_____ ✗ The woman left a message, but it was not written.

_____ ✓ **The woman says she left a message on the man's voicemail, which is only on a phone.**

3.

ANSWER ANALYSIS ▶

_____ ✗ The woman checks why the proposal was not completed and knows what the deadline was, but she told the man to do it.

_____ ✓ **The woman asks the man why he did not complete the proposal, which shows that he was responsible.**

_____ ✗ The CEO is mentioned only in connection to a meeting with Mr. Jenson, never in connection with the proposal.

_____ ✗ Mr. Jenson is the person who was supposed to receive the proposal, not complete it.

PROGRESSIVE PRACTICE: Go for the TOEIC® Test

Directions: Listen to a conversation between two speakers. Then choose the correct answers to the three questions about that conversation. Fill in the letter (A), (B), (C), or (D). You will hear each conversation only once. 🎧 Track 3-25

1. Where does the conversation take place?

(A) In a hotel

(B) In a restaurant

(C) In an airport

(D) In an office

2. What does the man want?

(A) A new printer

(B) A boarding pass

(C) Some identification

(D) Another room key

3. What will the man likely do next?

(A) Get on a plane

(B) Pay his bill

(C) Ask for directions

(D) Show his identification

4. What are the speakers discussing?

(A) Treating an illness

(B) Taking a vacation

(C) Completing a co-worker's assignments

(D) Hiring an assistant for the office

5. What does the woman offer to do?

(A) Cancel a meeting

(B) Assist the man

(C) Replace broken equipment

(D) Find new clients

6. When is the man's meeting?

(A) Tomorrow

(B) Wednesday

(C) Next Monday

(D) Later next week

7. Who most likely is Jim Carter?

(A) A secretary

(B) A real estate agent

(C) A doctor

(D) A salesman

8. When does Mr. Carter's meeting end?

(A) At 10:00

(B) At 10:15

(C) At 10:30

(D) At 11:00

9. What does the woman ask the man to do?

(A) Give a message to his boss

(B) Cancel a meeting that morning

(C) Schedule an appointment with a doctor

(D) Call her back in ten minutes

10. What are the speakers talking about?

(A) Next year's budget

(B) A job interview

(C) A new employee

(D) An accounting error

11. Why did the funding change?

(A) The company lost money.

(B) Fewer equipment purchases were approved.

(C) The retail department is expanding.

(D) Several clients were added.

12. What will the man likely do next?

(A) Visit the Accounting Department

(B) Check on a client

(C) Interview applicants

(D) Look at computer prices

13. What problem do the speakers discuss?

(A) A missed delivery

(B) A price increase

(C) A drop in sales

(D) A rescheduled meeting

14. What does the man want to do?

(A) Find a new supplier

(B) Reduce purchases by 10 percent

(C) Compare sales teams' numbers

(D) Raise the company's rates

15. What will the woman probably do next?

(A) Increase their rates

(B) Meet with the sales team

(C) Contact a different supplier

(D) Order more paper

16. Where are the speakers?

(A) In a restaurant

(B) At a train station

(C) In a hotel

(D) On a street corner

17. Why does the woman ask for advice?

(A) To get directions

(B) To choose transportation

(C) To get food recommendations

(D) To select the right train

18. How will the woman get to the convention center?

(A) On foot

(B) By car

(C) By taxi

(D) By train

TOEIC® Test Part 4: Talks

Part 4 of the TOEIC Listening test is very similar to Part 3. The main difference is that Part 4 features ten talks by a single speaker instead of conversations between two or more speakers. Each talk is followed by three questions that you will look at on the page as you listen. The talks are quite short and often last less than a minute each.

Topics for talks in Part 4 may include:

» *Weather and news reports*

» *Airport and train station announcements*

» *Voicemail messages*

» *Advertisements*

» *Office schedule listings*

» *Store sale announcements*

» *Speeches about business advice*

QUICK GUIDE: Talks

Definition	Part 4 is a test of your listening comprehension. It requires skills similar to those used in Part 3. You will listen to short talks by a single speaker, answer questions about central ideas and basic details, and draw conclusions based on the information you hear.
Targeted Skills	In order to correctly answer Part 4 questions, you must be able to: • understand the topic / main idea of a talk. • identify key facts from a talk. • make conclusions about a talk based on details. • understand paraphrased language in answer options. • pre-read questions to predict important information.
Question Types	• **Topic / Main Idea:** *Who is this talk for?* • **Detail:** *What time does the train leave?* • **Inference:** *What can be inferred from the talk?*
Answer Options	• **Topic / Main Idea Questions:** locations, occupations, audience, topics, etc. • **Detail Questions:** suggestions, instructions, times, quantities, etc. • **Inference Questions:** audience, contexts, feelings, meanings, etc.
Things to Watch For	• **Talk Distracters:** Answer options may repeat words or use words that sound similar to words used in the talk. Be careful! These types of words are often used to distract you from the correct answer option. • **Vocabulary Clues:** As in Part 3, some correct answers are not said directly in the talk. You must listen for vocabulary clues and paraphrased or slightly changed information to find the answer.

WALK THROUGH: Talks

A What You'll See

In Part 4, you will see the directions, the questions, and the answer options on the page. Read the sample questions below. Think about the types of information the questions are asking for. Is each answer related to an action? A location? A time or date? Look at the answer options. What kinds of key words might you listen for to choose the answer for each one?

QUICK TIP

As in Part 3, in Part 4 you should quickly pre-read the questions and answer options *before* you hear the talk. This will help you decide what types of information to listen for.

Part 4: Talks

Directions: Listen to a talk. Then choose the correct answers to the three questions about that talk. Fill in the letter (A), (B), (C), or (D). You will hear each talk only once.

1. Where is the speaker?

(A) In Los Angeles
(B) On an airplane
(C) At the airport
(D) At a travel agency

2. How long will the trip take?

(A) Three hours
(B) A little less than four hours
(C) A little more than four hours
(D) Eleven hours

3. What will happen next?

(A) There will be a sightseeing trip.
(B) A movie will be shown.
(C) The plane will be serviced.
(D) Drinks will be served.

B What You'll Hear

You will first hear a short talk and then three questions about it. Listen to the sample talk as you read along in the script. Underline the important information in the script. Circle and look up any words you don't know. 🎧 Track 4-01

SAMPLE SCRIPT ▶
(script not available in test)

Man: Good morning and welcome to Flight 83 to Los Angeles. Our trip today should take just under four hours, and we'll be arriving at Los Angeles International Airport at eleven o' clock local time. We have clear skies today and should be able to have a good view of the Rocky Mountains. I'll point them out, as well as other sights of interest, as we approach them. For your entertainment, we'll be showing an in-flight movie in about an hour. In a minute, the flight attendants will begin the beverage service, so sit back, relax, and enjoy your trip.

Glossary:

◀ POWERED BY COBUILD

approach: get closer to something

attendant: someone whose job is to serve or help people in a place, such as a gas station, parking lot, or coat room

beverage: any kind of drink

C What You'll Do

In the test, you will listen to the audio and choose the best answer for each question. Listen to the recording again and answer the questions in Part A. Use the information you underlined in Part B if needed. 🎧 Track 4-01

GET IT RIGHT: Tips and Tasks for Answering Correctly

QUESTION TYPES

Topic / Main Idea Questions

As in Part 3, topic / main idea questions in Part 4 of the Listening test require you to look at the details and context of the talk to find the main theme the speaker is talking about. Here are some possible topic / main idea questions.

> **Possible topic / main idea questions:**
>
> » *What is this report about?*   » *Where would you hear this announcement?*
>
> » *Who is this message for?*   » *What is the purpose of this talk?*

» **TIP 1 Pay attention to the beginning of the talk.** Just as in Part 3 conversations, important information about the main idea may be stated at the beginning of the talks in Part 4. The first one or two sentences set the context for the talk. Listen carefully to the beginning sentences in a talk, as they often give clues to the main idea. You can then look for the answer option that includes this same information.

TASK Pre-read the questions and answer options. Then listen to the start of each talk. Choose the topic or main idea of the talk.   🎧 Track 4-02

1. Who is this message for?

   (A) Computer technicians

   (B) Telephone operators

   (C) Electron Company staff

   (D) Computer users

2. Where would you hear this talk?

   (A) At a museum

   (B) On a tour bus

   (C) In a paint store

   (D) In an art class

3. What problem is the show about?

   (A) Dream analysis

   (B) Job hunting

   (C) Employment policy

   (D) Dressing for work

» **TIP 2 Learn to recognize synonyms.** The talk may not use any of the exact words you see in the answer options. Instead, the answer to a main idea question may contain a synonym of a word used by the speaker. A synonym is a word or expression that means the same as another word or expression. Learning to recognize common synonyms for words related to topics covered in Part 4 of the TOEIC test will help you find the correct answer choices. See the examples in the chart on page 69.

Examples of Synonyms Related to Common Topics	
Topic	**Topic-Related Words and Synonyms**
Shopping	*store:* shop, retailer, boutique, outlet, department store *clerk:* salesperson, sales rep *shopper:* buyer, consumer, customer
Dining out	*restaurant:* café, coffee shop, cafeteria, deli, bistro *eat:* have, consume, snack on, dine *meal:* breakfast, lunch, dinner, supper, snack, a bite to eat
Work	*job:* employment, position, work *employer:* boss, supervisor, manager, CEO, department head
Traveling	*trip:* journey, vacation, excursion, tour *travel:* go, visit, see, tour *arrive:* get to, land, disembark *leave:* depart, take off, board
Health	*healthy:* well, fit *sick:* ill, unwell, not well *sickness:* illness, disease *medicine:* pills, drugs, prescription, medication
Clothes	*clothes:* clothing, garment, attire, dress, outfit *wear:* have on, be dressed in
Music	*concert:* recital, musical performance *musician:* performer, instrumentalist, accompanist

TASK Read the word and write at least one synonym for it.

1. musical performance _____

2. disease _____

3. excursion _____

4. department head_____

5. consume _____

6. retailer_____

7. garment _____

8. depart _____

» **TIP 3 Learn key words that may give clues to topics and main ideas.** Some other topics often found in Part 4 of the TOEIC test are weather, sports events, news, prices, and business. Keep a list of the types of words associated with these topics. Then use a thesaurus to learn common synonyms for words related to those topics.

TASK Pre-read each question and its two answer options. Then listen to part of a talk as you read along in the script. Circle one word in the script that is a synonym of a word in one of the answer options. Then answer the question.   🎧 Track 4-03

1. Where would you hear this announcement?

   a. in a store   **b.** in a park

> **Man:** Welcome to Park Place, the city's largest retailer, where we treat our customers like royalty.

2. What is this review about?

   a. a play   **b.** a restaurant

> **Woman:** If you're looking for an inexpensive place for a delicious post-theater dinner, the Riverview Café might well suit your needs.

3. Who is this talk for?

a. vacation planners

b. shoppers

> **Man:** Do you need an escape from the stresses of work? Sign up for one of our weeklong excursions to the beaches of Mexico.

Try a TOEIC Test Question

Pre-read the question and answer options. Then listen to the audio as you read along in the script. In the script, underline important information given at the start. Circle one or more words in the script that are synonyms for words in one of the answer options. Then answer the question. 🎧 Track 4-04

SAMPLE SCRIPT ►
(script not available in test)

> **Woman:** The annual City Festival of Music will take place next weekend at the National Theater. The doors open on Sunday morning at 9:00 a.m., and there will be musical performances by local and national orchestras and bands all day until eight in the evening. This one-day-only event is a unique opportunity to hear performances by some of the country's top musicians. Don't miss it. Tickets are on sale at the National Theater box office. Order your ticket today.

1. What is this announcement about?

(A) A school party

(B) A musical

(C) A music school

(D) A day of concerts

Detail Questions

As in Part 3, Part 4 of the Listening test detail questions require you to listen carefully for key information in a talk. These questions are about specific rather than general information. Anything mentioned in a talk can be the basis of a detail question, including suggestions, instructions, times, quantities, and other items. The answer information is usually clearly stated in the talk.

QUICK TIP

Practice taking notes! Detail questions are one of the most common question types for Part 3 and Part 4 of the TOEIC Test. Practice listening for details and taking notes whenever possible before you take the test.

Possible topics for detail questions:

» *Suggestions, advice, instructions, or requests* » *Reasons or purposes*

» *Duration, frequency, quantity, or times* » *Locations*

Detail Questions About Suggestions, Advice, Instructions, or Requests

A speaker may instruct or advise listeners to do something, or the speaker may make a specific suggestion or request. Detail questions may ask about this type of information.

Possible detail questions about . . .

suggestions or advice:
» *What does the speaker suggest people do?*
» *What does the speaker offer as a solution?*

requests:
» *What is the speaker asking people to get?*
» *What does the announcement ask people to do?*

instructions:
» *What is the first step in the process?*
» *What does the speaker say NOT to do?*

» **TIP Recognize words and expressions used for suggestions, advice, instructions, or requests.**
Certain words and expressions are used to give advice and instructions or to make suggestions and requests. For example, the word *please* is often used with requests and instructions. Listen for words and expressions such as these as they may help you recognize key information.

Common Words and Expressions Used for Suggestions, Advice, Instructions, or Requests	
Words or Expression Types	**Examples**
please	*Please line up at the gate.* *We ask that you please present your ticket.*
Imperative verbs	*Drive carefully.* *Don't forget to visit our snack bar.*
Modals *should* and *must*	*You should pay for your ticket ahead of time.* *Customers must pay with cash.*
Certain expressions, such as *you'd better, it's better, it's a good idea*	*It's a good idea to call before 9:00.* *It's better to make a reservation first.*
Certain verbs, such as *suggest, recommend, advise, want, tell, ask, request*	*We suggest arriving early.* *We are asking all passengers to remain seated.*

TASK Read parts of talks. Underline one suggestion, piece of advice, instruction, or request in each.

1. **Woman:** We will allow first-class passengers to board first. Show your ticket to the gate agent when boarding the train.

2. **Man:** The icy weather has made road conditions very dangerous, and several accidents have already been reported. If you witness an accident, you should report it immediately to the local police.

3. **Woman:** It's a good idea to buy your ticket before the end of the month because the company will give you a ten percent discount.

4. **Man:** Please have your money ready for the cashier before you reach the head of the line. This will help the line move faster.

5. **Woman:** Visitors are asked to register with the receptionist before going upstairs. A visitor's pass will be issued at that time.

Try a TOEIC Test Question

Pre-read the question and answer options. Then listen to the audio as you read along in the script. Underline one suggestion. Then answer the question. ⌒ Track 4-05

SAMPLE SCRIPT ►
(script not available in test)

Woman: Don't know what to get your loved one for Valentine's Day? Then we have the answer for you! Stop by Norby's department store's annual jewelry sale! Today we're featuring any number of great deals on necklaces, earrings, and even diamond rings. They make great gifts that let your loved one know just how you feel. Norby's department store—gift solutions for people who really care.

What does the speaker NOT suggest people do?

(A) Buy their loved ones a gift

(B) Go shopping at Norby's department store

(C) Feature great deals

(D) Show people they care

Detail Questions About Duration, Frequency, Quantity, or Time

These types of questions ask *when, what time, how many, how much, how often,* or *how long.* When you see these kinds of questions, you need to listen carefully for numbers, times, or other key details. As in Part 3, the information needed to answer these questions in Part 4 may be paraphrased or restated in different ways.

Duration:
- » *How long will the road be closed?*
- » *How long must the people wait?*

Frequency:
- » *How often do the trains leave?*
- » *How many times a month does the club meet?*

Quantity:
- » *How many tickets are available?*
- » *How much are winter coats discounted this week?*

Time:
- » *When is the office open?*
- » *What time will the program begin?*

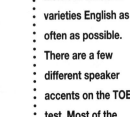

» **TIP Learn to distinguish between similar-sounding numbers and words.** Incorrect answer options may include numbers, days, quantity expressions, or time expressions that sound similar to the correct answer. Watch out for them! Here are some examples of commonly confused quantity and time words.

Commonly Confused Numbers and Time Words		
seven / eleven	*sixteen / sixty*	*Sunday / Monday*
thirteen / thirty	*seventeen / seventy*	*Tuesday / today / two days*
fourteen / forty	*eighteen / eighty*	*Wednesday / one day*
fifteen / fifty	*nineteen / ninety*	*fifth / sixth*

TASK Listen to parts of talks. For each talk, circle the word you hear. 🎧 Track 4-06

1. (A) Sunday   (B) Monday

2. (A) 50   (B) 60

3. (A) Two days   (B) Tuesday

4. (A) 13   (B) 30

5. (A) Fifth   (B) Sixth

QUICK TIP

Listen to different varieties English as often as possible.

There are a few different speaker accents on the TOEIC test. Most of the speakers are American or use American English grammar and vocabulary, but you may hear British, Australian or other Englishes as well.

Try a TOEIC Test Question

Pre-read the question and answer options. Then listen to the audio as you read along in the script. Underline one request. Next, circle one incorrect answer option with a number that sounds similar to the correct answer. Finally, answer the question. 🎧 Track 4-07

SAMPLE SCRIPT ▶
(script not available in test)

Man: For all passengers traveling on the 10:14 train to Cambridge, the train has been delayed 15 minutes due to engine problems. Repeat, the 10:14 train to Cambridge has been delayed 15 minutes and will now be departing at 10:29 a.m. Please adjust your travel plans accordingly.

1. How late is the train?

(A) 10 minutes

(B) 14 minutes

(C) 15 minutes

(D) 50 minutes

Inference Questions

Like Part 3, Part 4 of the Listening test has inference questions. This type of question asks you to make a conclusion based on facts and details from the talk. Inference questions often ask you to infer who a person is, where the speaker might be, or what might happen next. As in Part 3, the answers to these questions are usually not stated directly. You have to listen and choose the best answer using the information given.

> ### Possible inference questions:
>
> » *Who is probably giving the speech?*   » *What will probably happen after the talk?*
> » *Where might you hear this information?*

» **TIP Use vocabulary clues from the answer options and the audio to find the correct answer.**
Before you listen, pre-read the questions and answer options and think about the kinds of vocabulary you might hear for each option. Then listen carefully to the talk. Pay attention to the vocabulary clues given in the talk to help you answer inference questions. Remember, words can be used in more than one context. See pages 45, 46, and 69 for more information about topic-related vocabulary clues.

TASK Pre-read each question and its answer options. Notice the words in parentheses after each answer option—these are some vocabulary clues you might hear for that option. Then listen to part of a talk as you read along in the script. Circle the words in the script that match the three vocabulary clues in the correct answer. Then answer the question.   🎧 Track 4-08

1. Where might you hear this announcement?

   a. An airport *(gate, board, boarding pass)*

   b. A train station *(track, board, ticket)*

   c. A school *(bell, bus, line)*

   d. A bus *(fare, seat, driver)*

> **Woman:** Northeast 1782 to Wichita is now ready to board at Gate 17. Remember, only two carry-ons per passenger are permitted. Please have your boarding pass out and ready to present to . . .

2. Who is probably giving the talk?

   a. A salesperson *(customers, marketing, sell)*

   b. A secretary *(phone calls, desk, messages)*

   c. A consumer *(buy, discount, cash)*

   d. An accountant *(totals, profit and loss, monthly report)*

> **Man:** Thank you very much for joining us today on *Where to Get Great Deals*! I'm Herb Niedermayer, and I'm here to teach you how to buy what you want for less. One great trick is to always offer cash. By offering cash, many stores will offer you a discount — sometimes up to 25 percent! You can also save money by shopping during sales. Be sure to read your local newspapers to find out which stores are having sales right now. Another thing that can help is to . . .

Try a TOEIC Test Question

Pre-read the question and answer options. Then listen to the audio as you read along in the script. As you listen, circle three vocabulary clues in the script that help you identify the correct answer. Then answer the question. 🎧 Track 4-09

SAMPLE SCRIPT ▶
(script not available in test)

Woman: Hi, this is Jennifer Leska speaking. I'm calling to let you know that I'm very upset with the service I received at your store last week. I wanted to exchange a birthday gift I had gotten from a friend, but the salesperson who helped me was terrible. He had no idea what to do! It took about an hour, and in the end I still didn't get my gift because he couldn't find the right color and size. I'm extremely dissatisfied, so I'd like to speak with a manager. Please call me at . . .

What can you infer from this message?

(A) The salesperson was successful.

(B) The customer is not happy.

(C) The sales manager is not happy.

(D) The customer sent her friend a birthday gift.

TYPES OF TALKS

In Part 4 of the Listening test, you will hear different types of talks. Knowing what type of talk you are listening to will help you identify the information you need. Read the chart below to familiarize yourself with the types of talks you might hear in Part 4, along with a description of each type and sample audio and questions.

Types of Talks	Descriptions	Sample Phrases	Sample Test Questions
Announcements ☐	These give specific information listeners need. They may be related to travel, business, shopping, or other contexts.	*May I have your attention, please?* *Flight 10 will be leaving in fifteen minutes.*	*Where would you hear this announcement?* *What are passengers asked to do?*
Speeches ☐	These are short talks that you might hear at a meeting or conference.	*Welcome to the fifth annual Business Professionals Conference.* *I am happy to have the opportunity to speak with you today about a very important issue.*	*What is the speech about?* *What will the person talk about next?*
Tours ☐	These are informational talks by tour and museum guides.	*Welcome to the City Museum of Art.* *We will begin our tour in just a few minutes.*	*How long will the tour last?* *How much do the tickets cost?*

(continued)

Types of Talks	Descriptions	Sample Phrases	Sample Questions
Advertisements ☐	These usually promote stores or products. They may contain information about special sales.	*We are pleased to announce a storewide sale.*	*When is the sale over?*
		We look forward to seeing you at our store.	*How much are prices reduced?*
Reports ☐	These are short bits of information about weather, traffic, news, or business.	*This is your morning weather update.*	*When will the weather change?*
		City officials met yesterday to discuss the current budget crisis.	*What happened last Monday?*
Introductions ☐	These short talks may introduce a speaker or radio show guest.	*Our speaker today is an expert in international economics.*	*What is the speaker's occupation?*
		We are fortunate to have a very special guest with us tonight.	*What will the guest talk about?*
Voicemails ☐	These may be outgoing phone messages or phone messages left by a caller.	*Press "one" to hear our hours.*	*How can a caller find out about the schedule?*
		Please leave your name, number, and a brief message.	*What happens after a caller leaves a message?*
Instructions / Lectures ☐	These may be advice or information on topics, such as business, health, or travel.	*These tips will help you achieve your goals.*	*What advice does the speaker give?*
		Contact your bank immediately if you lose your credit card.	*What is the first step to take?*

TASK Listen to parts of eight talks and scan the information about talks. In the chart on pages 74 and 75, write the number of each talk next to the correct type of talk. 🎧 Track 4-10

PROGRESSIVE PRACTICE: Get Ready

Practice Set 1

A Pre-read the questions and answer options. Think about what type of information you should listen for to answer each question. Circle the correct information type from the options given. Then listen to the talk and mark the correct answers. 🎧 Track 4-11

1. What is the weather like now?   **Information Type:**   Weather Condition   Temperature

   (A) Clear

   (B) Cloudy

   (C) Rainy

   (D) Cold

2. What will the high temperature be today?   **Information Type:**   Temperature   Forecast

   (A) 8 degrees

   (B) 9 degrees

   (C) 14 degrees

   (D) 40 degrees

3. When might it snow?   **Information Type:**   Weather Condition   Day or Time

   (A) This afternoon

   (B) Tomorrow

   (C) Sunday

   (D) Monday

B Now check your answers. Read the explanations in the *Answer Analysis* boxes and look at the answer options. Note why each answer option is correct or incorrect. This will help you learn to identify incorrect answer options.

1. What is the weather like now?

   (A) Clear

   (B) Cloudy

   (C) Rainy

   (D) Cold

> ANSWER ANALYSIS ▶   *Information Type:* **Weather Condition**
>
>   ✓ **(A) The speaker says the sky is sunny, and there is not a cloud to be seen. For weather, that is the meaning of "clear."**
>
>   ✗ (B) The speaker says the word "cloud," but that does not describe the weather now.
>
>   ✗ (C) This is what the weather will be like later in the day.
>
>   ✗ (D) This is how the weather will be on the weekend, and it contradicts the speaker's statement that the current temperature is "relatively warm."

2. What will the high temperature be today?

   (A) 8 degrees

   (B) 9 degrees

   (C) 14 degrees

   (D) 40 degrees

ANSWER ANALYSIS ▶   *Information Type:* Temperature

   ✗ (A) This confuses the number eight with the similar-sounding word "late."

   ✗ (B) The speaker says the next weather report will be at 9:00, not that the temperature is 9 degrees.

   ✗ (C) This confuses the number 14 with the similar-sounding correct temperature, 40.

   ✓ **(D) The speaker states that the temperature "will reach a relatively warm 40 degrees."**

3. When might it snow?

(A) This afternoon

(B) Tomorrow

(C) Sunday

(D) Monday

ANSWER ANALYSIS ▶   *Information Type:* Day or Time

   ✗ (A) This is when it will rain.

   ✗ (B) This is when the rain will continue.

   ✓ **(C) The man says there may be some snow late in the weekend, and this is the second day of the weekend.**

   ✗ (D) This day is not mentioned, but it sounds similar to the correct answer.

Practice Set 2

A Pre-read the questions and answer options. Think about what type of information you should listen for to answer each question. Circle the correct information type from the options given. Then listen to the talk and mark the correct answers. ∩ Track 4-12

1. Who is this announcement for?   **Information Type:** Person's Name   Occupation Title

(A) Flight attendants

(B) Airline passengers

(C) Airplane pilots

(D) Boat passengers

2. How long will the trip last?   **Information Type:** Time of Day   Length of Time

(A) 15 minutes

(B) 50 minutes

(C) 3 hours

(D) 4 hours

3. What does the speaker ask listeners to do?   **Information Type:** Request   Quantity

(A) Stay in their seats

(B) Check the schedule

(C) Read a magazine

(D) Get up and move around

B Now check your answers. Read the explanations in the *Answer Analysis* boxes and look at the answer options. Note why each answer option is correct or incorrect. This will help you learn to identify incorrect answers.

1. Who is this announcement for?

(A) Flight attendants

(B) Airline passengers

(C) Airplane pilots

(D) Boat passengers

ANSWER ANALYSIS ▶ *Information Type:* **Occupation Title**

✗ (A) Part of the announcement informs listeners what the flight attendants will do, so it is probably not for flight attendants.

✓ **(B) The words "flight" and "flight attendant" suggest that the announcement is on an airplane. The speaker also mentions beverage service, or drinks given to airline passengers.**

✗ (C) This is probably the occupation of the person who is making the announcement, not who is listening to it.

✗ (D) The words "aboard" and "landing" could be used about a boat, but the word "flight" could not.

2. How long will the trip last?

(A) 15 minutes

(B) 50 minutes

(C) 3 hours

(D) 4 hours

ANSWER ANALYSIS ▶ *Information Type:* **Length of Time**

✗ (A) This is how much ahead of schedule they will arrive at their destination.

✗ (B) This number sounds similar to 15 but is not mentioned.

✓ **(C) The speaker says that the flight will take three hours.**

✗ (D) This sounds similar to the word "before" ("fifteen minutes before our scheduled arrival time").

3. What does the speaker ask listeners to do?

(A) Stay in their seats

(B) Check the schedule

(C) Read a magazine

(D) Get up and move around

ANSWER ANALYSIS ▶ *Information Type:* **Request**

✓ **(A) The speaker says, "We ask you to remain seated." The correct answer is a paraphrase of this.**

✗ (B) The speaker says the word "scheduled" ("fifteen minutes before our scheduled arrival time"), but it is not used to make a request.

✗ (C) This is something the passengers may do if they want to, but it is not a request.

✗ (D) This is what the passengers may do later if they want to, but they are requested not to do it now.

PROGRESSIVE PRACTICE: Get Set

Practice Set 1

A Pre-read the questions and answer options. Think about the type of information needed to answer each question. Then listen to the talk and mark the correct answers. 🎧 Track 4-13

1. What time did the speaker call the doctor's office?

(A) 2:00

(B) 7:00

(C) 7:30

(D) 11:30

2. Why did the speaker call?

(A) To make an appointment

(B) To cancel an appointment

(C) To speak with the doctor

(D) To arrange a trip

3. When will the speaker call back?

(A) This afternoon

(B) Wednesday morning

(C) On Saturday

(D) Next week

B Now check your answers. Look at the talk in the scripts at the back of this book. Then look at the explanations in the *Answer Analysis* box. Write the letter of each answer option from Part A next to the reason why it is correct or incorrect. This will help you learn to identify incorrect answer options.

1.

> ANSWER ANALYSIS ▶
>
> _____ ✓ **This is the time the caller says.**
> _____ ✗ This is the time of the caller's appointment, not when the person called.
> _____ ✗ This time is close to the correct answer, but it is wrong by half an hour.
> _____ ✗ This sounds similar to the correct answer, but the caller does not mention this time.

2.

> ANSWER ANALYSIS ▶
>
> _____ ✗ This is confused with the reason the caller can't go to her appointment.
> _____ ✓ **The speaker says she is calling about her appointment and that she won't be able to make it, which means that she has to cancel it.**
> _____ ✗ This repeats a word from the message, but the speaker says she will call back to do this next week.
> _____ ✗ The speaker mentions Dr. Kim, but she does not say that she wants to talk to the doctor directly.

3.

> ANSWER ANALYSIS ▶
>
> _____ ✗ The speaker mentions this in the message, but it is given as the current time, not when she will call back.
> _____ ✗ This is the time period of the appointment that the speaker needs to cancel.
> _____ ✗ This is when the speaker will return from her trip.
> _____ ✓ **The speaker says that she will "call again" at this time to reschedule.**

Practice Set 2

A Pre-read the questions and answer options. Think about the type of information needed to answer each question. Then listen to the talk and mark the correct answers. 🎧 Track 4-14

1. What is being advertised?

(A) Business suits

(B) Office supplies

(C) Luxury cars

(D) Dream homes

3. When is the sale over?

(A) Sunday

(B) Monday

(C) Tuesday

(D) Today

2. How much is the discount?

(A) Ten percent

(B) Fifteen percent

(C) Twenty percent

(D) Twenty-five percent

B Now check your answers. Look at the talk in the scripts at the back of this book. Then look at the explanations in the *Answer Analysis* box. Write the letter of each answer option from Part A next to the reason why it is correct or incorrect. This will help you learn to identify incorrect answer options.

1.

> ANSWER ANALYSIS ►
>
> _____ ✗ The speaker mentions this at the very beginning of the talk, but it is used to make a comparison.
>
> _____ ✓ **The speaker mentions special prices on "automobiles" and "vehicles," which are synonyms for "cars."**
>
> _____ ✗ This repeats a word from the last line of the talk, but it is mentioned as the place people can drive to in their new cars.
>
> _____ ✗ This repeats two words from the talk, but the speaker does not use these words together.

2.

> ANSWER ANALYSIS ►
>
> _____ ✓ **This is what the speaker says is the discount on luxury vehicles.**
>
> _____ ✗ The speaker suggests several possible discounts. This is the first one.
>
> _____ ✗ The speaker suggests several possible discounts. This is the second one.
>
> _____ ✗ The speaker suggests several possible discounts. This is the third one.

3.

> ANSWER ANALYSIS ►
>
> _____ ✗ This is when the speaker says that listeners should "come on down," that is, visit the dealership.
>
> _____ ✗ This day is not mentioned specifically.
>
> _____ ✗ This day is not mentioned specifically.
>
> _____ ✓ **The speaker says that the deals are good only through this day.**

Practice Set 3

A Pre-read the questions and answer options. Think about the type of information needed to answer each question. Then listen to the talk and mark the correct answers. 🎧 Track 4-15

1. How much do tickets cost?

(A) $0

(B) $1

(C) $2

(D) $3

2. Where does the tour take place?

(A) In a museum

(B) In a factory

(C) At a harbor

(D) On a boat

3. What does the guide suggest?

(A) Eating

(B) Drinking

(C) Taking pictures

(D) Buying souvenirs

B Now check your answers. Look at the talk in the scripts at the back of this book. Then look at the explanations in the *Answer Analysis* box. Write the letter of each answer option from Part A next to the reason why it is correct or incorrect. This will help you learn to identify incorrect answer options.

ANSWER ANALYSIS ▶

_____ ✗ When talking about tickets, the speaker says that listeners must have "one." This confuses a pronoun with a price information.

_____ ✗ This number sounds similar to the word "few," as when the speaker says the tour will begin "in just a few minutes."

_____ ✓ **The speaker says that tickets are "free." This means there is no cost.**

_____ ✗ This number sounds similar to the word "free," which is the correct answer.

ANSWER ANALYSIS ▶

_____ ✗ This is something visitors will see in the second exhibit, not where they will be.

_____ ✗ This is the subject of the first exhibit, not where the tour takes place.

_____ ✗ This is the subject of the second exhibit. Visitors are in a building, not at the water.

_____ ✓ **The speaker mentions the word "museum." She also mentions "artifacts," "exhibits," and "gift shop," which are associated with museums.**

ANSWER ANALYSIS ▶

_____ ✗ This is incorrect because the speaker says that photographing the exhibits is not permitted.

_____ ✓ **The speaker invites listeners to visit the gift shop to purchase pictures and souvenirs. "Buy" is a synonym for "purchase."**

_____ ✗ This is incorrect because the speaker says that drinks are not permitted.

_____ ✗ This is incorrect because the speaker says that food is not permitted.

PROGRESSIVE PRACTICE: Go for the TOEIC® Test

TOEIC® TEST PRACTICE

Directions: Listen to a talk. Then choose the correct answers to the three questions about that talk. Fill in the letter (A), (B), (C), or (D). You will hear each talk only once. 🎧 Track 4-16

1. What time does the bank close on Saturday?

(A) 5:00

(B) 8:00

(C) 9:00

(D) 12:00

2. How can you find out how much money is in your bank account?

(A) Press "1"

(B) Press "3"

(C) Hold the line

(D) Call back later

3. Who should press "2"?

(A) Customer service representatives

(B) People wanting to borrow money

(C) People wanting to invest money

(D) Owners of small businesses

4. Who is Mr. Peterson?

(A) A nature photographer

(B) A radio announcer

(C) A magazine editor

(D) A travel agent

5. What will Mr. Peterson talk about?

(A) His education

(B) His awards

(C) His book

(D) His trip

6. What will happen in the second half of the show?

(A) A new guest will speak.

(B) There will be a news report.

(C) The conversation will begin.

(D) Mr. Peterson will answer questions.

7. What is this talk about?

(A) Nutrition

(B) Exercise

(C) Office work

(D) Weight loss

8. According to the speaker, what should you eat for breakfast?

(A) Sweets

(B) Fruit

(C) Meat

(D) Pastries

9. What does the speaker advise?

(A) Avoid the elevator

(B) Eat lunch in the park

(C) Move slowly

(D) Take the bus

10. What event is this report about?

(A) A fire

(B) A traffic jam

(C) A car accident

(D) A hospital closure

11. What time did it happen?

(A) 3:00

(B) 6:00

(C) 8:00

(D) 10:00

12. Who talked with a reporter?

(A) A doctor

(B) A firefighter

(C) A truck driver

(D) A police officer

13. What has caused the train delay?

(A) Rain

(B) Snow

(C) Repairs

(D) An accident

14. When will the train leave?

(A) 8:30

(B) 9:00

(C) Around noon

(D) It is uncertain.

15. What are passengers asked to do?

(A) Buy tickets

(B) Have breakfast

(C) Pay for their meal

(D) Speak with the crew

16. Where would you hear these instructions?

(A) In a store

(B) In a hotel

(C) In a bank

(D) In a garage

17. What should the customer do first?

(A) Show a ticket

(B) Sign something

(C) Set a purchase on the counter

(D) Put a credit card in the machine

18. How can the customer ask for help?

(A) Use the star key

(B) Insert a card

(C) Press the beeper

(D) Turn on a light

Practice TOEIC® Test: Listening

TAKING THE PRACTICE TEST

The following Listening Practice Test will help you evaluate the TOEIC test-taking skills that you have learned for the Listening section of the test. The Listening Practice Test is divided into four parts, just as on the actual test. The level of difficulty of the audio and the written material is like that of the TOEIC test. The timing between question items is similar to the test, so you should try to keep up with the pace to prepare yourself. The complete Listening Practice Test should take you 45 minutes.

We advise you to simulate the actual test when you take the Listening Practice Test. Take the test in a quiet setting. Be sure to follow the directions exactly as instructed. Don't replay the audio or go back to previous pages in the book.

Use the answer sheet on page 85 to mark your answers as you will do on the actual test. You may remove it from the book or make a photocopy for reuse if you want to try the test again. Use a #2 pencil. Mark your answers by filling in the letters of your answer choices on the answer sheet.

For example, the **test taker** below has chosen "B."

Be sure you mark only one answer per item on your answer sheet. If you want to change an answer, be sure to erase it completely. Do NOT cross it out! On the actual test, this will be scored as two answers and the item will be marked as incorrect.

SCORING THE TEST

After you complete the Listening Practice Test, check your answers in the answer key that starts on page 212. Scores on the actual test are determined by the number of correct answers. This raw score is then converted to a scaled score. Only the scaled score is released to the test taker. While your score on this test is not a sure guarantee of your TOEIC® test score, you can calculate a comparable scaled score by referring to the scoring chart on page 246.

Listening Comprehension Practice Test Answer Sheet

1. (A) (B) (C) (D)	26. (A) (B) (C) (D)	51. (A) (B) (C) (D)	76. (A) (B) (C) (D)
2. (A) (B) (C) (D)	27. (A) (B) (C) (D)	52. (A) (B) (C) (D)	77. (A) (B) (C) (D)
3. (A) (B) (C) (D)	28. (A) (B) (C) (D)	53. (A) (B) (C) (D)	78. (A) (B) (C) (D)
4. (A) (B) (C) (D)	29. (A) (B) (C) (D)	54. (A) (B) (C) (D)	79. (A) (B) (C) (D)
5. (A) (B) (C) (D)	30. (A) (B) (C) (D)	55. (A) (B) (C) (D)	80. (A) (B) (C) (D)
6. (A) (B) (C) (D)	31. (A) (B) (C) (D)	56. (A) (B) (C) (D)	81. (A) (B) (C) (D)
7. (A) (B) (C) (D)	32. (A) (B) (C) (D)	57. (A) (B) (C) (D)	82. (A) (B) (C) (D)
8. (A) (B) (C) (D)	33. (A) (B) (C) (D)	58. (A) (B) (C) (D)	83. (A) (B) (C) (D)
9. (A) (B) (C) (D)	34. (A) (B) (C) (D)	59. (A) (B) (C) (D)	84. (A) (B) (C) (D)
10. (A) (B) (C) (D)	35. (A) (B) (C) (D)	60. (A) (B) (C) (D)	85. (A) (B) (C) (D)
11. (A) (B) (C) (D)	36. (A) (B) (C) (D)	61. (A) (B) (C) (D)	86. (A) (B) (C) (D)
12. (A) (B) (C) (D)	37. (A) (B) (C) (D)	62. (A) (B) (C) (D)	87. (A) (B) (C) (D)
13. (A) (B) (C) (D)	38. (A) (B) (C) (D)	63. (A) (B) (C) (D)	88. (A) (B) (C) (D)
14. (A) (B) (C) (D)	39. (A) (B) (C) (D)	64. (A) (B) (C) (D)	89. (A) (B) (C) (D)
15. (A) (B) (C) (D)	40. (A) (B) (C) (D)	65. (A) (B) (C) (D)	90. (A) (B) (C) (D)
16. (A) (B) (C) (D)	41. (A) (B) (C) (D)	66. (A) (B) (C) (D)	91. (A) (B) (C) (D)
17. (A) (B) (C) (D)	42. (A) (B) (C) (D)	67. (A) (B) (C) (D)	92. (A) (B) (C) (D)
18. (A) (B) (C) (D)	43. (A) (B) (C) (D)	68. (A) (B) (C) (D)	93. (A) (B) (C) (D)
19. (A) (B) (C) (D)	44. (A) (B) (C) (D)	69. (A) (B) (C) (D)	94. (A) (B) (C) (D)
20. (A) (B) (C) (D)	45. (A) (B) (C) (D)	70. (A) (B) (C) (D)	95. (A) (B) (C) (D)
21. (A) (B) (C) (D)	46. (A) (B) (C) (D)	71. (A) (B) (C) (D)	96. (A) (B) (C) (D)
22. (A) (B) (C) (D)	47. (A) (B) (C) (D)	72. (A) (B) (C) (D)	97. (A) (B) (C) (D)
23. (A) (B) (C) (D)	48. (A) (B) (C) (D)	73. (A) (B) (C) (D)	98. (A) (B) (C) (D)
24. (A) (B) (C) (D)	49. (A) (B) (C) (D)	74. (A) (B) (C) (D)	99. (A) (B) (C) (D)
25. (A) (B) (C) (D)	50. (A) (B) (C) (D)	75. (A) (B) (C) (D)	100. (A) (B) (C) (D)

Listening Practice Test

Listen to the following track for the entire test. 🎧 Track LPT-01

PART 1: PHOTOS

Directions: Look at each photo. You will hear four statements about the photo. The statements are not in your book. Mark the letter of the statement that best describes the photo. You will hear each statement only once.

1.

2.

3.

4.

Go to the next page ➔

5.

6.

7.

8.

Go to the next page ➔

9.

10.

This is the end of Part 1.

Look at the next page to start Part 2 →

PART 2: QUESTION-RESPONSE

Directions: Listen to the question or statement and three possible responses. You will hear them only one time, and they are not in your book. Choose the best response, and mark the corresponding letter on your answer sheet.

11. Mark your answer on your answer sheet.

12. Mark your answer on your answer sheet.

13. Mark your answer on your answer sheet.

14. Mark your answer on your answer sheet.

15. Mark your answer on your answer sheet.

16. Mark your answer on your answer sheet.

17. Mark your answer on your answer sheet.

18. Mark your answer on your answer sheet.

19. Mark your answer on your answer sheet.

20. Mark your answer on your answer sheet.

21. Mark your answer on your answer sheet.

22. Mark your answer on your answer sheet.

23. Mark your answer on your answer sheet.

24. Mark your answer on your answer sheet.

25. Mark your answer on your answer sheet.

26. Mark your answer on your answer sheet.

27. Mark your answer on your answer sheet.

28. Mark your answer on your answer sheet.

29. Mark your answer on your answer sheet.

30. Mark your answer on your answer sheet.

31. Mark your answer on your answer sheet.

32. Mark your answer on your answer sheet.

33. Mark your answer on your answer sheet.

34. Mark your answer on your answer sheet.

35. Mark your answer on your answer sheet.

36. Mark your answer on your answer sheet.

37. Mark your answer on your answer sheet.

38. Mark your answer on your answer sheet.

39. Mark your answer on your answer sheet.

40. Mark your answer on your answer sheet.

This is the end of Part 2.

Go to the next page to start Part 3 ➜

PART 3: CONVERSATIONS

Directions: Listen to a conversation between two speakers. Then choose the correct answers to the three questions about that conversation. Fill in the letter (A), (B), (C), or (D) on your answer sheet. You will hear each conversation only once.

41. Where is the man going?

    (A) His apartment

    (B) The dentist's office

    (C) Downtown

    (D) The mall

42. When is he going there?

    (A) This morning

    (B) At noon

    (C) This afternoon

    (D) In the evening

43. How will he get there?

    (A) Walking

    (B) In the woman's car

    (C) By train

    (D) By bus

44. What problem are they discussing?

    (A) The coffee machine is broken.

    (B) They need to order new supplies.

    (C) The cafeteria is closed.

    (D) The coffee pot is too small.

45. What will the man do?

    (A) Make a fresh pot of coffee

    (B) Get coffee at the cafeteria

    (C) Buy a new machine

    (D) Fix the machine

46. When will he do it?

    (A) Before lunch

    (B) At noon

    (C) On Sunday

    (D) On Monday

47. Who is the man?

    (A) A chef

    (B) A waiter

    (C) A customer

    (D) A dishwasher

48. How much does the woman owe?

    (A) $50

    (B) $55

    (C) $60

    (D) $65

49. How will she pay?

    (A) Cash

    (B) Check

    (C) Credit card

    (D) Money order

50. What time will the meeting start?

    (A) 7:00

    (B) 10:45

    (C) 11:00

    (D) 11:45

51. How many chairs will they need?

    (A) 8

    (B) 10

    (C) 12

    (D) 15

52. Who will bring the extra chairs?

    (A) The man

    (B) The woman

    (C) The director

    (D) The assistant

53. What is the problem with the hotel room?

(A) It is too noisy.

(B) It doesn't have a view.

(C) The bed isn't comfortable.

(D) It costs too much.

54. What will the man do about the problem?

(A) Nothing

(B) Charge her less

(C) Change her bed

(D) Give her a different room

55. When will the woman leave the hotel?

(A) This morning

(B) Tonight

(C) Tomorrow

(D) In four nights

---

56. Why was the man late?

(A) He had a meeting.

(B) His clock wasn't working.

(C) He had an appointment.

(D) He was stuck in traffic.

57. What time is it now?

(A) 9:30

(B) Just before 11:00

(C) 11:00

(D) Just after 11:00

58. Who wants to see the man now?

(A) His assistant

(B) His friend

(C) His boss

(D) His client

---

59. Why did the man change the time for his vacation?

(A) He has too much work.

(B) He couldn't get a hotel room.

(C) He has to go on a business trip.

(D) He doesn't have enough money.

60. Where will he take his vacation?

(A) In a city

(B) By a lake

(C) At the beach

(D) In the mountains

61. When will he take his vacation?

(A) This week

(B) Next week

(C) In September

(D) In November

---

62. What did the man do last weekend?

(A) Played tennis

(B) Met with a client

(C) Visited a friend

(D) Worked on a project

63. Where does the man play tennis?

(A) At a hotel

(B) At a school

(C) At a park

(D) At a club

64. When does the woman want to play tennis?

(A) Sunday

(B) Monday

(C) Friday

(D) Saturday

Go to the next page ➜

65. Where does this conversation take place?

(A) At a theater

(B) At a train station

(C) At a travel agency

(D) At a soccer game

66. How many tickets does the man want?

(A) 1

(B) 3

(C) 4

(D) 8

67. Where will the man sit?

(A) Near the front

(B) In the center

(C) In the back

(D) On the aisle

68. What will the woman do this afternoon?

(A) Look for her key

(B) See a new apartment

(C) Take the man to lunch

(D) Buy some new clothes

69. What time will she do it?

(A) 1:00

(B) 2:30

(C) 5:00

(D) 5:30

70. What does she say about her current apartment?

(A) It isn't very big.

(B) The rent is too high.

(C) It's too far from work.

(D) It doesn't have enough closets.

This is the end of Part 3.

Look at the next page to start Part 4 ➔

PART 4: TALKS

> **Directions:** Listen to a talk. Then choose the correct answers to the three questions about that talk. Fill in the letter (A), (B), (C), or (D). You will hear each talk only once.

71. What gate will the flight leave from?

(A) 5

(B) 15

(C) 16

(D) 92

72. What are passengers asked to do now?

(A) Check extra bags

(B) Board the plane

(C) Show their tickets

(D) Speak with assistants

73. Who will get on the plane first?

(A) People with high row numbers

(B) People with low row numbers

(C) People with small children

(D) People with first-class tickets

74. When will fares go up?

(A) September 1

(B) September 15

(C) December 1

(D) December 15

75. What happens if you press "1"?

(A) You hear about subways.

(B) You hear about buses.

(C) You hear about fares.

(D) You hear about the effects of weather.

76. How can you speak directly with a person?

(A) Press "2"

(B) Press "3"

(C) Press "4"

(D) Stay on the line

77. What event is this announcement about?

(A) An art exhibit

(B) A music class

(C) A museum tour

(D) A musical performance

78. What time does the event begin?

(A) 2:00

(B) 7:00

(C) 8:00

(D) 11:00

79. What will happen after the event?

(A) There will be a garden tour.

(B) Refreshments will be served.

(C) A chef will give a demonstration.

(D) Information about the museum will be provided.

80. What is this advertisement for?

(A) A hotel

(B) A restaurant

(C) A business lunch

(D) A party planning service

81. When is a reduced price available?

(A) Near the beginning of the month

(B) Near the end of the month

(C) Every Wednesday

(D) Tuesday through Saturday

82. What happens on Sunday?

(A) The business is closed.

(B) There are special deals for children.

(C) Customers are invited to a party.

(D) Breakfast is served.

Go to the next page ➔

83. What's the weather like now?

(A) Cloudy

(B) Windy

(C) Clear

(D) Chilly

84. How high will the temperature get today?

(A) 35 degrees

(B) 45 degrees

(C) 55 degrees

(D) 65 degrees

85. When will the weather change?

(A) This afternoon

(B) This evening

(C) Tomorrow

(D) Sunday

86. When will the tour begin?

(A) In four minutes

(B) In five minutes

(C) In nine minutes

(D) In ten minutes

87. What will happen after lunch?

(A) A trip to a museum

(B) A visit to the zoo

(C) A tour of monuments

(D) A ride to the park

88. What is NOT allowed on the bus?

(A) Eating

(B) Standing

(C) Taking photos

(D) Asking questions

89. What will Ms. Whitaker talk about?

(A) The Business Owners' Association

(B) Accounting services

(C) Financing a business

(D) A business conference

90. What will happen immediately after Ms. Whitaker's talk?

(A) She will read a chapter from her book.

(B) Refreshments will be served.

(C) There will be a slide show.

(D) John Jones will talk.

91. What time will next month's meeting begin?

(A) 2:00

(B) 7:30

(C) 8:00

(D) 8:30

92. Why are streets closed today?

(A) Construction work is in progress.

(B) There is a bad traffic jam.

(C) There will be a parade.

(D) The weather is bad.

93. What does the speaker suggest that listeners do?

(A) Use public transportation

(B) Follow the events on TV

(C) Park in designated areas

(D) Stay at home

94. When will streets reopen?

(A) At noon

(B) At 2:00 p.m.

(C) In the evening

(D) Tomorrow

95. What is the purpose of the call?

(A) To cancel an appointment

(B) To change an appointment

(C) To give a reminder about an appointment

(D) To explain the reason for an appointment

96. Who is the appointment with?

(A) A dentist

(B) A bank officer

(C) An office cleaning service

(D) A medical doctor

97. When is the appointment?

(A) Sunday

(B) Monday

(C) Friday

(D) Saturday

98. When is the museum open?

(A) Every day

(B) Weekends only

(C) Every day except Sunday

(D) Monday through Friday only

99. What will happen next week?

(A) There will be a new permanent exhibit.

(B) Gemstones will go on display.

(C) The planetarium will close.

(D) Classes for adults will begin.

100. How can you get more information about the museum?

(A) Press "1"

(B) Call back later

(C) Stay on the line

(D) Visit the Web site

This is the end of the Listening Test.

Guide to the TOEIC® Test
Reading Section

The second section of the TOEIC Listening and Reading Test is the Reading Section. It consists of three parts with a total of 100 questions. It is a test of your ability to comprehend written English in a business context. You will complete sentences and answer comprehension questions about reading passages.

QUICK GUIDE: Reading Section

Definition	The Reading Section tests your comprehension of written English and your ability to identify correct language use. There are three parts to this section. You will choose the correct words or phrases to complete sentences and answer comprehension questions about a variety of types of reading passages.
Targeted Skills	In order to do well on the Reading Section, you must be able to: • understand vocabulary pertaining to business and everyday activities. • identify correct grammatical forms. • identify correct word usage. • understand the main idea and details in a variety of types of reading passages. • make inferences about information you read. • read and answer questions within the time given.
The Parts of the Reading Section	**Part 5:** You will choose the best words or phrases to complete sentences. **Part 6:** You will read passages with incomplete sentences and choose the best words or phrases to complete these sentences. **Part 7:** You will read passages of varying types and lengths and answer comprehension questions about them. You will also read double passages and answer questions about both. (See below for more thorough descriptions of each part of the Reading Section.)
Question Types	**Parts 5 and 6:** Choose the correct grammatical form, word form, or vocabulary word to complete each sentence. **Part 7:** Answer main idea, detail, audience, and inference questions about a variety of reading passages.
Timing	The Reading Section of the TOEIC test lasts approximately 75 minutes. Because the content is printed in your test booklet, you can go back and check or adjust your answers as long as it's within the time allowed.

Parts of the TOEIC® Test Reading Section

Part 5

In Part 5 of the Reading Test, you will read sentences and complete them. There is a total of 40 items in this part of the test. For each sentence, you will choose among four answer options to complete the sentence. The sentence topics focus on common business and everyday themes. The sentences focus on different types of language issues.

Part 5 sentences may deal with themes such as:

- Office issues
- Financial issues
- Sales and marketing
- Business transactions
- Schedules

- Transportation
- Tourism
- Dining out
- Entertainment
- Weather

Part 5 items may focus on grammar issues such as:

- Verb tense
- Verb form
- Subject-verb agreement
- Pronouns
- Prepositions

- Transition words
- Comparative adjectives
- Adverbs
- Time clauses
- Conditionals

Part 5 items may focus on vocabulary issues such as:

- Word families (related words)
- Parts of speech

- Word meaning
- Commonly confused words

Part 6

Part 6 of the Reading Test consists of four reading passages. Three sentences in each passage are incomplete. For each of these incomplete sentences, you will choose among four answer options. There is a total of 12 questions in this part of the test.

The reading passages include a variety of types like those you might see in common business or everyday contexts. They may be of the following types:

- E-mails
- Memos
- Notices
- Advertisements

- Letters
- Instructions
- Articles

The incomplete sentences in Part 6 are similar to the incomplete sentences in Part 5. The difference is that they are presented within the context of a passage, or text. To complete some of the items, you may have to look at the surrounding sentences in order to choose the correct answer option.

Part 7

In Part 7 of the Reading Test, you will read passages of varying types and lengths and answer comprehension questions about them. The reading passages include types you might see in common business and everyday situations.

The passages may be of the following types:

- E-mails
- Letters
- Memos
- Agendas
- Advertisements
- Notices

- Articles
- Reports
- Forms
- Charts, tables and graphs
- Schedules

There is a total of 48 questions in Part 7. You will answer a variety of types of comprehension questions. Comprehension question types will include the following:

- **Main Idea:** *What is this report mainly about?*
- **Detail:** *Where does Ms. Kim work?*
- **Purpose:** *Why did Mr. Jones write the letter?*
- **Audience:** *Who is this article for?*
- **Inference:** *What can we infer about the writer of this e-mail?*
- **Vocabulary:** The word "insight" in line 10 is closest in meaning to

Part 7 begins with 7–10 single passages, each one followed by 2–5 comprehension questions, for a total of 28 questions. The single passages are followed by a series of double passages. Double passages are sets of two related reading passages followed by five comprehension questions for each set, for a total of 20 questions. Some of the questions require looking at the information in both passages and making the appropriate connections in order to answer correctly. The question types are the same as for the single passages, except that you normally won't see vocabulary questions for the double passages.

Here are some examples of double passage types:

- A train schedule and an e-mail about making travel arrangements
- A help-wanted ad and a letter asking for employment
- A page of course descriptions and a class registration form
- An invoice and a letter disputing the charges
- A meeting agenda and a meeting report

Challenges & Solutions

» **CHALLENGE 1: "The vocabulary in the Reading Test is even harder than in the Listening Test!"**

SOLUTION: The Reading Test does include higher-level vocabulary than the Listening Test, so it's important to become comfortable reading in English. Practice by reading advertisements, business letters (a "how-to guide" for writing business letters is a great source), newspaper articles, and business journals. There are many sources of reading material on the Internet. Most major business journals have websites, and you can learn a lot of vocabulary by reading the articles. Websites with information about tourism, shopping, restaurants, and so on will also expose you to many vocabulary words that are useful for the TOEIC test.

SOLUTION: Underline words you don't know as you go through the readings and questions in this book. Then look them up in a dictionary. This will help you get used to some of the language you may find on the test. (See also the *Guide to the TOEIC Test Listening Section* for more vocabulary expansion hints.)

SOLUTION: Learn common suffixes and prefixes to help you find the meanings of new words. Suffixes, or word endings, often indicate the part of speech of a word. Prefixes, or word beginnings, often add a specific meaning to a word. Learning the function and meaning of different suffixes and prefixes will help you expand your vocabulary. Here are some examples.

ⓔ POWERED BY COBUILD

Common Suffixes			
Suffixes	**Parts of Speech**	**Meanings**	**Examples**
-ation *-tion* *-sion*	nouns	refers to a state or process, or to an instance of that process	*examination, inflammation, protection, information, permission, confusion*
-ment	nouns	refers to the process of making or doing something, or to the result of this process	*replacement, government, environment, document, assessment*
-er *-or*	nouns	refers to a person who performs a particular action, often because it's his or her job	*carpenter, teacher, copier, vendor, inspector*
-ize	verbs	refers to the process by which things or people are brought into a new state	*civilize, modernize, realize*
-ify	verbs	refers to making something or someone different in some way	*beautify, glorify, terrify, signify*
-en	verbs	refers to the process of putting someone or something into a particular state, condition, or place	*brighten, enlighten, frighten*
-ate	verbs	refers to becoming or changing into	*educate, eradicate, obliterate*
-able	adjectives	indicates what someone or something can have done to them	*readable, reliable, believable, adorable*
-ive	adjectives	refers to a state of being related to something, or to having certain qualities	*creative, decisive, objective*
-al	adjectives	indicates what something is connected with	*regional, grammatical, magical, national*
fore-	verbs; nouns	refers to something being or coming before	*foretell, forefather, forethought*
inter-	adjectives	refers to things that move, exist, or happen between two or more people or things	*international, interact, intermingle, interdependent*
mis-	verbs; nouns	refers to something being done badly or incorrectly	*misspell, misquote, misunderstanding, mistreatment*
re-	verbs; nouns	refers to an action or process being repeated	*reread, redo, rebuild, rework*
in- *im-* *il-* *ir-*	various	forms words that have the opposite meaning of the root word	*inconsiderate, incapable, impossible, immoral, illiterate, illegal, irresponsible, irregular*

⊆ **POWERED BY COBUILD**

Common Prefixes			
Prefixes	**Parts of Speech**	**Meanings**	**Examples**
dis-	various	forms words that have the opposite meaning of the root word	*dishonest, disagree, displease, disorder, discomfort*
un-	various	forms words that have the opposite meaning of the root word	*uninteresting, unlawful, unpopular, unprofessional*
de-	verbs	forms words that have the opposite meaning of the root word	*defrost, decompress, deform, decompose*
sub-	nouns; adjectives	**nouns:** refers to things that are part of a larger thing or that are below something **adjectives:** refers to people or things that are at a lower standard or level	**nouns:** *subgroup, subtotal, submarine, subway, subzero* **adjectives:** *substandard, subtropical*

» **CHALLENGE 2: "There seems to be a big focus on grammar in the Reading Test, and I'm not that good at grammar."**

SOLUTION: Be sure to study the grammar points and activities for Part 5 in this book to help bring up your grammar skills. Then, when you are finished with the *Progressive Practice* section and practice test for Part 5, note which types of questions you got wrong (e.g., Did you miss a lot of questions about verb tenses? Did you have trouble choosing the right verb forms?). This will help narrow down problem areas where you need more practice. When you have identified your weak areas, you can then look for exercises in grammar books to help you practice and strengthen your skills in these areas.

SOLUTION: Read a lot, especially business-related materials. Seeing language and grammar in context will help you become more familiar with structure and word forms.

» **CHALLENGE 3: "I can't always find important information in the reading passages."**

SOLUTION: Before reading the passage, always read the questions first. This will give you an idea of what to look for in the passages. You can apply this technique when you do the *Progressive Practice* section and practice test for Part 7 of this book.

SOLUTION: Know how to spot specific question types, such as main idea, detail, vocabulary, or inference questions. Knowing the question type will help you know what sort of information to look for in the passage.

SOLUTION: Learn and practice the skimming techniques found on pages 137 to 139 of this book. Skimming means reading over a text very quickly to get a general understanding of the main ideas, how the passage is organized, and what types of information it contains. Being able to skim well will help you more quickly answer main idea, detail, and general questions.

» **CHALLENGE 4: "The passages can be pretty long! There's no way I can read them all and still have time to complete the questions."**

SOLUTION: Here again you can use your skimming skills. You can practice skimming with any reading text. Before reading, skim the text to get a general idea of the content. Make a guess about the main idea and some of the details. Then read the entire text more thoroughly to see how close your guesses came.

SOLUTION: Practice reading short texts about common TOEIC test topics and time yourself. You can read the text again later and try to do it in less time, or you can try to read texts of about the same length in the same amount of time or less. This will get you used to reading in a timed situation and help you read more quickly.

SOLUTION: When you're taking the test, quickly look for key words in the questions and answer options. Then go back to the passage and look for these key words in the text. The answer to the question will often be found in the general part of the text where the key words appear.

» **CHALLENGE 5: "The wording in the answer options doesn't match the wording in the passage."**

SOLUTION: The answer options on the reading comprehension section of Part 7 are often paraphrased, or reworded from the information in the passage. Study the paraphrasing skills on pages 47–53 of the Listening Section of this book to learn more about paraphrasing. You can practice paraphrasing when you read texts in English. After you read a sentence, write the idea again using your own words. This will help you get used to different ways of expressing the same idea.

SOLUTION: Quite often, some of the answer options do have the exact wording found in the text. Be sure to look very closely at these answer options and compare them to the information presented in the text. These answer options often contain factual information, but they do not actually answer the question.

» **CHALLENGE 6: "I can never decide what the correct answer option is!"**

SOLUTION: The questions after the passages are presented in the same order as the information in the passage. This will help you narrow down the possible places where an answer can be found.

SOLUTION: You'll probably notice that one or two of the answer options are clearly <u>not</u> the correct answers. Many students find that they can effectively narrow down the possible answers to two answer options. Carefully consider these two answer options, and if you still can't decide on the correct answer option, guess between the two. A fifty percent chance of getting the correct answer is always better than a twenty-five percent or thirty-three percent chance. On the TOEIC test, incorrect answers are simply not totaled with your score. You do not lose points for wrong answers.

SOLUTION: Don't spend too much time thinking about an answer. If you find yourself being indecisive, go with the answer you chose first. Often your first instinct is the right one.

» **CHALLENGE 7: "I'm very tired by the time I get to the last section of the test, so I don't do as well on that part."**

SOLUTION: Pace yourself. Try to work at a steady pace and avoid spending too much time worrying over any one question. If you find that you are lingering too long over a question, just make a guess and move on. Working at a steady pace will help you maintain your energy throughout the test.

SOLUTION: Do the test backward. Some students find it useful to start with the last, most difficult part of the test so that they can tackle those questions with greater energy. However, this solution doesn't work for everyone. The problem is that you may end up spending too much time on the last part, leaving yourself too little time for the earlier parts. You can try this out with practice tests and see if it works for you.

» **CHALLENGE 8: "I always worry that I won't be able to finish."**

SOLUTION: Again, pace yourself. When you practice at home, time yourself. Make sure you allow enough time to get through all the parts of the Reading Test. In the actual Reading Test, you <u>can</u> go back to the earlier parts, so leave enough time to go back to questions you weren't sure of.

TOEIC® Test Part 5: Incomplete Sentences

Part 5 of the Reading Test consists of 40 items—each one a sentence with a blank. You will choose the correct word or phrase to fill the blank. You will need to be able to identify the grammatical form or vocabulary word that correctly completes the sentence.

Topics for Part 5 sentences may include:

» *Office issues*

» *Financial issues*

» *Sales and marketing*

» *Business transactions*

» *Transportation*

» *Tourism*

» *Entertainment and dining out*

» *Schedules*

QUICK GUIDE: Incomplete Sentences

Definition	Part 5 is a test of your reading comprehension. It requires you to apply your knowledge of grammar and vocabulary to a reading context.
Targeted Skills	In order to correctly answer Part 5 questions, you must be able to determine what part of speech is missing. Then you must be able to identify the correct word or expression to complete the sentence.
Completion Types	All Part 5 items consist of a sentence with a blank and four choices for filling the blank. Items focus on the following types of issues. **Vocabulary:** • Words that seem similar but are different • Phrasal verbs **Word forms:** • Noun, pronoun, verb, adjective, and adverb use • Infinitive and gerund use **Grammar:** • Missing subject • Missing object or complement • Missing verb • Missing preposition or adjective
Things to Watch For	Distracters, or incorrect answer options, may include the following. • Words with similar sounds but different meanings (*prescription* vs. *subscription*) • Words with similar meanings but different usage (*allow* vs. *let*) • Words with similar meanings and similar usage (*some* vs. *any*) • Combinations for phrasal verbs (*turn over* vs. *turn in*) • Word form use (*comfort, comfortable, comforting,* etc.) • Grammar use (noun vs. gerund, etc.)

WALK THROUGH: Incomplete Sentences

A What You'll See

In Part 5, you will see the directions, the questions, and the answer options on the page. Below are three sample incomplete sentence fill-ins from Part 5. Review the sample sentences and notice the missing words. Think about the types of words that can be used to complete the sentences. What type of word is missing in each sentence?

Directions: Each sentence is missing a word or phrase. Four possible answer options are shown. Choose the best answer option and mark the corresponding letter on your answer sheet.

1. Although Mr. Jones _____ been working here for very long, he is completely familiar with all our office procedures.

   (A) isn't
   (B) wasn't
   (C) hasn't
   (D) haven't

2. Trees have been planted all along the local sidewalks as part of an effort to make the neighborhood _____.

   (A) beauty
   (B) beautify
   (C) beautiful
   (D) beautification

3. The doctor gave her a _____ for some medicine.

   (A) prescription
   (B) subscription
   (C) description
   (D) construction

QUICK TIP

Often you can eliminate an answer option right away. In Question 1 on this page, you have to choose the correct verb form to follow the subject, *Mr. Jones.* You can quickly see that choice **(D)** does not agree with the subject and therefore cannot be the correct answer.

B What You'll Do

In the test, you will choose the best word or phrase to complete each sentence. The first item in the sample questions above focuses on a grammar issue, the second one is about word forms, and the third question is about word meanings. Choose the correct words or phrases to complete the sentences in Part A. You will need to use the words around the blanks to help you choose the best answer for each sentence.

Glossary:

(€ POWERED BY COBUILD)

familiar: describing something you know or understand well

procedure: a way of doing something, especially the usual or correct way

sidewalk: a path with a hard surface by the side of the road

GET IT RIGHT: Tips and Tasks for Answering Correctly

FILL-IN TYPES

Vocabulary Completions

Vocabulary-based sentence completions require you to choose the appropriate word to complete the sentence. Some vocabulary items focus on word meanings only. In those cases, you will see four answer options that have similar but distinct meanings (e.g., *transmit / expand*). Some other vocabulary items focus on word form. In those cases, you will see answer options that appear similar (e.g., *attention / detention*). Here is an example of a vocabulary-based sentence completion.

Helen gave a brief _____ before discussing the project.
× beginning
✓ introduction
× reduction
× inspector

In this example, all of the words are nouns, so you must choose the word that best fits the context.

» **TIP 1 Learn how to recognize answer options that seem similar but have different meanings.**
The answer options for vocabulary fill-ins always include four different words with distinct definitions. However, the answer options may be similar word forms or may have some of the same word parts.

Answer options may be similar because they use the same prefix or suffix. Learn the differences in meaning among answer options that look similar. Study these charts of common prefixes and suffixes.

Common Prefixes		
Prefixes	**Meanings**	**Examples**
a-	forms adjectives with *not, without,* or *opposite* in their meaning	*That behavior was **atypical** and wasn't like him at all.*
bi-	forms adjectives, nouns, or verbs that mean *two, double,* or *twice*	*The store is having a **biannual** sale—the next sale will occur in six months.*
de-	forms verbs that mean *remove, away,* or *down*	*After the snowstorm, they had to **de-ice** the roads in order to prevent accidents.*
ex-	forms adjectives, adverbs, nouns, and verbs that mean *out, former,* or *remove*	*Ms. Umani is the **ex-president** of YEO Financial.*
im-/in-/il-	forms adjectives and adverbs that mean *not, without,* or *opposite*	*The cord was **improperly** connected, leading the system to fail.*
mis-	forms adjectives, adverbs, nouns, and verbs that mean *wrong* or *bad*	*The editor apologized for the **misprint** and published a correction.*
pre-	forms adjectives, nouns, and verbs that mean *before*	*Customers must **prepay** for the merchandise before shipment.*
re-	forms verbs that mean *again* or *back*	*Mr. Wu hired an expert to **redecorate** his home.*
sub-	forms adjectives, nouns, and verbs that mean *under* or *incomplete* or that describe a later action	*The product was returned because of its **substandard** quality.*
un-	forms adjectives, nouns, and verbs that mean *not, without,* or *remove*	*It was **unusual** for her to go out to lunch. She typically ate at her desk.*

Common Suffixes		
Suffixes	**Meanings**	**Examples**
-able/-ible	forms adjectives that means *able to be*	*His homework was so messy, it wasn't **readable**.*
-acy/-cy	forms nouns that show a state or quality of something	*They added walls in the office to give the employees more **privacy**.*
-ast	forms nouns that show a person connected with a certain activity	*She was a **gymnast** in her youth.*
-ate	forms adjectives, nouns, and verbs that mean *make* or *put in order*	*The banker said the man could **activate** the credit card the same day he received it.*
-er/-or	forms nouns that show a person or thing connected with a certain activity	*The **director** was pleased with the outcome.*
-ful	forms adjectives that show that something has certain qualities	*The vacation was **wonderful,** and everyone had a great time.*
-hood	forms nouns that describe a group of people or a condition	*He visited the area many times during his **childhood**.*
-ish	forms adjectives that say what a person, object, or action is like	*The old paper was **yellowish**.*
-less	forms adjectives that mean *not* or *without*	*He was fired because he made too many **careless** mistakes.*
-ment	forms nouns that show an action, process, or result	*She received **encouragement** from her supervisor.*
-ness	forms nouns that show a quality or condition	*His **alertness** suffered because he had worked for eighteen hours straight.*

TASK 1 In each sentence, circle the underlined word that is used incorrectly. What word should replace it? Choose a word from the box and write the new sentence on the line. How many of the words in the box do you know?

delayed   doable   erasable   mismarked   prevent
projector   redo   remarkable   repeated

1. My <u>meeting</u> was <u>relayed</u> <u>until</u> the week <u>after</u> next.

_____

2. The <u>marker</u> <u>left</u> a <u>stain</u> that is not <u>eraser</u>.

_____

3. Due to several <u>problems</u>, I had to <u>undo</u> the <u>project</u> over <u>again</u>.

_____

Part 5 may also include distracters that are commonly confused words. This chart shows word pairs that are often confused. Be sure to note their definitions and parts of speech.

Confusing Word Pairs		
Words	**Definitions**	**Examples**
ad<u>mit</u> / per<u>mit</u>	admit - v. to accept that something is true	John **admitted** that he had accidentally set off the fire alarm.
	permit - v. to allow something to occur	The manager **permitted** the employees to listen to music during work hours.
<u>a</u>ffect / <u>e</u>ffect	affect - v. to influence or cause to change	The weather may **affect** our plans.
	effect - n. a result	The recent economic climate has had an **effect** on spending.
ac<u>c</u>ept / ex<u>c</u>ept	accept - v. to take something that is offered	Rita Hallow **accepted** the award for designer of the year.
	except - conj. not including	Everyone **except** the accounting staff must attend the meeting.
chicken / kit<u>chen</u>	chicken - n. a bird raised for its meat and eggs	The **chicken** looked for worms in the yard.
	kitchen - n. a room in which food is prepared for eating	He spent all day in the **kitchen** cooking the meal.
<u>conscious</u> / <u>conscience</u>	conscious - adj. to understand what is happening	It is part of a supervisor's tasks to be **conscious** of everything that happens during the shift.
	conscience - n. awareness about something being good or bad	The human resources manager always complied with fair hiring practices, which helped him keep a clear **conscience.**
de<u>c</u>ent / des<u>c</u>ent	decent - adj. having good manners and morals	The customer did the **decent** thing by bringing the wallet to the lost and found.
	descent - n. the process of moving downward	The company's **descent** into bankruptcy occurred over the last decade.
<u>experi</u>ence / <u>experi</u>ment	experience - n. the process of doing things that add to one's knowledge or skills	Sara has ten years of **experience** as a sales representative.
	experiment - n. a scientific test that is meant to determine how something works	The **experiment** showed that calcium is an important part of the human diet.
pre<u>scription</u> / sub<u>scription</u>	prescription - n. a piece of paper on which a doctor writes the name of a medicine	I have to go to the drugstore to fill my **prescription**.
	subscription - n. a request to receive something regularly	I just got a **subscription** to my favorite magazine.
precede / proceed	precede - v. to come before	The vice president's speech **preceded** the president's.
	proceed - v. to continue	After a short break, the tour **proceeded.**

Confusing Word Pairs *(continued)*		
Words	**Definitions**	**Examples**
receipt / *recipe*	*receipt - n.* a document that shows items or services that have been purchased and the amount paid for them	*After the customer paid for the meal, the cashier gave her the **receipt**.*
	recipe - n. a document that gives instructions for making food	*Sammy enjoyed the meal so much that he asked the hostess for the **recipe** so he could make it himself.*
sensible / *sensitive*	*sensible - adj.* having common sense	*The company is looking for employees who are **sensible** and independent.*
	sensitive - adj. aware of the feelings of others	*Clients respond well to Bob because he is **sensitive** to their needs.*

TASK 2 Choose the correct word to complete each sentence.

1. I had to (admit / permit) that I was wrong.

2. I mixed the ingredients together as directed in the (receipt / recipe).

3. She canceled her (prescription / subscription) to the magazine.

Finally, some answer options may appear similar because they are homophones, which are sets of words that share the same pronunciation but have different meanings and slightly different spellings. Study the list of common homophones, making note of the definition and part of speech for each word.

Common Homophones		
Words	**Definitions**	**Examples**
aloud / *allowed*	*aloud - adv.* in a speaking voice	*Please read the paragraph **aloud**.*
	allowed - past form of the verb allow	*The manager **allowed** everyone to leave early.*
board / *bored*	*board - n.* a group that gives advice	*The **board** will meet on June 1 to discuss the new plans.*
	bored - adj. not interested	*Everyone was **bored** during the long meeting.*
brake / *break*	*brake - n.* the device that stops a vehicle	*She quickly stepped on the **brake** to avoid hitting the squirrel in the road.*
	break - v. to destroy or make unusable	*You didn't **break** the copier.*
complement / *compliment*	*complement - v.* to go well with something	*The beverage **complemented** the flavors of the meal.*
	compliment - v. to say something nice about someone or something	*Gregory **complimented** his assistant on her work.*
council / *counsel*	*council - n.* a group that makes rules or advises about something	*The safety **council** decided that the product was not suitable for children.*
	counsel - v. to give advice	*The lawyer **counseled** her client to think carefully before responding.*

(continued)

Common Homophones *(continued)*		
Words	**Definitions**	**Examples**
do / due	*do - v.* to perform or make	*They **do** very good work.*
	due - adj. owed or required	*The report isn't **due** until Tuesday.*
ensure / insure	*ensure - v.* to guarantee	*I read the report three times to **ensure** that there were no mistakes in it.*
	insure - v. to provide insurance for something	*The owner **insured** the car before driving it.*
there / their / they're	*there -* indicates a place	*My sister is over **there**.*
	their - belonging to a group of people	*Here are **their** shoes.*
	they're - the contraction for *they are*	***They're** arriving at 10:00.*
wood / would	*wood -* a hard substance from trees	*The table is made of **wood**.*
	would - a modal verb	***Would** you like to join us for lunch?*

TASK 3 Write the correct word from the box to complete each sentence. Five words are not used.

brake	aloud	there	break	board
their	bored	due	allowed	do

1. All employees are permitted to take a fifteen-minute _____ .

2. Peter yawned because he was _____ .

3. I have several things _____ before the end of the week.

4. Employees have to pay for _____ uniforms.

5. We are not _____ to check personal e-mails at work.

» **TIP 2 Learn how to recognize words with similar meanings but different usage.** Answer options on Part 5 may include words that have similar meanings but that differ in the way they are used grammatically. Study the words in the chart and analyze how they are different.

Words with Similar Meanings but Different Usage

Words	Meanings	Examples of Correct Use
allow / let	to permit to do something	*Allow me to introduce myself.* *Let me introduce myself.*
yearly / annual	occurring once a year	*The sales meeting is held yearly.* *The sales meeting is annual.*
have / take	to accept	*She'll have the chicken and potatoes for dinner.* *I couldn't take the call because I was busy.*
tell / say	to use the voice to express something	*I'll tell him about the change when he arrives.* *I said I wouldn't be able to come because I'm sick.*
do / make	to act in order to bring about a certain result	*I did the laundry over the weekend.* *I made a mistake.*
lay / lie	in a horizontal position	*I usually lay the blanket on the grass before sitting down.* *I often lie awake thinking about my work.*

TASK Choose the correct word to complete each sentence.

1. Our bosses never (allow / let) us take calls at work.

2. When did you (tell / say) her to call back?

3. He was feeling sick, so he asked to (lay / lie) down.

» **TIP 3 Familiarize yourself with special word forms that have different meanings but similar usage.**
See the chart for a list of words that have different meanings but similar uses.

Words with Different Meanings but Similar Usage

Words	Usage Notes	Examples
some / any	Use *some* with count nouns in positive statements. Use *any* with noncount nouns in negative statements and in questions.	*I don't need more coffee, thanks. I have some.* *I'd like some more cookies, though. I don't have any.*
many / much	Use *many* with count nouns. Use *much* with noncount nouns.	*We didn't see many people in the conference room.* *There isn't much time left before the plane leaves.*
a few / a little	Use *a few* for count nouns. Use *a little* for noncount nouns.	*I had a few chips for lunch, but I'm hungry now.* *There was a little milk left in the jug.*
a lot of	Use with both count and noncount nouns.	*There were a lot of papers on the desk.* *There was a lot of paperwork to complete before Sean could leave work.*

TASK Choose the correct word to complete each sentence.

1. There isn't (some / any) paper in the copy machine.

2. Do you have (many / much) vacation days left?

3. Maybe we can ask our boss for (a few / a little) more time to finish the report.

» **TIP 4 Learn how to recognize phrasal verbs and their correct meanings.** A phrasal verb is a special type of verb that combines a verb and a preposition or an adverb. Phrasal verbs may consist of two or three words. For example, *cut out* and *put up with* are both phrasal verbs.

In the answer options on Part 5 of the test, you may encounter phrasal verbs that use the same verb but alternate the adverbs or prepositions the verb is combined with. In order to choose the correct answer in these cases, you must know the meanings of different phrasal verbs. The following chart lists a few confusing phrasal verbs and some of their meanings.

QUICK TIP

. English has thousands

. of different phrasal

. verbs. Keep a list

. of phrasal verbs

. and their meanings.

. Organize the list by

. main verb, and note

. the various particles.

. Include meanings and

. examples.

Confusing Phrasal Verbs		
Phrasal Verbs	**Meanings**	**Examples**
• *back down*	• to withdraw	• *The sales representative **backed down** and let the customers browse without him.*
• *back out /* *back out of /* *back out on*	• to withdraw	• *Once you sign, you cannot **back out of** the agreement.*
• *back up*	• to support	• *My manager **backs me up** on all sales decisions.*
• *cut down /* *cut down on*	• to decrease	• *The company **cut down on** spending by finding a new distributor.*
• *cut in / cut in on*	• to interrupt	• *The assistant **cut in on** the meeting to give Ms. Sterling a message.*
• *cut up*	• to cut into many pieces	• *He **cut up** the old credit card so nobody else could use it.*
• *fill in / fill in for*	• to be a substitute for	• *Mary is **filling in for** Annie, who is sick.*
• *fill out*	• to complete	• *The man **filled out** the job application.*
• *fill up /* *fill up on /* *fill up with*	• to fill to the top	• *He **filled up** his tank with gas.*
• *pull down*	• to lower	• *Jessica **pulled down** the shade in the conference room.*
• *pull out /* *pull out of*	• to withdraw	• *The company **pulled out of** the deal one day before the contracts were signed.*
• *pull through*	• to survive	• *He was in a terrible accident, but he **pulled through.***
• *run across*	• to find	• *I **ran across** a problem in your report.*
• *run into*	• to meet unexpectedly	• *I **ran into** James at the conference.*
• *run out / run out of*	• to not have any of something	• *We've **run out of** ink.*

Try a TOEIC Test Question

Read the sentence and answer options. Choose the best answer option to complete the sentence.

1. Riverview Township _____ a pamphlet each year that includes a guide to local attractions and maps of the main areas of the town.

(A) announces

(B) decides

(C) publishes

(D) investigates

Word-Form Completions

Word-form completions present answer options that are different parts of speech but that come from the same root word. This chart provides a description of the different parts of speech in English.

Review of the Basic Parts of Speech			
Parts of Speech	**Functions**	**Example Words**	**Example Sentences**
Nouns / Pronouns	person, place, or thing	**nouns:** *sister, house, T-shirt* **pronouns:** *she, it, they*	*Our new **apartment** is really great! **It** was pretty cheap.*
Verbs	action or linking word	**action verbs:** *run, eat, touch* **linking verbs:** *be, become, seem*	*Jada **knocked** on the door, but nobody **seemed** to be home.*
Adjectives	modify a noun or pronoun	*big, yellow, happy*	*He bought a **wooden** desk for his **small** office.*
Adverbs	modify a verb, adjective, or adverb	*quickly, sadly, importantly, very, usually*	*Petra **quickly** climbed up the stairs before entering the office **quietly.***
Prepositions	indicate the relationship between different words in a sentence, typically in terms of location or time	**prepositions of location:** *to, by, around* **prepositions of time:** *at, on, in*	*She walked **around** the building.* *He arrived **at** 3 o'clock.*

You can recognize word-form completions because the answer options share the same root. Here is an example of a word-form completion.

Mr. Hu's new office was small but _____.
- ✗ comfortably
- ✗ comforted
- ✓ comfortable
- ✗ comfort

» **TIP 1 Learn how to identify what part of speech is missing from the sentence.** In order to correctly answer word-form completions, you will need to be able to recognize the part of speech of the missing word or phrase. Then you will know what to look for when you read through the answer options and will be able to eliminate incorrect answers more easily. Study the chart for some hints on determining the missing part of speech.

How to Recognize the Basic Parts of Speech		
Parts of Speech	**Tips**	**Examples**
Nouns / Pronouns	• usually go before a verb • nouns often appear after *a/an* or *the* • nouns may go after an adjective pronouns replace nouns	*The black **cat** <u>jumped</u> onto the table.* ***We** <u>have</u> an important meeting today.*
Verbs	• usually follow a noun or pronoun	*The <u>copier</u> **is** on the fourth floor. <u>It</u> **makes** thirty copies a minute.*
Adjectives	• usually come before a noun • often follow a linking verb	*The **new** <u>manager</u> seemed **tired.***

(continued)

How to Recognize the Basic Parts of Speech *(continued)*		
Parts of Speech	**Tips**	**Examples**
Adverbs	• usually end with *-ly* • can appear after a verb • can appear before a subject	*They <u>talked</u> **quietly** among themselves.* ***Soon** <u>they</u> will open for business.*
Prepositions	• always followed by a noun	*Gerald found the document **in** <u>the folder</u>.*

TASK Choose which part of speech will be needed in each of the blanks.

1. Because of its _____ plot, the book sold millions.

    a. adjective   **b.** noun   **c.** adverb

2. The mail carrier put the stack of letters _____ a sack.

    a. verb   **b.** preposition   **c.** noun

3. Dr. Maxwell _____ an appointment at 3 o'clock.

    a. adjective   **b.** verb   **c.** adverb

» **TIP 2 Understand how different parts of speech are formed.** One way to change the part of speech for a word is by adding a different suffix to the root. Learn the common endings used to create each word form in order to quickly identify the part of speech of each answer option.

Common Suffixes for English Word Forms		
	Suffixes	**Examples**
Nouns	*-acy* *-al* *-ance/-ence* *-dom* *-ity* *-ness* *-ship* *-sion/-tion*	*private (adj.)* → *priv<u>acy</u> (n.)* *renew (v.)* → *renew<u>al</u> (n.)* *permanent (adj.)* → *perman<u>ence</u> (n.)* *wise (adj.)* → *wis<u>dom</u> (n.)* *able (adj.)* → *abil<u>ity</u> (n.)* *expressive (adj.)* → *expressive<u>ness</u> (n.)* *friend (n.)* → *friend<u>ship</u> (n.)* *intrude (v.)* → *intru<u>sion</u> (n.)*
Verbs	*-ate* *-en* *-ify* *-ize*	*fix (v.)* → *fix<u>ate</u> (v.)* *fat (adj.)* → *fatt<u>en</u> (v.)* *electric (adj.)* → *electr<u>ify</u> (v.)* *central (adj.)* → *central<u>ize</u> (v.)*
Adjectives	*-able/-ible* *-al* *-ful* *-ic* *-ious/-ous* *-ish* *-ive* *-less*	*escape (v.)* → *escap<u>able</u> (adj.)* *society (n.)* → *societ<u>al</u> (adj.)* *faith (n.)* → *faith<u>ful</u> (adj.)* *cycle (n.)* → *cycl<u>ic</u> (adj.)* *grace (n.)* → *grac<u>ious</u> (adj.)* *self (n.)* → *self<u>ish</u> (adj.)* *effect (n.)* → *effect<u>ive</u> (adj.)* *odor (n.)* → *odor<u>less</u> (adj.)*

TASK Underline the suffixes in the bolded words. Then use the suffixes you underlined to determine the part of speech of each bolded word. Write *noun*, *verb*, or *adjective* on the line.

1. The salary for the position is **negotiable.** _____

2. The company **reinstated** a former policy. _____

3. The **authorship** of the novel was questioned. _____

4. Harry **organized** his desk before leaving for the weekend. _____

5. While not enormous, the sign was still quite **impressive.** _____

» **TIP 3 Know when to use infinitives and gerunds.** *To read, to ask,* and *to eat* are all examples of infinitives that can be used as nouns. A gerund is another type of noun that is formed by adding *-ing* to a verb. *Working, sleeping,* and *eating* are all examples of gerunds. The chart shows a partial list of verbs that are followed by infinitives, gerunds, or either.

Verbs Followed by Infinitives		Verbs Followed by Gerunds		Verbs Followed by Either Infinitives or Gerunds
agree	offer	acknowledge	have	attempt*
appear	persuade	admit	imagine	begin
arrange	plan	advise	involve	continue
ask	prepare	allow	mind	forget*
be able	promise	appreciate	miss	keep
beg	propose	avoid	permit	like
choose	refuse	can't help	postpone	love
decide	request	complete	practice	need
deserve	say	consider	quit	prefer
expect	start	delay	recall	regret*
fail	strive	deny	report	remember*
get	threaten	detest	resent	start
hesitate	use	enjoy	resist	stop*
hope	wait	escape	resume	try
hurry	want	excuse	risk	
intend	wish	finish	suggest	*meaning changes depending on whether the infinitive or gerund is used
neglect		forbid	tolerate	
Examples:		**Examples:**		**Examples:**
✓ We <u>agreed</u> **to meet** at seven.		✓ The company <u>forbids</u> **using** the phone during work hours.		✓ We'll <u>continue</u> **to discuss** this after the break.
✗ We agreed meeting at seven.		✗ The company forbids to use the phone during work hours.		✓ We'll <u>continue</u> **discussing** this after the break.
				✓ I <u>remember</u> **to turn off** the light before I leave.
				✓ I <u>remember</u> **turning off** the light before I left.

If you see both an infinitive and a gerund among the answer options, be sure to look at the verb that comes before the blank—you may be able to eliminate an incorrect answer option!

TASK Choose the correct word to complete each sentence.

1. We delayed (to print / printing) the notice due to some changes.

2. Mr. Wallace hesitates (to ask / asking) for help because he knows how busy everyone is.

3. Timothy offered (to review / reviewing) my report before I submitted it.

» **TIP 4 Understand the difference between possessive adjectives and possessive pronouns.** While both forms indicate ownership, a possessive adjective <u>modifies a noun,</u> while a possessive pronoun <u>replaces a noun</u>. Look at these examples.

I put **my** <u>keys</u> on the table. (possessive adjective)
The <u>keys</u> on the table are **mine**. (possessive pronoun)

Possessive adjectives and possessive pronouns have very similar forms. Use the chart to help you learn the form for each type. Make sure you know the difference between the two on the day of the test.

Singular		Plural	
Possessive Adjective	**Possessive Pronoun**	**Possessive Adjective**	**Possessive Pronoun**
my	*mine*	*our*	*ours*
your	*yours*	*your*	*yours*
her *his* *its*	*hers* *his* –	*their*	*theirs*

TASK Choose the correct possessive form to complete each sentence.

1. These books must belong to (her / hers).

2. (Our / Ours) philosophy is that the customer is always right.

3. I don't mind trying (their / theirs) as long as it is good.

» **TIP 5 Watch out for irregular adverbs.** Typically, adverbs are created by adding *-ly* to the adjective form of the word. However, there are a number of irregular adverbs that do not follow this rule. Study this chart of irregular adverbs.

Irregular Adverbs						
Adverb Shares Form with Adjective					**Adverb and Adjective Have Different Forms**	
daily	*far*	*hard*	*late*	*low*	<u>Adjective</u> → <u>Adverb</u>	
early	*fast*	*high*	*long*	*much*	*good*	*well*

TASK Choose the correct word to complete each sentence.

1. Allison worked (hard / hardly) on the project.

2. Yuri did a (good / well) job on the report.

3. Tom drives (fast / fastly).

Try a TOEIC Test Question

Read the sentence and answer options. Choose the best answer option to complete the sentence.

1. The company _____ record losses this quarter.

(A) report

(B) reported

(C) reportedly

(D) reportable

Combination Completions

Combination completions test your knowledge of vocabulary and word forms. You can identify a combination completion because the answer options will include features of both vocabulary completions and word-form completions. Here is an example of a combination completion.

Dara was _____ to learn that her report had not arrived late after all.
× retrieved
× retrieval
✓ relieved
× relief

The answer options for the example above include two different parts of speech: two nouns (*retrieval* and *relief*) and two adjectives (*retrieved* and *relieved*). You must pick the correct part of speech to go in the blank. Additionally, once you choose the correct part of speech, you have to choose between two words that have different meanings—in this case, *retrieved* and *relieved.* Therefore, you must use the skills you learned for vocabulary <u>and</u> word-form completions in order to choose the correct answer.

Try a TOEIC Test Question

Read the sentence and answer options. Choose the best answer option to complete the sentence.

1. The computer did not function correctly because the new software was _____ with the system.

(A) incompatible
(B) incompatibility

(C) incomplete
(D) incompletely

Grammar Completions

Grammar completions test your knowledge of a number of grammatical concepts, including the following.

- Parts of speech
- Sentence parts (subject, object, complement, etc.)
- Gerunds
- Infinitives
- Participles
- Verb tense and voice
- Comparative and superlative adjectives
- Conjunctions

Here is an example of a grammar completion sentence.

While the company is based in Brazil, English is _____ by many of the employees.
× speak
× speaking
× spoke
✓ spoken

When you encounter a grammar completion sentence, it is helpful to start by asking yourself if the missing word or phrase is the subject, object, verb, complement, or another sentence part. This chart shows sentence parts and their functions.

Review of Sentence Parts			
	Definitions	**How to Identify**	**Example Sentences**
Subject	the person, place, or thing that is doing or being something	• A subject typically comes before a verb. • Ask yourself, "Who or what is [verb + *-ing*]?" The answer to this question is the subject.	*Maxine* <u>completed</u> the form. The **company picnic** <u>was</u> canceled due to rain.
Verb	an action or state of being	• A verb usually follows a subject.	<u>They</u> **traveled** to Japan for the conference. <u>The weather</u> **was** beautiful throughout the trip.
Object	the person, place, or thing that the verb is acting upon	• An object typically comes after a verb. • Ask yourself, "Who or what is affected by the verb?" The answer to this question is the object.	*Neal* <u>opened</u> **the package.**
Complement	a word or phrase that is necessary in order to complete the meaning of the subject or object of a sentence	**subject complement:** • often follows a linking verb • may be an adjective or noun clause that describes the noun **object complement:** • may follow the direct object of the sentence • can be a noun or adjective form	**subject complement:** *Learning* **English** *can improve one's job prospects.* **object complement:** *Gina followed Herman* **into the office.**

Missing Subject

» **TIP 1 Remember what parts of speech can be the subject of a sentence.** In English, the subject of a sentence can be a noun, pronoun, gerund, or an infinitive.

Parts of Speech That Can Be Subjects		Parts of Speech That Can't Be Subjects	
Nouns	*The <u>employees</u> met in the conference room.*	**Verbs**	✗ *<s>The print will have to be replaced soon.</s>* ✓ *The <u>printer</u> will have to be replaced soon.*
Pronouns	*<u>She</u> submitted her application yesterday.*		
Gerunds	*<u>Preparing</u> for the meeting was difficult.*	**Adjectives**	✗ *<s>The <u>wise</u> of the decision was questioned.</s>* ✓ *The <u>wisdom</u> of the decision was questioned.*
Infinitives	*<u>To read</u> the report was his priority.*		

If the blank is the subject of the sentence, you can eliminate answer options that are verbs or adjectives.

TASK Underline the subject in each sentence. Then write the specific part of speech of the subject.

1. Training is often facilitated by real-world examples. _____

2. To finish the project is their goal. _____

3. Ms. Tazi was promoted to regional director last month. _____

» **TIP 2 Know the subject personal pronouns and when to use them.** Personal pronouns replace proper or common nouns in a sentence. If a personal pronoun is used as a substitute for a noun that is the subject of a sentence, be sure to use the following forms.

Subject Personal Pronouns	
Singular	**Examples**
I	*I went to the store.*
you	*You have keys to the office.*
he/she/it	*She lives on the fourth floor.*
Plural	**Examples**
we	*We are invited to the office party.*
you	*You can sit at this table.*
they	*They forgot to lock the office.*

TASK Replace the underlined part of each sentence with the correct subject personal pronoun.

1. <u>Ms. Reynolds</u> called William and Alice into her office. _____

2. <u>Eric, Wendy, and I</u> are visiting the corporate office tomorrow. _____

3. <u>My brother</u> turned on the computer. _____

» **TIP 3 Understand how gerunds can be used as the subject of a sentence.** A gerund is a noun form that is created by adding *-ing* to a verb. *Talking, reading,* and *filing* are all gerunds. See the following examples of sentences with gerunds as subjects. Note that subject gerunds always take a singular verb and are not preceded by an article (*a/an* or *the*).

✓ Talking <u>is</u> not permitted in the library.
✗ ~~Talking <u>are</u> not permitted in the library.~~
✓ Walking <u>is</u> a good way to improve one's health.
✗ ~~<u>A walking</u> is a good way to improve one's health.~~

TASK Circle one error in each sentence. Then correct the sentence.

1. Jogging are a healthy and fun activity for many people.

_____

2. Attending bimonthly staff meetings are required.

_____

3. Buy new equipment will cost the company a lot of money.

_____

» **TIP 4 Know the sentence construction in which infinitives can serve as the subject.** *To ask, to e-mail,* and *to talk* are all infinitives. While it is not common, the following sentence construction allows infinitives to be used as subjects: infinitive + linking verb + complement.

To ask <u>was</u> the best way to find out.
To teach <u>is</u> very fulfilling.
To talk <u>seems</u> impolite.
To succeed <u>can be</u> difficult.

TASK Underline the subjects in the sentences. Place a check mark (✓) next to each sentence that uses an infinitive as the subject.

1. ☐ To walk is the fastest way to get there.
2. ☐ I gave the letter to Marcia.
3. ☐ To start the project immediately will be important.

» **TIP 5 Use your knowledge of nouns to recognize the correct usage of participles as adjectives.**
Participles are adjectives that use the -ing and -ed forms of verbs. Remember that adjectives describe nouns. See the chart for more information about participles.

Types	Forms	Usage	Examples
Present Participle	verb + -ing*	• The present participle modifies a noun that affects someone or something. • If the subject is active, use the present participle.	*Ms. Jenkins gave an* **interesting** *lecture.* *Marcos thought the movie was* **exciting.**
Past Participle	regular verb** + -ed	• The past participle modifies a noun that is affected by someone or something. • If the subject is passive, use the past participle.	*Please call if you are* **interested** *in purchasing the item.* *Paula was* **excited** *about her upcoming vacation.*

* The present participle has the same form as the gerund. The difference is that present participles function as adjectives, while gerunds function as nouns.
**The past participle form varies for irregular verbs.

TASK Choose the correct participle form to complete each sentence.

1. All employees are required to watch the (training / trained) video.
2. Ruben forgot his (jogging / jogged) shoes at home.
3. Consumers are (concerned / concerning) about the rising prices.

Missing Verb

» **TIP 1 Make sure that the verb you choose agrees with the subject.** In English, verbs must agree with their subjects. Agreement is determined on the basis of three features: number, tense, and voice. This chart is a summary of subject-verb agreement.

Subject-Verb Agreement		
Types of Agreement	**Explanations**	**Examples**
Number	refers to whether the noun and the corresponding verb are singular or plural	✓ *Mr. Wang* **is waiting** *in the lobby.* ✗ *Mr. Wang are waiting in the lobby.*
Tense	refers to whether the verb agrees with time markers introduced in the sentence	✓ *Martha* **traveled** *to Belgium last week.* ✗ *Martha travels to Belgium last week.*
Voice	refers to whether the verb supports a passive or active interpretation	✓ *They* **were lectured** *by their boss about tardiness.* ✗ *They lectured by their boss about tardiness.*

In most cases, it is easy to figure out if the verb agrees with the subject. However, there are some instances in which it is hard to determine whether the subject takes a singular or plural verb. This chart is a guide for special cases of number agreement.

Special Cases of Number Agreement		
Use a singular verb if . . .	**Use a plural verb if . . .**	**Special Cases**
one of these quantifiers is the subject: *one, somebody, something, anybody, anyone, anything, everybody, everyone, everything, nobody, no one, nothing.* ✓ *Anyone who <u>wants</u> to attend the party must contact Ms. Riley by Friday.* ✗ *Anyone who <u>want</u> to attend the party must contact Ms. Riley by Friday.*	one of these quantifiers is the subject: *many, several, few, both (of the), a number of, a couple of, a variety of.* ✓ *A number of the employees <u>are</u> working on that account.* ✗ *A number of the employees <u>is</u> working on that account.*	If the subject and the verb are far away from each other in the sentence, they still have to agree. ✓ *The **consultant** from Savalas and Associates <u>is</u> waiting in the lobby.* ✗ *The **consultant** from Savalas and Associates <u>are</u> waiting in the lobby.*
the subject is a gerund or noun clause. ✓ *<u>Reviewing an application</u> **takes** him one hour.* ✗ *<u>Reviewing an application</u> **take** him one hour.*	there are two subjects connected by *and.* ✓ *Melissa and Marcus <u>are</u> in agreement about the contract.* ✗ *Melissa and Marcus <u>is</u> in agreement about the contract.*	When two parts of the subject are connected with *or*, the verb agrees with the second one. ✓ *Maggie's employees or Jesse <u>is</u> picking up the materials tomorrow.* ✗ *Maggie's employees or Jesse <u>are</u> picking up the materials tomorrow.*

TASK Choose the verb that agrees with the subject.

1. Many of the managers at the company (is / are) trained using Wilson's method.
2. A membership card or two forms of identification (is / are) needed to access the materials.
3. Something they will need to talk about (is / are) the terms of the contract.
4. The shipping and sales departments (is / are) meeting today.

» **TIP 2 Understand when to use the base form of a verb.** The base form of a verb is one that doesn't include any special endings to indicate tense, and it is the one you would encounter in a dictionary entry. Here is a list of situations in which you would use the base form of a verb in a sentence.

When to Use the Base Form of a Verb	
Rules	**Examples**
When there is a modal before a verb blank	✓ *Ella must <u>call</u> her client.* ✗ *Ella must calls her client.*
In imperative sentences	✓ *Go to the store.* (no subject) ✗ *Goes to the store.*
After *that* clauses that start with the following verbs: advise insist recommend demand necessary request essential order require important propose suggest	✓ *He **advised** that we **leave** before dark.* ✗ *He **advised** that we **left** before dark.* ✓ *The store **requires** that employees <u>give</u> every customer a receipt.* ✗ *The store **requires** that employees <u>gives</u> every customer a receipt.*

(continued)

When to Use the Base Form of a Verb *(continued)*	
Rules	**Examples**
After some causative verbs in the following construction: causative verb + object + base verb **Causative Verbs:** *let, make, have, get*	✓ We <u>had</u> Jack **finish** the report. ✗ ~~We <u>had</u> Jack **finishes** the report.~~ ✓ Jeffrey <u>let</u> Max **write** the press release. ✗ ~~Jeffrey <u>let</u> Max **writes** the press release.~~
After some verbs of perception in the following construction: verb of perception + object + base verb **Verbs of Perception:** *feel, hear, listen, look, notice, observe, see, smell, taste, touch, watch*	✓ They <u>saw</u> Mr. Anaya **present** at a conference. ✗ ~~They <u>saw</u> Mr. Anaya **presented** at a conference.~~

TASK Underline one error in each sentence. Then write each sentence with the correct form.

1. Asks for an extra pamphlet.

_____

2. I observed Liana trains the new employees.

_____

3. Yolanda let Tim takes Friday off.

_____

Missing Object

» **TIP 1 Remember what parts of speech can be an object.** The object of a sentence can be a noun, pronoun, gerund, or infinitive. Remember that all of these function as nouns. Look at the chart for more information about objects.

Parts of Speech That Can Be Objects		Parts of Speech That Can't Be Objects	
Nouns	Allison mailed the <u>letter</u>.	**Verbs**	✗ ~~Rupert asked for <u>promote</u>.~~ ✓ Rupert asked for <u>a promotion</u>.
Pronouns	I talked to <u>him</u>.		
Gerunds	The position involves <u>typing</u>.	**Adjectives**	✗ ~~Stefanie thinks <u>amazing</u>.~~ ✓ Stefanie thinks her <u>job is amazing</u>.
Infinitives	Kelly is trying <u>to sleep</u>.		

If you see a verb or an adjective as an answer option for a sentence that is missing an object, be sure to eliminate those choices.

TASK Underline the object in each sentence. Then write the specific part of speech of the object.

1. The company launched a new product last month. _____

2. Stacy read the biography. _____

3. Mr. Humphrey invited us to the grand opening. _____

4. Our client called to complain. _____

5. His assistant considered quitting. _____

» **TIP 2 Familiarize yourself with the different usage of pronouns.** There are different types of pronouns, or words that replace nouns in sentences, that can function as the object of a sentence. This chart has more information about object pronouns.

Types of Pronouns That Can Be Objects	
Personal Pronouns	**Reflexive Pronouns**
• Replace a common or proper noun that serves as an object in the sentence • May follow a preposition **Singular** *me* *you* *him, her, it* **Plural** *us* *you* *them*	• Used when the object of the sentence is the same as the subject • Reflexive form must agree with the subject • May go after a preposition **Singular** *myself* *yourself* *himself, herself, itself* **Plural** *ourselves* *yourselves* *themselves*
Examples: *Jake gave* **Wilma** *the stapler.* → *Jake gave* **her** *the stapler.* *Jason met* **Olivia and Peter** *outside.* → *Jason met* **them** *outside.*	**Examples:** *I listened to* **myself** *speak in the recording.* *Alex and Penny taught* **themselves** *French.* *Ted and I went to the meeting by* **ourselves.**

TASK Complete each sentence with the correct pronoun. Use the pronoun for the word in parentheses.

1. I can't believe I locked (I) _____ out of the house for the second time this week.
2. Dr. Wittles wrote (Laura) _____ a prescription for her ear infection.
3. We could hear (Paul) _____ talking about the new contract in the next room.

» **TIP 3 Watch out for the fake object *it*.** In the following construction in English, *it* can serve as an object despite not receiving an action.

subject + verb + fake object *it* + complement + infinitive / *that* clause

Stella finds **it** difficult <u>to concentrate</u> when it is noisy.
James made **it** clear <u>that</u> he expected the documents today.

TASK Unscramble the sentences.

1. [found] [that none of the meeting rooms were available.] [it hard to believe] [Mr. Perez]

_____

_____

2. [thinks] [Roberta] [that the company will hire new employees soon.] [it unlikely]

_____

_____

_____

3. [Kayla's positive attitude] [it easy] [to see why people love to work with her.] [makes]

_____

_____

_____

Missing Complement

» **TIP 1 Learn the different types of complements and their uses.** A complement is a word or phrase that provides information that is necessary in order to understand the meaning of the subject or object. This chart gives information about subject and object complements.

Types of Complements	How They Are Used	Examples
Subject Complements	• Come after a linking verb • Give more information about the subject • May be a noun, gerund, infinitive, adjective, or participle	*Mr. Williams is* **planning** *to leave by one o'clock.* *Anne* **seems** *unsure about what to do.*
Object Complements	• Give more information about the object • May be a noun, gerund, infinitive, adjective, or participle	*Mr. Quinn* **expects** *Jackie to meet with the clients today.* *They* **held** *a teleconference in order to include the international managers.*

TASK Decide whether the underlined part of each sentence is a subject or an object complement.

1. The negotiations have <u>finally ended</u>.
   a. subject complement
   b. object complement

2. The company's primary concern is to keep its clients <u>happy</u>.
   a. subject complement
   b. object complement

3. The receptionist called Ms. Wendell <u>to remind her about her appointment</u>.
   a. subject complement
   b. object complement

Missing Adjective or Preposition

» **TIP 1 Memorize common verb-preposition collocations.** Collocations are words that often occur together. Unfortunately, there are no rules for how collocations are formed, so you must take time before the test to study common verb-preposition collocations. This chart shows some common collocations.

Common Collocations			
about	*at*	*for*	*in*
ask about	*arrive at*	*admire for*	*arrive in*
care about	*smile at*	*ask for*	*believe in*
complain about	*stare at*	*excuse for*	*participate in*
dream about	*contact at*	*forgive for*	*succeed in*
worry about	*e-mail at*	*search for*	*decline in*
of	*on*	*to*	*with*
accuse of	*comment on*	*apply to*	*argue with*
consist of	*concentrate on*	*belong to*	*compare with*
get rid of	*count on*	*contribute to*	*discuss with*
remind of	*decide on*	*explain to*	*help with*
take care of	*insist on*	*respond to*	*provide with*

TASK Use the words in the box to complete the sentences.

for	of	to	with

1. My assistant will take care _____ the arrangements.
2. The prospective employee had three days to respond _____ the job offer.
3. We helped him search _____ the keys.
4. The representative provided me _____ a sales brochure.

» **TIP 2 Know the comparative and superlative forms of adjectives.** Comparatives and superlatives are forms of adjectives that allow comparisons of two or more nouns. Comparatives are used to compare two nouns, while superlatives express that a noun has the highest or lowest degree of something.

<u>This job</u> is **harder than** <u>the one</u> I had before. (comparative)
Harriet is **the tallest** in her family. (superlative)

This chart shows rules for forming comparatives and superlatives.

How to Form Comparatives and Superlatives			
	Comparatives	**Superlatives**	**Examples**
For adjectives with one syllable	add -*er*	add -*est*	*cold / colder / coldest*
For adjectives with two syllables that end in -*y*	change -*y* to -*i* and add -*er*	change -*y* to -*i* and add -*est*	*lazy / lazier / laziest*
For adjectives with two syllables that do <u>not</u> end in -*y*	add *more*	add *most*	*awkward / more awkward / most awkward*
For adjectives with three or more syllables	add *more*	add *most*	*wonderful / more wonderful / most wonderful*
Irregular adjectives	–	–	*bad / worse / worst* *good / better / best* *little / less / least*

TASK Write the correct comparative or superlative adjective in each blank. Use the word in parentheses.

1. Samuel's speech was slightly (short) _____ than the speech that followed.
2. The company has the (good) _____ reputation in the industry.
3. Maggie has the (large) _____ office in the building.
4. Dr. Bevel made one of the (amazing) _____ discoveries of the decade.
5. He couldn't be (happy) _____ to help you with the problem.

Try a TOEIC Test Question

Read the sentence and answer options. Choose the best answer option to complete the sentence.

1. Hiring decisions are made by qualified professionals who are _____ to seek out employees who will fit in with the company.

(A) train
(B) trains
(C) trained
(D) training

PROGRESSIVE PRACTICE: Get Ready

Choose the best answer to complete each sentence. Then check your answers in the *Answer Analysis* boxes. Read the explanations and note why each answer option is correct or incorrect. This will help you learn to identify correct and incorrect answer options.

1. Our company usually _____ a party for the entire staff at the end of the year.

(A) give

(B) gives

(C) have given

(D) were giving

ANSWER ANALYSIS ▶

✗ (A) This verb does not agree with the subject.

✓ **(B) This verb agrees with the third person singular subject "company."**

✗ (C) This verb does not agree with the subject, and the tense is incorrect. The sentence is about an action that usually happens, so it requires simple present tense.

✗ (D) This verb does not agree with the subject, and the tense is incorrect.

2. If we walk _____, we can get to the station before the train leaves.

(A) quickness

(B) quicken

(C) quickly

(D) quick

ANSWER ANALYSIS ▶

✗ (A) This is a noun where an adverb is needed.

✗ (B) This is a verb where an adverb is needed.

✓ **(C) This is an adverb of manner that modifies the verb "walk."**

✗ (D) This is an adjective where an adverb is needed.

3. Mr. Simms was late for work because _____ car broke down.

(A) his

(B) he's

(C) him

(D) he

ANSWER ANALYSIS ▶

✓ **(A) "His" is a possessive adjective that refers to a man. In this sentence, it refers to the fact that the car belongs to Mr. Simms.**

✗ (B) This is a contraction for "he is."

✗ (C) This is an object pronoun.

✗ (D) This is a subject pronoun.

4. We expect _____ this project before the end of the month.

(A) finish

(B) finishing

(C) to finish

(D) will finish

ANSWER ANALYSIS ▶

✗ (A) This is the base form of the verb.

✗ (B) This is a gerund.

✓ **(C) The main verb "expect" is followed by an infinitive verb.**

✗ (D) This is the future form of the verb.

5. I always carry an extra set of keys _____ my coat pocket.

(A) for

(B) to

(C) on

(D) in

ANSWER ANALYSIS ▶

✗ (A) "For" in this sentence would mean that the keys are for opening the pocket, which doesn't make sense.

✗ (B) "To" means "in the direction of," which doesn't make sense in this context.

✗ (C) "On" means "on top of," which is not a logical meaning for this sentence.

✓ **(D) "In" means "inside." The keys are inside the pocket.**

6. Sarah won the tennis competition last week, and they gave her a fifty-dollar gift certificate as her _____.

(A) price

(B) prize

(C) pride

(D) pries

ANSWER ANALYSIS ▶

✗ (A) "Price" refers to the cost of something. It looks similar to the correct answer, but the meaning does not fit the context.

✓ **(B) A "prize" is something awarded for winning a competition.**

✗ (C) "Pride" is the noun form of "proud." It looks similar to the correct answer, but the meaning does not fit the context.

✗ (D) "Pries" is the third person singular form of "pry," a verb with several meanings, none of which fit the context.

7. Get _____ the bus at Main Street and then walk two blocks north to our office.

(A) in

(B) up

(C) on

(D) off

> **ANSWER ANALYSIS ▶**
> ✗ (A) "Get in" refers to entering a car or similar vehicle, so it does not fit this context.
> ✗ (B) "Get up" means "to arise," so it does not fit this context.
> ✗ (C) "Get on" refers to boarding a bus, train, or airplane, so it does not fit this context.
> ✓ **(D) The phrasal verb "get off" means to exit a bus, train, or airplane.**

8. We _____ work on the project after tomorrow's meeting.

(A) will start

(B) starting

(C) have started

(D) started

> **ANSWER ANALYSIS ▶**
> ✓ **(A) The future form of the verb is required because the action will take place "after tomorrow."**
> ✗ (B) This is part of a present continuous verb that can be used for future meaning, but the auxiliary is missing.
> ✗ (C) This is a present perfect verb, which cannot be used to refer to a future action.
> ✗ (D) This is a past tense verb and refers to a past action.

9. We are looking for a new office that is _____ than our current one.

(A) large

(B) largely

(C) larger

(D) largest

> **ANSWER ANALYSIS ▶**
> ✗ (A) This is the adjective without a comparative ending.
> ✗ (B) This is an adverb.
> ✓ **(C) This sentence compares two offices—the new one and the current one. The word "than" is a cue that a comparative adjective is needed.**
> ✗ (D) This is the superlative form of the adjective.

10. The office is closed today _____ it is a holiday.

(A) although

(B) because

(C) after

(D) but

> **ANSWER ANALYSIS ▶**
> ✗ (A) "Although" introduces a contradiction. There is no contradictory situation here.
> ✓ **(B) "Because" introduces a reason. The holiday is the reason the office is closed.**
> ✗ (C) "After" introduces a time clause.
> ✗ (D) "But" introduces a contradiction. There is no contradictory situation here.

PROGRESSIVE PRACTICE: Get Set

Answer the question. Then read the explanations in the *Answer Analysis* box. Write the letter of each answer option next to the reason why it is correct or incorrect. This will help you learn to identify incorrect answer options.

1. Prices will continue to _____, and everything will become more expensive.

   (A) up

   (B) high

   (C) rise

   (D) above

   ANSWER ANALYSIS ▶

   _____ ✗ This is an adjective.

   _____ ✓ **This is a verb. The meaning of the verb is "to go up."**

   _____ ✗ This can be either a preposition or an adverb.

   _____ ✗ This can also be either a preposition or an adverb.

2. If you walk _____ the lobby, you will see the elevators on the other side.

   (A) through

   (B) between

   (C) under

   (D) on

   ANSWER ANALYSIS ▶

   _____ ✗ This means "to have one on each side."

   _____ ✗ This means "beneath."

   _____ ✗ This means "on top of."

   _____ ✓ **This means "to go from one end to the other."**

3. _____ every day is the best way to improve your health.

   (A) Exercise

   (B) To exercise

   (C) Must exercise

   (D) Exercising

   ANSWER ANALYSIS ▶

   _____ ✗ This is a modal plus a main verb and cannot be used without a subject.

   _____ ✗ This is an infinitive verb.

   _____ ✓ **This is a gerund used as the subject of the sentence.**

   _____ ✗ This is the base form of the verb.

4. You can't spend all day trying to make up your mind; it's better to be _____.

(A) decide

(B) decision

(C) decisive

(D) decisively

ANSWER ANALYSIS ▶

_____ ✓ **This is an adjective following the linking verb "be" and describing the person addressed.**

_____ ✗ This is a verb.

_____ ✗ This is an adverb.

_____ ✗ This is a noun.

5. Those snacks on the table _____ for this afternoon's staff meeting.

(A) is

(B) are

(C) has

(D) was

ANSWER ANALYSIS ▶

_____ ✗ This is the past tense third person singular form of "be."

_____ ✗ This is the third person singular form of "have."

_____ ✗ This is the third person singular form of "be."

_____ ✓ **This plural verb agrees with the plural subject "snacks."**

6. The closing of the factory had a bad _____ on the local economy.

(A) effect

(B) affect

(C) deflect

(D) perfect

ANSWER ANALYSIS ▶

_____ ✗ This is an adjective that means "ideal."

_____ ✓ **This is a noun that means "result" or "consequence."**

_____ ✗ The meaning of this word is similar to the correct answer, but it is a verb, not a noun.

_____ ✗ This is a verb that means "to repel."

7. _____ the document carefully before you sign it.

    (A) Read

    (B) To read

    (C) Reading

    (D) Should read

ANSWER ANALYSIS ▶

_____ ✓ **This is an imperative verb used to give advice or instructions.**

_____ ✗ This is a modal plus verb. It needs a subject.

_____ ✗ This is an infinitive verb form. It cannot be the subject in this case, because there is no main verb.

_____ ✗ This is a gerund. It cannot be used as the subject in this case, because there is no main verb.

8. If nobody answers the phone, please call _____ later.

    (A) on

    (B) up

    (C) back

    (D) off

ANSWER ANALYSIS ▶

_____ ✗ This forms a phrasal verb meaning "to make a phone call."

_____ ✓ **This forms a phrasal verb meaning "to call again."**

_____ ✗ This forms a phrasal verb meaning "to cancel."

_____ ✗ This forms a phrasal verb meaning "to visit."

9. I will be out of town next week, _____ I won't be able to attend the meeting.

    (A) though

    (B) so

    (C) since

    (D) or

ANSWER ANALYSIS ▶

_____ ✗ This introduces a contradiction.

_____ ✗ This introduces a reason.

_____ ✗ This introduces a choice.

_____ ✓ **This introduces a result.**

10. Several clients are visiting from out of town, and I asked _____ to join us for dinner tonight.

   (A) it

   (B) him

   (C) they

   (D) them

ANSWER ANALYSIS ▶

_____ ✓ **This is a third person plural object pronoun. It follows the main verb of the clause and refers to "clients."**

_____ ✗ This is a third person singular pronoun and would refer to a thing, not to people.

_____ ✗ This is a third person plural pronoun, but it is a subject pronoun, not an object pronoun.

_____ ✗ This is a singular, not a plural, pronoun. It refers to one man.

11. We don't have a large budget for this trip, so we really shouldn't plan to stay in _____ expensive hotel.

   (A) more

   (B) most

   (C) mostly

   (D) the most

ANSWER ANALYSIS ▶

_____ ✗ This is an adverb where an adjective is needed.

_____ ✓ **This is a superlative adjective describing one noun ("hotel") out of a group (all the hotels in the area).**

_____ ✗ This is used for comparative, not superlative, adjectives.

_____ ✗ This is missing the word "the," which is needed as part of the superlative adjective.

12. Some people might _____ at the meeting late, so let's wait before we close the door.

   (A) to arrive

   (B) arrive

   (C) arriving

   (D) will arrive

ANSWER ANALYSIS ▶

_____ ✗ This is a gerund or present participle.

_____ ✗ This is an infinitive form.

_____ ✗ This is another modal plus verb. The sentence already has one modal.

_____ ✓ **A modal is followed by the base form of the verb.**

13. Mr. Kim speaks French fluently because he _____ in France for so many years.

(A) will live

(B) is living

(C) lived

(D) lives

ANSWER ANALYSIS ▶

_____ ✓ **This is simple past tense. We know he lived in France in the past. We don't know if he still lives there, so simple past fits the sentence.**

_____ ✗ This is the future form of the verb. It doesn't fit the context.

_____ ✗ This is the present continuous form of the verb. It doesn't fit with the prepositional phrase "for so many years."

_____ ✗ This is the simple present form of the verb. It doesn't fit the context.

14. One of the most important characteristics of a good manager is that she takes _____ for her own mistakes.

(A) response

(B) responsible

(C) responsibly

(D) responsibility

ANSWER ANALYSIS ▶

_____ ✗ This is an adjective.

_____ ✓ **This is a noun. It is the object of the verb "takes."**

_____ ✗ This is an adverb.

_____ ✗ This is a noun, but it has the wrong meaning for this context. It means "answer" or "reaction."

15. We can send you an application by mail, _____ you can download one from our Website.

(A) or

(B) so

(C) since

(D) when

ANSWER ANALYSIS ▶

_____ ✗ This introduces a time clause.

_____ ✗ This introduces a result.

_____ ✓ **This indicates a choice between two actions.**

_____ ✗ This introduces a cause or reason.

PROGRESSIVE PRACTICE: Go for the TOEIC® Test

Directions: Each sentence is missing a word or phrase. Four possible answer options are shown. Choose the best answer option and mark the corresponding letter on your answer sheet.

1. The director is meeting with investors, as the company would like to _____ operations.

   (A) expend

   (B) expand

   (C) expanse

   (D) expense

2. Ms. Brown is a gifted speaker, and everybody _____ listening to her talks.

   (A) are enjoying

   (B) have enjoyed

   (C) enjoys

   (D) enjoy

3. The contractor will start the work as soon as we _____ the necessary forms.

   (A) will sign

   (B) signing

   (C) signed

   (D) sign

4. _____ more than the amount that is budgeted for this project.

   (A) Don't spend

   (B) Not spend

   (C) Doesn't spend

   (D) Won't spend

5. It is _____ to see sales drop somewhat at this time of year.

   (A) type

   (B) typify

   (C) typical

   (D) typically

6. We don't expect a large number of people to show _____ for the afternoon meeting.

   (A) up

   (B) in

   (C) out

   (D) off

7. It is very important to sign the application form _____ you submit it to the Human Resources Office.

   (A) after

   (B) before

   (C) as soon as

   (D) until

8. Ms. Jackson is interested in reading the marketing report and asked us to send _____ a copy.

   (A) she

   (B) herself

   (C) hers

   (D) her

9. All the employees working in this department _____ a formal evaluation at the end of the year.

   (A) has received

   (B) is receiving

   (C) receives

   (D) receive

10. Our office is conveniently located directly across the street _____ the subway station.

    (A) from

    (B) of

    (C) to

    (D) on

11. We have to pay taxes when we _____ parts from overseas to use in manufacturing our products.

    (A) report

    (B) import

    (C) deport

    (D) export

12. There aren't _____ chairs for the meeting, so we will have to get some from the other room.

    (A) much

    (B) number

    (C) enough

    (D) quantity

13. You really should _____ a lawyer before you sign any of those documents.

    (A) consult

    (B) to consult

    (C) consulting

    (D) consultation

14. We _____ interview most of the job applicants next week.

    (A) are going to

    (B) going to

    (C) are

    (D) to

15. We will probably have to ask for an _____ because it looks like we won't be able to meet the deadline.

    (A) extent

    (B) extend

    (C) extensive

    (D) extension

16. _____ we made our travel plans at the last minute, we were still able to get a good deal on the tickets.

    (A) Since

    (B) Despite

    (C) Although

    (D) Because

17. This printer cost much less than our other printers, but it works just _____.

    (A) well

    (B) good

    (C) as well

    (D) as good

18. We are considering _____ several temporary employees to help us with the extra workload.

    (A) hire

    (B) hiring

    (C) to hire

    (D) might hire

19. Shirley is one of our most _____ staff members; we can count on her for just about anything.

    (A) reluctant

    (B) relieved

    (C) relocated

    (D) reliable

20. If it _____ next weekend, we will have to cancel our plans for going to the beach.

    (A) rains

    (B) raining

    (C) will rain

    (D) has rained

TOEIC® Test Part 6: Text Completion

Part 6 of the Reading Test consists of four short reading passages, or texts. In each passage, there are three sentences that are incomplete. You will choose the correct word or phrase to complete each of those sentences. As in Part 5, you will need to be able to identify the grammatical form or vocabulary word that correctly completes the sentence. You may also need to refer to the context of the surrounding sentences to answer some of the questions.

Topics for Part 6 reading passages may include:

» *Letters and memos*

» *Ads*

» *E-mails*

» *Instructions*

» *Articles*

» *Notices*

QUICK GUIDE: Text Completion

Definition	Part 6 is a test of your reading comprehension. It requires you to apply your knowledge of grammar and vocabulary to reading and to understand meaning and usage in context.
Targeted Skills	In order to correctly answer Part 6 questions, you must be able to identify appropriate usage of English grammar and vocabulary, as well as correct use of words and expressions in context.
Completion Types	Part 6 items consist of incomplete sentences within a reading text, such as a letter, article, or notice. Completion items in Part 6 focus on the same types of vocabulary, word forms, and grammar items as Part 5 of the Reading Test. In addition, Part 6 questions may have the following focus. **Words in Context:** Choose the correct word among four words that all fit within a sentence grammatically. You must examine the context in which the word will be placed to choose the correct answer.
Things to Watch For	Distracters, or incorrect answer options, will often be the same as in Part 5—words that are similar but different, incorrect phrasal verbs, incorrect word forms, and incorrect grammar forms. For some questions, all answer options will be grammatically correct, but the distracters will not fit within the context of the sentence.

WALK THROUGH: Text Completion

A What You'll See

In Part 6, you will see a short reading text with three incomplete sentences. There will be four answer options for filling each blank to complete the sentence. Look at this sample text.

Glossary:

⊜ POWERED BY COBUILD

association: an official group of people who have the same job, aim, or interest

network: to try to meet new people who might be useful to you in your job

---

Third Annual City Business Owners' Conference

The Association of City Business Owners is pleased to announce that its third annual conference will take place at the Highbury Hotel on November 3. There will be a full schedule of workshops, a lunch, and an awards dinner. _____ this opportunity to meet and network

1. (A) Miss
   (B) Not miss
   (C) Missing
   (D) Don't miss

with other business owners like you. This conference is open to the public. Membership in the Association of City Business Owners is not _____. For more information about the

2. (A) required
   (B) appropriate
   (C) uncommon
   (D) appealing

conference and the association, please visit the website at _____ time.

3. (A) no
   (B) some
   (C) any
   (D) over

B What You'll Do

For Part 6, you will choose the best answer option to complete each sentence. The first sentence completion in the sample text above focuses on grammar, the second is about word meaning, and the third is about word use. Study the sentences in the sample text in Part A. Then mark the correct answers. You will need to use the words around the blanks to help you choose the best answer for each sentence completion.

GET IT RIGHT: Tips and Tasks for Answering Correctly

PASSAGE TYPES

In Part 6, you will have to choose an answer option that completes a sentence that is part of a longer passage. See the following chart for more information about the passage types that appear in Part 6.

Passage Types	
Letters	• Formal • Typically used for official communication outside of the company, such as correspondence between a company and a customer or between employees at two different companies
E-mails	• Informal • Often used for communication within the company, such as correspondence between two employees at the same company
Memos	• Usually addressed to multiple people at the same company • Provide information about an office-related topic, such as policy changes, company-wide announcements, or notices of closure
Ads	• Inform readers about an item or service • Often emphasize special promotions, product features, or low prices
Instructions	• Provide basic information about using a product or service or about how to do something, such as returning an item
Articles	• Similar to texts that appear in a newspaper or magazine • Topics may include financial news, information about research studies, or industry-specific news
Notices	• Give information about upcoming events

QUICK TIP

In order to skim effectively,

• you should first figure out the passage type. Knowing the purpose of the passage will help you determine the intended audience and locate information.

• do <u>not</u> pay attention to adjectives and articles (*a*, *an*, and *the*).

• make a mental note of the type of vocabulary used. This will help you make logical guesses about unfamiliar words and specialized vocabulary.

• look for transition words and the ideas that they connect.

• notice whether the passage has numbers, dates, proper names, and scientific or technical terms.

» **TIP 1 Skim the passage.** Regardless of the passage type, the first thing you should do before you try to answer the questions is skim the text. When you skim, you quickly read through the passage, paying attention only to the main ideas and how the passage is organized and written.

TASK 1 Look quickly at the passage on page 139. Do <u>not</u> read it completely. Then read each question and make a check mark (✓) next to the correct answer.

1. What type of passage is this?

_____ an e-mail _____ a personal letter _____ a business letter _____ an article

2. What types of dates and times does the passage have? (check all types)

_____ times of day _____ months _____ days of the week

3. Does the passage have other numbers?

_____ yes _____ no

4. Does the passage have any business names?

_____ yes _____ no

5. Does the passage have names of cities?

_____ yes _____ no

June 7

Donald Evans,

We spoke last Tuesday about the problem with several products we received in our last shipment from Tool Right Products. I am writing to ask that you send replacement products as soon as possible for the 22 missing ball-peen hammers and 17 damaged Phillips-head screwdrivers that we are returning in a separate package.

We had similar problems with previous shipments in January and March, and this is not acceptable. Please make certain that you work on improving your company's QC in the shipping department. If this continues, we will have to search for another merchandise supplier.

I trust that you will send the replacements before Friday of this week, as we need to restock merchandise for an upcoming sales event scheduled for the July 4 holiday week. If you foresee any problems with fulfilling this request, it is imperative that you call me.

Carol Buchanan
Vice President
Hill Brothers Hardware

TASK 2 Now skim the passage in Task 1. Then answer these questions. Do <u>not</u> use a dictionary.

1. Who is the letter written to?

a. Tool Right Products   **b.** Hill Brothers

2. What is the letter about?

a. a new product order   **b.** problems with shipments

3. What are Phillips-head screwdrivers?

a. computer hardware   **b.** a type of tool

4. Which context word might help you figure out what *QC* means?

a. *improving*   **b.** *shipping*

5. Why is July 4 mentioned?

a. because of a sale   **b.** because of a vacation

Try a TOEIC Test Question

Now read this sentence from the letter in Task 1. Choose the correct answer. Don't look back at the passage to find the answer!

> I trust that you will send the replacements before Friday of this week, as we need to
> _____ merchandise for an upcoming sales event scheduled for the July 4

1. (A) refuse

(B) restock

(C) record

(D) reward

holiday week.

QUESTION TYPES

Grammar-Based Questions

The majority of the grammatical concepts that appear in Part 6 are also tested in Part 5. It is important to review all of the grammar points for Part 5 in preparation for Part 6. Additionally, be sure to familiarize yourself with these grammar points.

» **TIP 1 Learn common phrasal verbs.** Phrasal verbs are two- or three-word phrases that include a verb and a preposition. In Part 6, you may encounter four different phrasal verbs as answer options. The chart below has a few of the many phrasal verbs that are commonly used in business settings. (See page 112 for another list of common phrasal verbs.)

Common Business Phrasal Verbs		
apply for (a job)	draw up (a contract)	report in at (the office)
bank on (something happening)	finish up (the report)	report off from (work)
call in (sick)	go over (the sales figures)	report to (work)
close on (a deal)	look for (a replacement)	send out (a package)
draw on (previous experience)	look into (a problem)	turn in (the report)

TASK Choose the correct phrasal verb to complete each sentence.

1. Greg will receive a commission once we (close on / look for) the deal with Weber Electronics.

2. Ms. Brennan (applied for / drew up) a job in Tokyo.

3. By working over the weekend, the team was able to (report off from / finish up) the report.

» **TIP 2 Become familiar with common business collocations.** Collocations are pairs or series of words that often appear together. In Part 6, you may have to choose among answer options to complete a common business collocation. See the following chart for a list of common business collocations.

Collocations / Definitions	Examples
brief absence - out for a short time	After a **brief absence** due to illness, Curtis is back to work.
flexible schedule - a schedule that can be changed easily	Many employees are attracted to the company because it offers **flexible schedules**.
glowing recommendation - a very good recommendation	Oliver received a job offer quickly thanks to the **glowing recommendation** from Ms. Tanner.
grounds for termination - reasons for firing an employee	Sharing confidential information about the company is **grounds for termination**.
heavy workload - a lot of work	Sheila hired a new assistant to help her manage her **heavy workload**.
leading competitor - a main rival	The company usually matches the prices set by its **leading competitor**.
on-the-job training - learning the skills for a job while at work	Thanks to his **on-the-job training**, Terry is now familiar with the software.
sales figures - the value of completed sales	Jayla compiled a report that included the **sales figures** for the entire quarter.
take-home pay - the amount of money an employee earns after taxes	A large percentage of Pamela's **take-home pay** is used to pay for housing.
up for promotion - to be eligible for a better position	After three years on the job, Harry is **up for promotion**.

TASK Unscramble the sentences.

1. [Tara knew] [a glowing recommendation.] [Mr. Finely would write her]

_____

2. [Amparo was not aware of the changes in the office.] [her brief absence,] [Due to]

_____

3. [its leading competitor] [last year.] [Terrance Industries outearned]

_____

» **TIP 3 Look for transitions in the passage to understand organization and find information.**
Transitions are words that give the reader clues as to how a paragraph or an entire passage is organized. See the chart for more information about transitions.

Functions	Transition Language		Examples
Indicates cause and effect	when as long as in order to because of due to therefore	for this reason as a result thus accordingly consequently so	_**Due to** the change in management, we will be closing two offices._ _**Consequently**, sales have fallen._
Indicates sequence	first second third eventually next	since then until prior to afterward	_**First**, be sure to turn off all the lights._ _**Second**, . . ._ _**Eventually**, we plan to open a second office._
Continues the same line of thinking	again additionally furthermore similarly	and equally likewise	_Always greet customers politely._ _**Likewise**, we expect employees to be cordial with co-workers._
Shifts the focus	although despite regardless in spite of	instead even so however	_This has been one of our best years ever. **Even so**, we expect sales to continue to improve._

TASK Choose the correct transition word or phrase to complete each sentence. Use the words in the box. There are two extra expressions.

Consequently	Due to	Equally	Regardless	Therefore

_____ rising production costs, the company was forced to raise its prices. _____, many customers were unhappy. _____, the company remained the most popular producer of consumer appliances in the region.

Try a TOEIC Test Question

Directions: Read the passage. Four answer options are given below each of the incomplete sentences. Choose the best answers to complete the sentences. Mark (A), (B), (C), or (D).

To: Front Desk Personnel <directoryfrontdesk@watersonhotels.com>
From: Richard Winters <mtnc.management@watersonhotels.com>

I am happy to announce a department-wide bonus for all front desk employees. The extra amount _____ on the paycheck for the next pay period. As you may

    1. (A) to appear
       (B) appeared
       (C) will appear
       (D) will have appeared

know, Waterson Hotel was recently named *Journey Magazine's* "Hotel of the Year." In particular, the magazine praised our front desk staff, which the writers described as "a winning combination of helpful, professional, and courteous." _____, the bonus is the hotel's way of saying thank you for a job well done

2. (A) However
   (B) Although
   (C) Accordingly
   (D) Similarly

this year and for helping the hotel earn this prestigious honor. Again, thank you very much for your excellent performance, and _____ the good work!

    3. (A) keep up
       (B) add up
       (C) catch up
       (D) end up

Sincerely,
Richard Winters, General Manager

Contextual Questions

Part 6 also includes contextual questions. All of the answer options for this question type fit grammatically, so you cannot depend on your grammar knowledge to choose the correct answer. Instead, you will have to use context clues.

» **TIP 1 Understand the key concepts of the passage.** If you know what the main idea of the passage is, you will be able to identify vocabulary that is related to the main topic. For example, if the passage is about the banking industry, you would expect to see common banking words, such as *balance*, *deposit*, or *checking account*. Don't forget to skim the entire passage—the main ideas and helpful clues are <u>not</u> always in the same paragraph as the blank.

TASK Write the vocabulary from the box under the correct headings.

loan	expense	ad campaign	hiring manager	recruit	target customer
checkbook	receipt	résumé	withdraw	billboard	balance sheet

Banking	Employment	Marketing	Accounting
1. _____	1. _____	1. _____	1. _____
2. _____	2. _____	2. _____	2. _____
3. _____	3. _____	3. _____	3. _____

» **TIP 2 Consider whether the answer options have positive or negative connotations.** By thinking about the positive or negative connotation, or meaning, of each choice, you may be able to eliminate options that do not fit the overall meaning of the sentence, passage, or paragraph. Look at this example.

Lisa was pleased about her recent _____.

(A) misfortune

(C) promotion

(B) dispute

(D) confusion

Choices (A), (B), and (D) all have negative meanings. It doesn't make sense that Lisa would be pleased about something negative, so you can eliminate those three answer options. Therefore, (C) is the correct answer.

TASK Place a check mark (✓) next to words with positive meanings and an "X" next to words with negative meanings. If you aren't sure of a word's definition, look it up in a dictionary.

_____ **1.** too expensive _____ **4.** luxurious _____ **7.** earn a raise

_____ **2.** preferable _____ **5.** overworked _____ **8.** on vacation

_____ **3.** stuck in traffic _____ **6.** award recipient _____ **9.** drowsy

» **TIP 3 Look for time markers in the nearby sentences.** Time markers are verbs or other words that indicate when an event took place. If you notice time markers near the blank, make sure that the answer you choose agrees with the time specified. For example, if the verb in the sentence before the blank is past tense, your answer choice should have a past tense meaning as well. Here are some common time markers.

Happened in the Past	Happens Habitually	Will Happen in the Future
• past tense suffix *-ed* • *yesterday* • *last week/month/year* • *a few minutes/hours/days/ weeks/months/years ago* • *before*	• simple present tense • *every morning* • *every day* • *all of the time* • *currently* • *always*	• *will* + verb • *going to* + verb • *tonight* • *tomorrow* • *next week/month/year*

Try a TOEIC Test Question

Directions: Read the passage. Four answer options are given below each of the incomplete sentences. Choose the best answers to complete the sentences. Mark (A), (B), (C), or (D).

Preventative Care: Key to Saving on Health Care in the Workplace?

A study conducted by a leading university revealed that the single most effective measure that a small business can take to prevent illness in the workplace is to _____ preventative care.

1. (A) predict
(B) challenge
(C) promote
(D) create

Preventative care involves taking action to avoid _____ before they occur. See the

2. (A) illnesses
(B) losses
(C) costs
(D) competition

following tips for preventing sickness in the workplace.

• **Place signs around the office reminding employees to wash their hands often.**
_____ hand washing prevents the spread of harmful, illness-causing germs.

3. (A) Expected
(B) Standard
(C) Careless
(D) Frequent

PROGRESSIVE PRACTICE: Get Ready

Questions 1–3

A Read the passage and look at the blanks. What types of words are missing? Write the number of each question next to the correct type of word needed to fill the blank. There is one extra word type.

_____ a gerund form of a verb   _____ a past tense verb

_____ an adjective   _____ a singular pronoun

Louise Howland
Milford Enterprises
73 Orford Street
Lyme, WA 20720

Dear Ms. Howland:

I am interested in applying for a job as an accountant at your company. I understand that you have several entry-level positions open in your Accounting Department. I recently _____ from the university with a degree in accounting. While I was

      1. (A) exited
          (B) launched
          (C) graduated
          (D) removed

still a student, I worked for two years as an assistant at Smith and Jones, Inc. _____ was a very interesting place to work, and I learned a lot while I was there.

2. (A) It
   (B) He
   (C) Him
   (D) They

I am enclosing my résumé and two letters of reference. I look forward to _____

                               3. (A) hear
                                  (B) hearing
                                  (C) will hear
                                  (D) heard

from you.

Sincerely,
Robert Carlson

B Choose the best answer to complete each sentence in Part A. Then check your answers and read the explanations in the *Answer Analysis* boxes. This will help you learn to identify correct and incorrect answer options.

1. I recently _____ from the university with a degree in accounting.

   (A) exited

   (B) launched

   (C) graduated

   (D) removed

ANSWER ANALYSIS ▶

   ✗ (A) "Exited" means "left." It is not usually used in the context of finishing school.

   ✗ (B) "Launched" means "started something new." This meaning does not fit the context.

   ✓ **(C) "Graduated" means "finished school."**

   ✗ (D) "Removed" means "took something out of." This meaning does not fit the context.

2. _____ was a very interesting place to work, and I learned a lot while I was there.

   (A) It

   (B) He

   (C) Him

   (D) They

ANSWER ANALYSIS ▶

   ✓ **(A) "It" refers back to "Smith and Jones, Inc.," the company where the writer of the letter worked. A company is a thing, not a person, so "it" is the correct pronoun.**

   ✗ (B) "He" refers to a man and cannot be used as a pronoun for a company.

   ✗ (C) "Him" refers to a man and cannot be used as a pronoun for a company. In addition, "him" is an object pronoun, but a subject pronoun is needed here.

   ✗ (D) "They" is a plural pronoun, but the pronoun needed here is singular.

3. I look forward to _____ from you.

   (A) hear

   (B) hearing

   (C) will hear

   (D) heard

ANSWER ANALYSIS ▶

   ✗ (A) "Hear" is a base form verb where a gerund is required.

   ✓ **(B) The expression "look forward to" is followed by a gerund.**

   ✗ (C) "Will hear" is a future form where a gerund is required.

   ✗ (D) "Heard" is a past tense verb where a gerund is required.

PROGRESSIVE PRACTICE: Get Set

Questions 1–3

A Read the passage and look at the blanks. What types of words are missing? Make a list.

For Rent:

Small office (300 square feet) in a downtown building that is conveniently _____ close to bus and subway lines.

    1. (A) locate
       (B) locally
       (C) located
       (D) location

Parking is also available. The office is on the second floor of a four-story building and has new paint and carpets. It is ready for a new _____ to move in on the first of next

    2. (A) tenant
       (B) landlord
       (C) customer
       (D) neighbor

month. Call Mr. Greene at 593-555-2911 for an appointment to see this office. Do you need more space? We also have several _____ offices available. Call for more information.

    3. (A) largely
       (B) largest
       (C) larger
       (D) as large as

B Answer the questions in Part A. Then read the explanations in the *Answer Analysis* boxes. Write the letter of each answer option next to the reason why it is correct or incorrect. This will help you learn to identify incorrect answer options.

1.

ANSWER ANALYSIS ▶

_____ ✗ This is a noun.
_____ ✓ **This is an adjective describing a characteristic of the building.**
_____ ✗ This is an adverb.
_____ ✗ This is a verb.

2.

ANSWER ANALYSIS ▶

_____ ✗ This word refers to someone who lives or works nearby.
_____ ✗ This word refers to someone who buys a product or service.
_____ ✗ This word refers to the owner of a building that has rental space.
_____ ✓ **This word refers to a person who rents space in a building.**

3.

ANSWER ANALYSIS ▶

_____ ✓ **This is a comparative adjective. The sentence compares the size of other offices to the office described in the ad.**

_____ ✗ This is a superlative adjective.

_____ ✗ This is an adverb.

_____ ✗ This is a comparison of equality. It doesn't fit the context, because the offices are not equal in size.

Questions 4–6

A Read the passage and look at the blanks. What types of words are missing? Make a list.

From:	m_wilson@inkinc.com
Date:	June 10
To:	s_wylie@inkinc.com
Subject:	Seoul visitors

Seymour,

Mr. Cho and Ms. Kim will be arriving from the Seoul office tomorrow afternoon. Their flight gets in at 1:30. Would you please pick them up at the airport? As soon as they arrive, they _____ to come directly to the office for a 2:00 meeting, so please bring

4. (A) needed

(B) will need

(C) to need

(D) are needing

them here. While they are in the meeting, you can _____ their luggage at their hotel.

5. (A) drop off

(B) pick up

(C) find out

(D) get in

They will probably want to rest before dinner, so you can take them back to the hotel after the meeting. I have invited them to dinner on their first night here, so please make dinner _____ for us. Most of the restaurants in this neighborhood serve great

6. (A) reservations

(B) resources

(C) requirements

(D) retailers

food, so please choose any one. Please make the reservation for 8:00. Thank you for your help.

Marcia

B Answer the questions in Part A. Then read the explanations in the *Answer Analysis* box. Write the letter of each answer option next to the reason why it is correct or incorrect. This will help you learn to identify incorrect answer options.

4.

ANSWER ANALYSIS ▶

_____ ✗ This is a past tense verb where a future verb is required.

_____ ✗ This is a present continuous verb where a future verb is required.

_____ ✗ This is an infinitive verb where a future verb is required.

_____ ✓ **The entire sentence is about the future. The first clause is the time clause, so it has a present verb. The main clause needs to be completed with a future verb.**

5.

ANSWER ANALYSIS ▶

_____ ✗ This means "to enter."

_____ ✗ This means "to claim" or "to retrieve."

_____ ✓ **This means "to deliver."**

_____ ✗ This means "to discover."

6.

ANSWER ANALYSIS ▶

_____ ✓ **This noun refers to calling ahead to hold a spot.**

_____ ✗ This noun refers to the skills and education needed to do a job.

_____ ✗ This noun refers to the group of businesses and people who sell things to the public.

_____ ✗ This noun refers to useful or valuable things.

PROGRESSIVE PRACTICE: Go for the TOEIC® Test

Directions: Read the passages. Four answer options are given below each of the incomplete sentences. Choose the best answers to complete the sentences. Mark (A), (B), (C), or (D).

Questions 1–3 refer to the following notice.

Notice to All Building Users

This is to inform you that repairs will be made to all the elevators in the building starting next week. The north elevators will be out of _____ from midnight Monday

1. (A) operate
   (B) operator
   (C) operation
   (D) operable

until midnight Tuesday. In order to avoid _____ the

2. (A) crowd
   (B) crowding
   (C) to crowd
   (D) might crowd

other elevators, we ask you to use the stairs whenever possible during that time. Work on the south elevators will begin at a later date to be determined. Thank you for your understanding. We regret any _____ this may cause.

3. (A) indefinite
   (B) inconsistence
   (C) inexperience
   (D) inconvenience

Questions 4–6 refer to the following letter.

Dear Customer,

We at Stateside Bank are excited about some new services we will be offering preferred customers such as you. As a small business owner, you may have wondered where to turn for financial _____. Now Stateside Bank is here to offer you the

        4. (A) advise

           (B) advice

           (C) advisor

           (D) advisable

support you need to keep your business in good financial health. When our new Small Business Section opens next month, we will have _____ counselors available to

        5. (A) expired

           (B) expensive

           (C) experienced

           (D) experimented

help you make decisions about investments and loans. We can help you develop a sound business plan, and we can show you how to invest your money to ensure the success of your business. Statistics tell us that the majority of small businesses fail within the first five years. _____ doesn't have to be one of them. Call Stateside

        6. (A) Ours

           (B) Yours

           (C) Mine

           (D) Theirs

Bank today to find out how we can help you stay successful.

Sincerely,
Roger Moorehead
Small Business Manager

Questions 7–9 refer to the following memo.

To: All staff
From: Mark Spyri
Re: Staff meeting

This is to remind you that the monthly staff meeting will take place next Friday afternoon from 1:00–3:00 in the conference room. Attendance at this meeting is _____. If there is an urgent reason why you cannot attend, I need to know

7. (A) mandatory
   (B) attractive
   (C) professional
   (D) punctual

about it ahead of time, so please discuss it with me _____ the meeting. The

8. (A) after
   (B) while
   (C) during
   (D) before

meeting agenda includes a discussion of certain personnel procedures, so you should _____ your copy of the employee manual with you. A complete

9. (A) bring
   (B) bringing
   (C) to bring
   (D) can bring

agenda will be made available on the day of the meeting.

Thank you.

Questions 10–12 refer to the following ad.

Parkside Hotel

Whether you are traveling for business or pleasure, the Parkside Hotel offers you all the _____ of home, from clean and cozy rooms to delicious meals in our café and

10. (A) comforts
    (B) comforting
    (C) comfortable
    (D) comfortably

restaurant, and warm and friendly service from our professionally trained staff. Our convenient downtown location makes it easy to _____ public transportation,

11. (A) acquire
    (B) assess
    (C) assure
    (D) access

museums, restaurants, theaters, and the new City Convention Center. Call or e-mail us today to reserve a room at the Parkside Hotel. You won't regret _____!

12. (A) us
    (B) it
    (C) you
    (D) them

TOEIC® Test Part 7: Reading Comprehension

Part 7 of the Reading Test consists of reading passages of varying lengths accompanied by reading comprehension questions. In the first section of Part 7, you read approximately ten single passages with a total of 28 questions. In the second section, you read four pairs of passages, each with a set of five questions that apply to both passages in the pair. There are a total of 48 questions in Part 7.

Topics for Part 7 reading passages may include:

» *E-mails, letters, and memos*

» *Advertisements*

» *Notices*

» *Articles and reports*

» *Forms*

» *Charts, tables, graphs, and schedules*

QUICK GUIDE: Reading Comprehension

Definition	Part 7 is a test of your reading comprehension. It requires you to read and comprehend main idea and detail information in a variety of passage types.
Targeted Skills	In order to correctly answer Part 7 questions, you must be able to: • understand the main idea of a reading passage. • identify details in a reading passage. • make inferences based on details. • skim to get the general idea of a reading passage. • scan for specific information. • identify correct definitions of vocabulary words.
Question Types	• **Main Idea:** *What is this article mainly about?* • **Detail:** *What time does the last train leave?* • **Inference:** *What will probably happen next week?* • **Vocabulary:** *The word "spectacle" in line 7 is closest in meaning to*
Things to Watch For	Because these are comprehension questions, you will need to be careful that you have identified the correct information within the passage. You will also need to watch for the following in questions and answer options. • **Paraphrases:** *noon* vs. *12:00* • **Negative Questions:** *Which product is NOT available online?* • **Audience:** *Who is this information for?* • **Double Passages:** You may need to confirm or compare information in two passages.

WALK THROUGH: Reading Comprehension

A What You'll See

In Part 7, you will see the directions, a complete reading text, and questions and answer options on the page for each passage. Single passages are followed by two to four comprehension questions each. Double passages are followed by five comprehension questions for each pair of texts.

Questions 1–3 refer to the following article.

Community Colleges: The Right Choice!

If you are looking for enthusiastic and reliable employees for your business, you may have to look no further than your local community college. Many community colleges provide training in skills that are applicable to a variety of business situations. Students at these institutions may be trained in such things as bookkeeping and basic accounting, sales and marketing, and data management, or they may have something more specialized, such as paralegal training. Whatever the requirements of your business, a well-trained recent community college graduate will have the necessary skills to contribute to its successful operation. Hiring locally trained staff is also a way of giving back to your community. It is a win-win situation all the way around.

Glossary:

⊜ POWERED BY COBUILD

enthusiastic: showing how much you like or enjoy something by the way you behave and talk

reliable: trusted to work well or behave in the way you want it to

contribute: say or do something to help to make something successful

1. Who is this article for?

(A) Community college students

(B) Business owners

(C) Staff trainers

(D) Employment agencies

2. What is recommended?

(A) Hiring staff from the local community

(B) Studying at a community college

(C) Getting training in business skills

(D) Being clear about business requirements

3. The word "applicable" in line 4 is closest in meaning to

(A) common

(B) understood

(C) avoidable

(D) useful

B What You'll Do

For Part 7, you need to choose the best response for each question based on the information in the passage. Now, try to answer the questions in Part A.

GET IT RIGHT: Tips and Tasks for Answering Correctly

PASSAGE TYPES

In Part 7 of the Reading Test, you will encounter different types of passages. Knowing how a passage is organized can help you find the information you need to answer questions quickly.

» **TIP Learn to recognize passage types.** Review the chart below to familiarize yourself with the different types of passages you may be asked to read in Part 7.

Descriptions of Passage Types	Typical Organization
General Correspondence ☐ • Letters are usually formal and are used for official communication outside of the company. • E-mails are typically informal and are used for communications within the company. • Memos are usually addressed to multiple people at the same company.	**Header:** may include the address of the recipient and the writer (in letters), the subject (in e-mails and memos), and the date **Greeting:** indicates who the correspondence is being directed to **First Paragraph:** describes what the correspondence is mainly about **Body Paragraphs:** give important details **Final Paragraph:** may describe what action the recipient needs to take **Signature:** indicates who the correspondence is from
Advertisements ☐ • provide information about products or services • often include information about special events, such as sales or grand openings	**Header:** describes the special event and the company making the offer **Body:** includes important details, such as the event's date, time, location, contact information, and business hours
Notices ☐ • announce special problems/warnings or information about upcoming events • often posted in public places, such as libraries, community centers, or bookstores	**Header:** indicates the problem, warning, or event being described in the notice **Body Paragraphs:** include important details like date, time, and location or reasons for the notice
Articles ☐ • texts that appear in newspapers or magazines • may include the results of studies • often describe news about businesses or community members	**Headline:** describes the main idea of the article / report **First Paragraph:** includes information that answers who, what, when, where, why, and how **Body Paragraphs:** provide additional details relating to the main topic
Instructions ☐ • provide information about using a product or service or how to do something, such as applying for a position	**Header:** describes what the instructions are for **Body Paragraphs:** give directions, often with sequence words like *first, second, third, before, next, then,* and *after*

Descriptions of Passage Types	Typical Organization *(continued)*
Forms ☐ • often include information that is completed by a customer or an evaluator • may consist of customer surveys, warranty registrations, and employee evaluations	**Header:** describes the purpose of the form **Body:** includes blanks to be completed with personal information or questions and answer boxes for the user to check off
Graphical Texts ☐ • may include both text and charts, tables, graphs, and schedules • may give information on a variety of topics, such as sales figures and consumer preferences • describe when and where events will take place	**Headers:** often include multiple headers **Fine Print:** additional information, usually in smaller text, often marked with an asterisk (*)

TASK Read the sample passages below. Then match the sample passages to the passage types in the chart on pages 154–155. Write the letter (a–g) in the white box next to each passage type.

a.

Blue Alps Ski Lodge Calendar of Events

December 17	Opening Day
December 20	Local Appreciation Day - All Blue Alps Village residents receive 50% off the daily lift tickets.
January 3	Ski Bunny Camp (for beginners only)

b.

Sales Increase for Whoop

The Chicago-based toy company Whoop has reported a twenty-five percent sales increase in the last month. According to a senior executive at the company, the increase resulted from the debut of the "Kiddy Baker" toy series, which made up nearly eighty-five percent of all sales for September.

c.

```
Dear Mr. Miller:

I am writing to confirm our meeting on January 28 at 3 p.m.
at my office. Please let me know if this is correct. If you
would like to reschedule, please contact my assistant at
555-325-1120.

Sincerely,
Beverley Simmons
```

d.

Griffin Bed and Breakfast
Customer Satisfaction Survey

Please rate your satisfaction with each of the following:	Excellent	Average	Poor
Overall satisfaction		✓	
Timeliness of check-in		✓	
Value for money	✓		

e.

Announcement

Don't miss a talk by Louise Foster, president of Treble Music Company. Ms. Foster will be speaking on December 4 in Gerber Hall at City University. E-mail events@city.edu for information and tickets.

f.

How to Use Your New Humidifier

First, remove the humidifier from the package. Second, fill the water tank with water and place the tank on the unit. Next, plug in the machine. Finally, turn on the machine.

g.

Edwinton Premium Vehicles

If you are looking for a new car, visit Edwinton Premium Vehicles today, southern Colorado's number one car dealership. There's a reason that people trust Edwinton Premium Vehicles—when you buy from us, you will receive outstanding service every step of the way. That means you will not only receive assistance from knowledgeable sales representatives when you're making your decision, but you will also have support from our award-winning automotive shop if anything ever goes wrong with your car.* So don't wait—visit us today and see what great deals are waiting for you!

*With purchase of warranty only

Double Passages

The Reading Test includes double passages at the end of Part 7. Double passages have comprehension questions that are based on two separate but related passages. Any combination of the passage types may be found in the double passages. For example, the first passage may be a letter requesting information about an event and the second a schedule for the event. Five questions appear for each double passage. You may find any of the question types that appear with the typical Part 7 passages. At least one question requires you to use information from <u>both</u> passages to identify the correct answer option.

QUICK TIP

Be sure to allow enough time to get through all of the parts of the Reading Test. You <u>are</u> permitted to go back to previous parts, so you can always go back to answer questions you weren't sure of.

» **TIP 1 Identify the information in <u>both</u> passages that can help you choose the answer.** Start by reading the question carefully in order to get a good understanding of the information you need. Then skim both passages and locate the relevant information. By doing this, you can confirm that the answer is based on information from both sources and make sure your answer is correct.

TASK Notice the highlighted information in each passage and how it is connected to Question 1. Then use the highlighted information to choose the correct answer.

Moore Sporting Goods Sale!

Spring is almost here, which means outdoor fun for everyone. Moore Sporting Goods wants to help you get ready for your spring trips by offering the lowest prices on camping gear! From March 8 to March 15 only, enjoy the lowest prices of the season on select items, including:

Your choice of tents for $80. Whether you need a summer tent or a 3-season tent, one that sleeps 2 or 8, it's only $80!* Our employees will help you choose the right tent for you.

Camping stoves for only $25. Because when you're camping, nothing is as satisfying as a warm meal.

10% off SleepReady** sleeping bags. These sleeping bags will keep you warm even on the chilliest nights.

And don't forget, you'll get a free tent light with any purchase! Don't miss this sale!

*Limited supplies
**Regular price $40

Notice to Moore Sporting Goods Shoppers

Please be advised that the advertisement published in the March 5 edition of the *Taylortown Daily* contained incorrect information for the following advertised specials:

- The advertisement says that you will receive a free tent light with any purchase. It should read "a free tent light with any purchase over $50."

- SleepReady sleeping bags are advertised as 10% off the original price. The ad should read $10 off the original price.

We apologize for any inconvenience this may have caused.

---

1. What is the correct price for SleepReady sleeping bags during the sale?

(A) $10

(B) $30

(C) $36

(D) $40

» **TIP 2 Read both passages carefully and completely.** Passages may include information that doesn't seem significant. However, it is important to consider all of the available information when answering questions. This chart shows seemingly unimportant information that is commonly used for questions that connect content from both passages.

QUICK TIP

When you scan a passage for extra information, look first for an asterisk. This is the most common way to present this extra information.

Information Types	Definitions	Found in . . .
Fine Print	• Fine print is text that is noticeably smaller than the rest of the text. • It may be marked with an asterisk (*). • Fine print gives additional details about a product or an offer, such as eligibility requirements or special terms and conditions. • Fine print may explain the sources of information.	• Advertisements • Notices • Instructions • Forms • Graphical texts
Special Pricing	• Special pricing includes coupons or discounts. • Watch out for conditions on special pricing. For example, special pricing may only apply if customers spend over a certain amount or make a purchase by a certain date.	• Correspondence • Advertisements • Notices • Forms

TASK Look at the correction notice on page 157. Underline the sentence in the correction notice that describes the correct special pricing for the tent light. Then in the advertisement, underline the prices listed for the four items in the answer options in number 1. Analyze the information in the two passages and choose the correct answer.

1. Which of the following items would qualify the customer for a free tent light?

    a. a tent   **b.** a camping stove   **c.** a sleeping bag   **d.** a cooler

» **TIP 3 Watch out for possible rewordings of time references, numbers, or alternate choices.** Double passage questions based on time references (such as times or dates), numbers (such as prices), or alternate choices often present this information in different ways. Typically, the first passage gives specific details, while the second passage discusses the same details in more general terms. For example, if the first passage gives specific dates, the second might refer to the dates in more general terms (e.g., *two days after X, a month prior to X*). This chart shows common ways of rewording time references, numbers, and alternate choices.

	What You May See in the First Passage	**What You May See in the Second Passage**
Time References	• *at 3:00* • *on January 4* • *until 10 p.m.*	• *in the afternoon* • *early in the year* • *late in the evening*
Numbers	• *50% off* • *25% increase* • *only $10 per person*	• *half-price* • *a quarter increase* • *$20 for two*
Alternate Choices	• *available in black and red* • *The first option is taking a cab. The second option is riding the bus.*	• *I bought the black, but I wish I had gotten one in the <u>other</u> color.* • *While the <u>former</u> is probably more convenient, I think the <u>latter</u> is probably less expensive.*

TASK Match the information (1–3) with the correct rewordings (a–c).

___ **1.** 12 p.m.   **a.** April 1

___ **2.** Two for the price of one   **b.** Buy 1 get one free

___ **3.** On the first of the month   **c.** Noon

QUESTION TYPES

Main Idea Questions

In Part 7, main idea questions ask you about the main themes of the reading passage. Main idea questions are usually the first in a question set. Expect to see no more than one main idea question per passage. You will encounter different subtypes of main idea questions. The chart shows different types of main idea questions.

Subtypes of Main Idea Questions		
Descriptions of Subtypes	**Answer Options**	**Examples**
Main Topic Ask about the main topic of the reading. This may include the heading choice.	include noun phrases	*What is being discussed in the memo?* *What is the advertisement for?* *What is the letter about?*
Place Ask about where the passage might appear or about the place that is being discussed.	include noun phrases describing places	*What kind of business is X?* *What kind of company does X work for?* *Where was this report probably published?*
Purpose Ask about the goal of the passage or why an author wrote the passage. This is the most common type of main idea question.	often begin with a *to* infinitive	*What is the purpose of the notice?* *Why did X write the letter?* *For whom is the report intended?*

This question type is similar to the topic / main idea questions in Parts 3 and 4 of the Listening Section. Therefore, in addition to studying the tips that follow it is advisable to review the notes for this question type in the Listening Section as well.

» **TIP 1 Know where to look for the main idea.** Depending on the passage type, you should be able to find the information you need to answer this question type by skimming a specific part of the passage. This chart gives information about where to find the main idea in different passage types.

Passage Types	Types of Main Idea Questions	Where to Find the Main Ideas
Correspondence	topic, place, purpose	first paragraph
Advertisements	place, purpose	header
Notices	topic, place, purpose	header
Articles / Reports	topic, place, purpose	headline and first paragraph
Instructions	place, purpose	header
Forms	topic, place	header
Graphical Texts	topic, place	header

TASK Match the title, headline, or introductory sentence (1–3) to the sample passage (a–c) that it best describes.

___ **1.** Manufacturing Giant to Buy Shipping Company

___ **2.** Top Ice Cream Flavors Sold

___ **3.** Follow these steps to set up your voice mailbox.

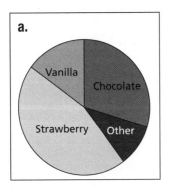

a.

b.

Press and hold down the pound key (#) for three seconds. You will then be prompted to enter a four-digit password. You will use this password to access your voice mailbox in the future, so be sure to choose a number that is easy to remember.

c.

Gregory Manufacturing announced plans to buy out the Banner Shipping Company. According to officials, the buyout will be finalized by the end of April.

» **TIP 2 Watch out for paraphrased information.** The correct answer option will likely contain reworded, or paraphrased, information from the passage.

TASK Mark the answer choice that correctly paraphrases the information in each sentence.

1. Please call our offices on Monday morning for an update.

    a. Updates about the offices will be available on Monday.

    b. For new information, contact the company at the beginning of the week.

2. The store will open its doors for the first time on February 10.

    a. The store's grand opening will take place in early February.

    b. On February 10, the store will open its doors early.

3. The bank will be closed next Friday due to a holiday.

    a. The holiday will cause numerous closures.

    b. The bank will not be open on the holiday.

QUICK TIP

If you see a choice that is worded almost the same as to the information in the passage, read it carefully because it is probably <u>not</u> the correct answer.

» **TIP 3 Eliminate answer options that focus on minor details.** Main idea questions are always about the entire passage, not just one or two points. Therefore, if you see an answer option that mentions only a minor detail, you should eliminate it.

TASK Read part of a passage. Check (✓) one main idea and make an X next to three minor ideas.

> ☐ A new study shows that performance-based payment may not be as effective as experts once believed. ☐ In a recent survey, researchers asked employees at companies that offer performance-based payment for feedback. ☐ Out of one hundred employees surveyed, only ten reported being "very happy" with the system. ☐ The majority of employees (nearly seventy percent) reported being "unhappy" or "very unhappy" with the system.

» **TIP 4 For main idea questions about place, pay attention to letterheads, addresses, and job titles.** The letterhead is the information about the business sending the correspondence. A letterhead typically includes the company's name and address. This chart includes information about letterheads, addresses, and titles and where to find them in passages.

Letterheads	Addresses	Job Titles
• The letterhead is usually located at the very top of any document issued by a company, including a letter, an invoice, or a receipt.	• In letters, the address of the recipient is usually on the top left part of the passage. • You may also find addresses in the final paragraph of correspondence, particularly if the writer wants to be contacted at a certain address.	• Job titles usually follow names in signatures.

Use letterheads, addresses, and job titles to figure out where the passage probably appeared. For example, if the company's name is Dream Tours, you can guess that the company may be a travel agency.

TASK Write the correct business type for each letterhead, address, or job title. Use the words in the box.

> shoe store   grocery store   pharmacy

Sneakers and Things 1. _____	Sincerely, *Gina Hauser* Gina Hauser, Pharmacist 2. _____	Keller and Sons Grocery 2305 N. Alameda Road Santa Fe, NM 87501 3. _____

» **TIP 5 For main idea questions about purpose, think about who the writer and the audience are.** By understanding who is probably writing the passage and the intended recipient, you will be able to eliminate answer choices that are illogical. For example, if the passage is a memo written by a staff coordinator to employees, it is unlikely that the purpose of the memo is to advertise a new product. You should also look for key phrases that signal purpose in passages.

> **Key Phrases That Signal Purpose**
>
> *I'm writing to (ask / inform / inquire) . . .*
> *I wanted to alert you that . . .*
> *I need to (explain / clarify / describe) . . .*
> *This letter serves as notice that . . .*

TASK Read the sample passage. Underline one sentence that signals the author's purpose. Then answer the question about the relationship between the writer and the recipient.

Roger Griffin
3425 Hallow Street
Benton, ID 83809

Dear Mr. Griffin:

I am writing to inquire about the assistant position advertised in the classified section of last Sunday's edition of *The Harrington Tribune*. I understand that it is a part-time position, which is perfect because I am currently a fourth-year student at Harrington College working on my thesis. This gives me great flexibility, and I am available to work at least twenty hours a week, though I may be able to work more depending on your needs. I believe that I am the ideal candidate for a number of other reasons as well. For one, last semester I worked as a personal assistant for Professor Hartley at the university. In this capacity, I answered phones and made appointments and travel arrangements for Professor Hartley. These skills, and others I gained during this experience, are undoubtedly very important for any assistant.

If you have any questions or would like to schedule an interview, please contact me by phone at 407-555-2831.

Sincerely,
John King

---

1. Which of the following best describes the relationship between Mr. Griffin and Mr. King?

    a. professor-student   **b.** employer-job candidate   **c.** writer-employee

Try a TOEIC Test Question

Questions 1–3 refer to the following letter.

Retro Diner
306 Martin Boulevard
Clarkston, AL 35295

Heller Uniforms and More
Jessica Heller, Owner
75 West Elm Street
Waterville, VA 24212

Ms. Heller:

I am writing in regard to my recent online purchase (confirmation #2301A012). According to my bill, I paid a total of $200 for ten shirts. I understand that the regular price is $20 per shirt; however, according to your website, the cost per shirt should have been $10 when purchasing more than five shirts. Therefore, I was overcharged by $100. I would like for your company to refund the $100 immediately. Please contact me via e-mail at jhill@retrodiner.com if you have any questions.

Sincerely,
Jane P. Hill

---

1. What is the purpose of the letter?

    (A) To request a copy of the invoice   (C) To complain about the quality of a product

    (B) To correct a billing error   (D) To confirm an online order

Detail Questions

Detail questions ask about specific information from the passage. They are the most common type of question in Part 7 and are used for all of the passage types. You may encounter between one and three detail questions per passage. There are two different subtypes of detail questions. This chart has more information on the subtypes.

Subtypes of Detail Questions		
Descriptions of Subtypes	Answer Choices	Examples
Wh- Questions: ask about specific facts and typically begin with any of the following *wh-* words: *who, what, when, where, why, how,* and *how much/many*	*who*: proper nouns, noun phrases *what*: nouns, noun phrases *when*: adverbial phrases starting with *in* (range of time or specific year), *at* (specific time), or *on* (day or date) *where*: places, adverbial phrases starting with *in* or *at* *why*: adverbial phrases beginning with *to* *how*: adverbial phrases starting with *by* *how much/many*: numbers, time references	*Who* is responsible for maintaining the machinery? *What* is one of the company's policies? *When* is the package scheduled to arrive? *Where* are the extra supplies stored? *Why* is Mr. Traynor going out of town? *How much* is the total?
Negative Fact Questions: ask you whether a given detail is true or false	nouns, noun phrases	*Which of the following is NOT true about X?* *Which product is NOT available from the online store?* *What is NOT a requirement?*

QUICK TIP

Look for the word *NOT* in capital letters in negative questions.

In addition to the tips that follow, be sure to review the tips for detail questions in Parts 3 and 4 of the Listening Section.

» **TIP 1 Read the questions first, paying special attention to key words.** By reading the questions first, you will know what information you need in order to choose the answer. Then you can scan the passage and quickly find the key words. Also, remember which key words are associated with certain *Wh-* questions.

Wh- Questions	What Types of Key Words to Look For
Who	names, job titles
When	time, date
Where	locations
Why	explanations, cause and effect relationships
How	explanation of a process
How much	numbers, times, prices, discounts, percentages

TASK Underline the *Wh-* word and other key words in each question below. Then circle the type of information you need to find in the passage.

1. When will the conference take place?

    a. a time   **b.** a place

2. Why did Ms. Bybee mention the airport in her memo?

    a. a suggestion   **b.** a reason

3. How much did Mr. Tan pay for the jacket?

    a. a size   **b.** a price

4. Which of the following is NOT true about Bloomfield Industries?

    a. a fact   **b.** an opinion

5. Where is the company's headquarters?

    a. a time   **b.** a place

» **TIP 2 For negative fact questions, watch out for lists.** The answer choices for negative fact questions are often based on lists, and the fact or detail that is <u>not</u> mentioned in the list is the correct answer.

TASK In each list, place a check mark (✓) next to the items that are mentioned in the passage.

From...	Sue Costa
To...	Max Moeller
Cc...	
Subject:	Office Supplies

Send

Max,

We have run out of a few essential items around the office. Please purchase the following by tomorrow: paper and ink for the printer and standard-sized envelopes. I know we're running low on pens, but I get a special deal on them from our supply company, so I'd rather hold off on those. Also, I can reimburse you for whatever you spend on these items. Just be sure to leave the receipt and a purchase form on my desk.

Thanks!
Sue

QUICK TIP

Train your eyes to see negative words like *not* and *no*. Whenever you see one of these words, slow down and read carefully. Watch for other negative words, such as *never, none,* or *nothing* and negative prefixes like *un-*.

List 1
☐ **1.** printer ink
☐ **2.** envelopes
☐ **3.** boxes
☐ **4.** printer paper
☐ **5.** pens

List 2
☐ **1.** provide the receipt
☐ **2.** reimburse the author for the purchase
☐ **3.** leave the purchase form on the desk

» **TIP 3 For negative fact questions, take your time.** When you see a negative fact question, make sure to read all of the answer choices carefully and confirm the facts in the passage. Eliminate any choices that <u>are</u> supported by the passage. The remaining answer option is the correct choice.

TASK The questions below are based on the e-mail in the Tip 2 Task. Read the questions and answer options carefully and eliminate any answer choices that are supported by the passage. Then circle the correct answers.

1. Max was NOT instructed to buy which of the following items?

    a. printer ink   **c.** printer paper

    b. envelopes   **d.** pens

2. What does Max NOT need to do?

    a. provide the receipt   **c.** get a reimbursement

    b. get a special deal   **d.** leave the receipt and a purchase form on the desk

Try a TOEIC Test Question

Questions 1–2 refer to the following letter.

William Henley
74 W Quarter Street
New Haven, CT 06501

Mr. Henley:

Thank you for your interest in McKinnon Industries. Your application for employment has been received by the Human Resources Department and will be forwarded to the division that you applied to for further review. Therefore, if you have any questions about your application, please contact the Engineering Department directly, not Human Resources. If one of the hiring managers expresses an interest in your skills, you will be contacted directly by a representative of that department.

Please note that due to the number of inquiries that we receive, my department is not able to return any materials that you may have submitted as part of your application, including CVs, portfolios, and samples.

Sincerely,
Roger Jackson, Human Resources Generalist
McKinnon Industries

---

1. Why is the company unable to return application materials to job applicants?

    (A) The materials become property of the company once submitted.

    (B) The company receives too many materials to return them all.

    (C) The materials are sent to different departments within the company.

    (D) The company needs the materials to make hiring decisions.

2. Which of the following is NOT true about Mr. Jackson?

    (A) He will personally contact Mr. Henley with a job offer.

    (B) He works in the Human Resources Department.

    (C) He regularly receives applications for employment.

    (D) He is unable to answer questions about an application status.

Inference Questions

Inference questions ask about information that is strongly implied in the passage. The correct answers for inference questions are <u>not</u> stated directly. However, the passage will provide enough information for you to draw the correct conclusion. There are two different subtypes of inference questions. The chart gives more information on the subtypes.

Subtypes of Inference Questions		
Descriptions of Subtypes	**Answer Choices**	**Examples**
General Inference: asks you to draw conclusions about facts that are strongly implied but not stated outright in the passage	nouns, noun phrases, complete sentences	*What is suggested about X?* *What can be inferred about X?* *What will most likely occur?* *What will X probably do?*
Intended Audience: asks you to infer who the passage is written for	nouns, noun phrases referring to people or groups of people, job titles	*Who is the memo written for?* *Who will likely read the notice?*

In addition to the tips that follow, be sure to review the tips for inference questions in Parts 3 and 4 of the Listening Section.

» **TIP 1 Pay attention to information about dates and locations.** Inference questions often use specific information about dates and locations in the passage. You will then have to choose an answer option that generalizes that specific information. For example, the passage may give the exact date that an event is taking place. The correct answer may then involve determining that something took place before or after the date given.

TASK Read the sample brochure below. Circle four references to times or dates and four references to locations.

Holiday Cruises

Travel in style on our popular Caribbean Cruise.

- Ten nights
- Choose from three departure dates: March 4, March 23, April 5
- The cruise departs from Fort Lauderdale, Florida
- Ports of call in Mexico, Belize, and the Cayman Islands

» **TIP 2 Make sure your answer choice is supported by information in the passage.** Although the passage won't give you the answer directly, it will provide enough clues for you to be able to choose the correct answer. Once you have chosen an answer, return to the passage and find the parts that support your answer. If you can't find information to support your answer, reconsider your choice.

TASK These inferences are based on the brochure in the Tip 1 Task. Place a check mark (✓) next to each correct inference and underline the information in the brochure that supports the statement.

☐ 1. The Caribbean cruise lasts more than one week.

☐ 2. The company offers several cruise dates in the summer.

☐ 3. The cruise makes at least three stops.

Try a TOEIC Test Question

Questions 1–2 refer to the following webpage.

Making Your Profile at RealJobs.com Work for You

Congratulations! By creating a profile at RealJobs.com, you've taken the first step toward finding the job of your dreams. Now you'll be able to search through over one million job listings in fifty major cities around the world. Here are some tips for getting the maximum benefits from the website, which has been specially designed to help you find a job you love.

- Upload a current résumé. It's the only way that recruiters can see what skills you have to offer and contact you if they have a position that's right for you.

- Complete the preference page. Just log into your account and click on the "preference" tab at the top right side of the page. On this page, you'll be able to enter the industries you're interested in and the cities you'd prefer to work in.

- Sign up for RealJobs.com's monthly newsletter. Our newsletter will give you updates about the site and offer great tips for finding jobs.

---

1. Who is the webpage meant for?

(A) Web designers

(B) Job hunters

(C) Business executives

(D) Real estate agents

2. What is probably true about people who are contacted by recruiters?

(A) They posted their résumés on the website.

(B) They signed up for the monthly newsletter.

(C) They set their preferences on the website.

(D) They live in one of the preferred cities.

QUICK TIP

To find the word, count down from the top of the passage. The title of the passage is often included in the line numbering, so look up or down one more line if you don't spot the word right away.

Vocabulary Questions

Vocabulary questions ask you to choose the answer option that has the same meaning as a word or phrase from the passage. The question will provide the word in quotation marks and will give you the line where that word can be found in the passage. In text with more than one paragraph, you may be given both the paragraph and line number.

Description of Question	Answer Choices	Example
Vocabulary: asks you to choose the word or phrase that has the same meaning as a word from the passage	nouns, verbs, adjectives, adverbs	*The word "X" in line 1 is closest in meaning to*

» **TIP 1 Find the word in the passage.** The question will tell you the line or the paragraph and line where the word can be found. Once you have located the word, read the sentence that it appears in as well as the surrounding sentences, paying special attention to any context clues that will help you understand the definition of the word. The chart has some helpful tips for using context clues.

Strategies for Using Context Clues		
Strategies	**Key Words**	**Examples**
Pay attention to **examples** that appear near the vocabulary word. If you are familiar with the examples, you can use them to determine the meaning of the vocabulary word.	*such as* *including* *consists of* *this includes* *along with* *like*	*They keep copies of* ***contracts*** *in a safe place* <u>*along with other important documents.*</u>
Look for key words that signal a **contrast** from a previous idea. If you know the meanings of the words from surrounding sentences, you will know that the question word has an opposite meaning.	*Unlike X, . . .* *On the other hand, X . . .* *while . . .* *But* *However*	<u>*While Lisa was always on time*</u>, *Gertrude was regularly* ***tardy.***

TASK Use the underlined context clues to help you choose the correct word to complete each sentence.

1. The price for the new version is (considerably / hardly) higher, <u>almost twice as much as the first edition</u>.

2. <u>Unlike Walter's office, which is always a comfortable temperature</u>, Yolanda's office always feels (moderate / frigid).

3. The company offers a number of (financial / essential) services, <u>including market updates and low-cost trading</u>.

» **TIP 2 Try replacing the vocabulary word with each of the answer options.** If you aren't sure about the correct answer for a vocabulary question, try each answer option in place of the given vocabulary word. You should eliminate any answer options that do not support the main ideas of the passage or are illogical when placed in the passage.

TASK One word in each of the sentences is illogical. Draw a line through the incorrect word. Then write the word from the box that should replace it.

candidates	renovations	suspicious

1. The lobby will be closed for several months due to renewals.

_____

2. There were reports of limited activity in the parking lot.

_____

3. Mr. Howard will be interviewing job terminals this afternoon.

_____

QUICK TIP

Improve your business vocabulary by reading business magazines and newspapers. When you encounter an unfamiliar word, make sure to look it up in a dictionary. Don't forget to learn all of the definitions of a word, as you may be asked about an uncommon usage.

Try a TOEIC Test Question

Questions 1–3 refer to the following reviews.

Reviews for Allen 1000-Watt Steamer

By: cleaningdad100   ★★★★

This product has changed the way I clean my house. I can use it to sanitize just about anything—toilets, showers, sinks, even my upholstered sofa. The best part is that I can clean my house without using any harmful chemical cleaners, which is important to me because I have two young children and a dog. It produces steam for about forty-five minutes, which is more than enough time to do everything I need to do. However, I am giving this product four stars instead of five stars because I found that the cord is much too short. Other than this slight shortcoming, I am completely happy with the steam cleaner.

Reviews for Allen 1000-Watt Steamer

By: RhondaS   ★★

To be honest, I expected a lot more from this product. It works fine on fabric surfaces like curtains or carpets, but when I tried it on the tile in my bathrooms, it didn't work at all. Plus, it is very loud when in use, which really bothered me. This model is $25 more than the other popular models, and I really thought that for the extra money, I'd get a higher-quality machine. I'll be returning this to the store and getting a more reasonably priced model tomorrow.

---

1. In the first review, the word "sanitize" in line 1 is closest in meaning to

   (A) fill

   (B) stain

   (C) replace

   (D) clean

2. In the first review, the word "shortcoming" in line 8 is closest in meaning to

   (A) limitation

   (B) danger

   (C) advantage

   (D) excess

PROGRESSIVE PRACTICE: Get Ready

Questions 1–3

A Read the advertisement and look at the questions. Write the number of each question next to the circled piece of information that answers it. Then answer the questions.

Sale! Sale! Sale!

Pringle's Downtown Shop Announces Its Semiannual Sale.

You'll find great discounts throughout the store.

- Women's Blouses .... 15% off
- Men's Trousers .... 15% off
- Men's and Women's Sportswear .... 20% off   **a.** _____
- Men's and Women's Office Attire .... 15–25% off
- Men's, Women's, and Children's Ski Outfits .... 35% off

Sale Dates: Monday, April 10 to Friday, April 14   **b.** _____

Don't miss these great discounts—your last chance for incredible prices on our entire stock of winter clothes.   **c.** _____

Come see our new line of summer clothing starting Saturday, April 15.

---

1. What is on sale?

  (A) Skis

  (B) Clothes

  (C) Office supplies

  (D) Sports equipment

2. What is offered at a 20% discount?

  (A) Blouses

  (B) Trousers

  (C) Sportswear

  (D) Office attire

3. What day does the sale end?

  (A) Monday

  (B) Wednesday

  (C) Friday

  (D) Saturday

B Now check your answers and read the explanations in the *Answer Analysis* boxes. This will help you learn to identify correct and incorrect answer choices in Part 7.

1.

ANSWER ANALYSIS ▶

  ✗ (A) This is confused with "ski outfits," which means clothes you wear for skiing.

  ✓ **(B) "Blouses," "trousers," "sportswear," "attire," and "outfits" are all words that refer to clothes.**

  ✗ (C) This is confused with "office attire," which means clothes you wear to the office.

  ✗ (D) This is confused with "sportswear," which means clothes you wear in informal situations.

2.

ANSWER ANALYSIS ▶

   ✗ (A) Blouses have a 15% discount.

   ✗ (B) Trousers have a 15% discount.

   ✓ **(C) Men's and women's sportswear is listed as 20% off.**

   ✗ (D) Office attire has a 15–25% discount.

3.

ANSWER ANALYSIS ▶

   ✗ (A) Monday is the first day of the sale.

   ✗ (B) Wednesday is not mentioned anywhere in the ad.

   ✓ **(C) The sale goes from Monday, April 10 to Friday, April 14.**

   ✗ (D) Saturday is the day after the sale ends, when new summer clothes will be sold.

Questions 4–6

A Read the schedule and look at the questions. Write the number of each question next to the circled piece of information that answers it. Then answer the questions.

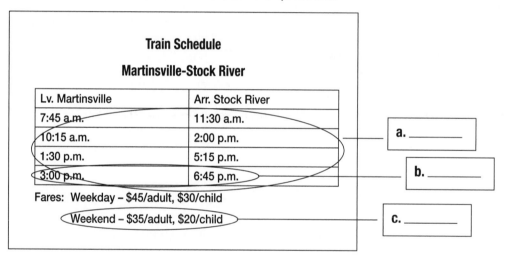

Train Schedule

Martinsville-Stock River

Lv. Martinsville	Arr. Stock River
7:45 a.m.	11:30 a.m.
10:15 a.m.	2:00 p.m.
1:30 p.m.	5:15 p.m.
3:00 p.m.	6:45 p.m.

Fares: Weekday – $45/adult, $30/child
          Weekend – $35/adult, $20/child

a. _____

b. _____

c. _____

4. How many trains a day travel between Martinsville and Stock River?

  (A) Two

  (B) Four

  (C) Six

  (D) Eight

5. How much does an adult ticket cost on a Saturday?

  (A) $20

  (B) $30

  (C) $35

  (D) $45

6. What time does the last train of the day get to Stock River?

  (A) 7:45 a.m.

  (B) 11:30 a.m.

  (C) 3:00 p.m.

  (D) 6:45 p.m.

B Now, check your answers and read the explanations in the *Answer Analysis* boxes. This will help you learn to identify correct and incorrect answer choices in Part 7.

4.

ANSWER ANALYSIS ▶

✗ (A) This is the number of columns on the schedule.

✓ **(B) There are four trains listed on the schedule.**

✗ (C) This number isn't mentioned anywhere.

✗ (D) This is confused with the number of times shown. There are two times for each train—the time it leaves and the time it arrives.

5.

ANSWER ANALYSIS ▶

✗ (A) This is the weekend child fare.

✗ (B) This is the weekday child fare.

✓ **(C) The weekend adult fare is $35.**

✗ (D) This is the weekday adult fare.

6.

ANSWER ANALYSIS ▶

✗ (A) This is the time the first train leaves Martinsville.

✗ (B) This is the time the first train arrives in Stock River.

✗ (C) This is the time the last train leaves Martinsville.

✓ **(D) The last train of the day leaves Martinsville at 3:00 p.m. and arrives in Stock River at 6:45 p.m.**

PROGRESSIVE PRACTICE: Get Set

Questions 1–3

A Read the notice and study the questions. Circle the information in the notice that answers each question. Then answer the questions.

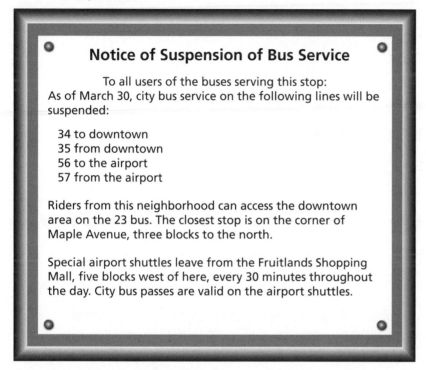

Notice of Suspension of Bus Service

To all users of the buses serving this stop:
As of March 30, city bus service on the following lines will be suspended:

34 to downtown
35 from downtown
56 to the airport
57 from the airport

Riders from this neighborhood can access the downtown area on the 23 bus. The closest stop is on the corner of Maple Avenue, three blocks to the north.

Special airport shuttles leave from the Fruitlands Shopping Mall, five blocks west of here, every 30 minutes throughout the day. City bus passes are valid on the airport shuttles.

1. What will happen on March 30?

(A) Buses will be added to some routes.

(B) Some bus routes will stop running.

(C) The cost of bus passes will increase.

(D) A new bus stop will be built.

2. What can bus riders do at the shopping mall?

(A) Buy a bus pass

(B) Catch the 23 bus

(C) Get a ride to the airport

(D) Take the bus to Maple Avenue

3. The word "access" in line 9 is closest in meaning to

(A) view

(B) return

(C) depart

(D) reach

B Now read the explanations in the *Answer Analysis* boxes. Write the letter of each answer option next to the reason why it is correct or incorrect. This will help you learn to identify incorrect answer options.

1.

ANSWER ANALYSIS ▶

_____ ✗ A bus stop is mentioned but not a new one.

_____ ✓ **Some bus lines "will be suspended," that is, they will no longer be in service.**

_____ ✗ Bus passes are mentioned, but their cost is not.

_____ ✗ This is the opposite of the correct answer. Buses will be removed from service, not added.

2.

ANSWER ANALYSIS ▶

_____ ✓ **The notice states, "Special airport shuttles leave from the Fruitlands Shopping Mall . . ."**

_____ ✗ This mentions the name of the street where the 23 bus stops.

_____ ✗ Bus passes can be used on the airport shuttles, which leave from the mall, but there is no mention made of where to buy them.

_____ ✗ This can be done on Maple Avenue.

3.

ANSWER ANALYSIS ▶

_____ ✗ This means "see."

_____ ✗ This means "go back."

_____ ✓ **Bus riders can "reach" or "get to" the downtown area on the 23 bus.**

_____ ✗ This means "leave."

Questions 4–6

A Read the letter to the editor and look at the questions. Circle the information in the letter that answers each question. Then answer the questions.

Dear Editor,

For a long time, our city was without a public park that was clean and safe for families. Now, thanks to the City Parks and Recreation Department and our mayor, we have a beautiful city park that every citizen can enjoy. And this was done without great cost to our city. Some politicians suggested building a completely new park at a cost of millions of dollars. Instead, at a much smaller cost, the mayor wisely decided to clean up the city park that already existed.

The park was closed for nearly all of last year while the improvements were being made. The Parks and Recreation Department has done a beautiful job. They removed all the trash, planted gardens, and installed new playground equipment. The presence of police and the new lighting system have ensured the safety of citizens using the park. While the park has already been open for a month, a special celebration was held last week. There was a very large turnout.

The newly improved park is a point of pride for our city. I invite all citizens who have not yet seen it to visit it soon.

Sincerely,
Nicholas Charles

---

4. Why did Mr. Charles write the letter?

(A) To praise the work done on the park

(B) To suggest building another park

(C) To complain about the cost of the park

(D) To invite people to a picnic in the park

5. How has the park been improved?

(A) It is bigger.

(B) It is cleaner and safer.

(C) It has more playgrounds.

(D) It has new fountains.

6. When was the park reopened?

(A) Last year

(B) A month ago

(C) Last week

(D) Yesterday

B Now read the explanations in the *Answer Analysis* boxes. Write the letter of each answer option next to the reason why it is correct or incorrect. This will help you learn to identify incorrect answer options.

4.

ANSWER ANALYSIS ▶

_____ ✗ This is what some politicians suggested, but Mr. Charles does not agree with it.

_____ ✓ **The main idea of the letter is that the park is much better now than it was before.**

_____ ✗ This is what Mr. Charles does at the end of the letter, but it is a detail, not the main point.

_____ ✗ Mr. Charles is happy about the low cost of improving the park. He says, "Instead, at a much smaller cost, the mayor wisely decided to clean up the city park that already existed."

5.

ANSWER ANALYSIS ▶

_____ ✓ **In the past, the park was not clean or safe. Now improvements include less trash, a police presence, and a better lighting system.**

_____ ✗ New playground equipment is mentioned, but the number of playgrounds is not.

_____ ✗ There is no mention of any change in the size of the park.

_____ ✗ Gardens are mentioned, but fountains are not.

6.

ANSWER ANALYSIS ▶

_____ ✗ This is when there was a celebration.

_____ ✗ This is not mentioned anywhere in the letter.

_____ ✓ **Mr. Charles writes, "While the park has already been open for a month . . ."**

_____ ✗ This is when the park was closed.

Questions 7–11

A Read the schedule AND the e-mail and look at the questions. Circle the information in the schedule or e-mail that answers each question. Then answer the questions.

Green Island Ferry Schedule

To Green Island

Leave Mainland	Arrive Green Island
7:00 A.M.	8:30 A.M.
9:30 A.M.	11:00 A.M.
2:30 P.M.	4:00 P.M.
5:00 P.M.	6:30 P.M.

To Mainland

Leave Green Island	Arrive Mainland
9:00 A.M.	11:30 A.M.
12:00 P.M.	1:30 P.M.
4:30 P.M.	6:00 P.M.
8:00 P.M.	9:30 P.M.

Fares

Foot passengers	$15 (one way)	$25 (roundtrip)
Passenger with car	$40 (one way)	$70 (roundtrip)

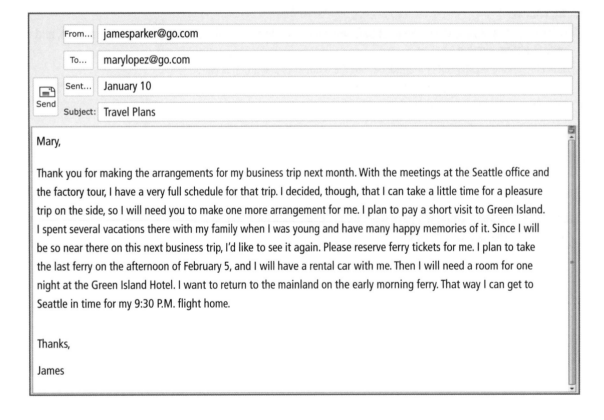

From... jamesparker@go.com

To... marylopez@go.com

Sent... January 10

Subject: Travel Plans

Mary,

Thank you for making the arrangements for my business trip next month. With the meetings at the Seattle office and the factory tour, I have a very full schedule for that trip. I decided, though, that I can take a little time for a pleasure trip on the side, so I will need you to make one more arrangement for me. I plan to pay a short visit to Green Island. I spent several vacations there with my family when I was young and have many happy memories of it. Since I will be so near there on this next business trip, I'd like to see it again. Please reserve ferry tickets for me. I plan to take the last ferry on the afternoon of February 5, and I will have a rental car with me. Then I will need a room for one night at the Green Island Hotel. I want to return to the mainland on the early morning ferry. That way I can get to Seattle in time for my 9:30 P.M. flight home.

Thanks,

James

7. How many scheduled ferries travel every day from the mainland to Green Island?

(A) Three

(B) Four

(C) Eight

(D) Sixteen

8. Why is James going to Green Island?

(A) To have fun

(B) To visit family

(C) To see a factory

(D) To meet colleagues

9. How much will his ferry ticket cost?

(A) $15

(B) $25

(C) $40

(D) $70

10. What time will his ferry to Green Island leave?

(A) 7:00 a.m.

(B) 9:30 a.m

(C) 5:00 p.m.

(D) 8:00 p.m.

11. What will James do on the evening of February 6?

(A) Stay at the Green Island Hotel

(B) Fly back home

(C) Ride the ferry

(D) Have a business meeting

B Now read the explanations in the *Answer Analysis* boxes. Write the letter of each answer option next to the reason why it is correct or incorrect. This will help you learn to identify incorrect answer options.

7.

ANSWER ANALYSIS ▶

_____ ✗ This is the number of ferries traveling in both directions, but the question asks about one direction only.

_____ ✓ **This is the number of ferries shown in the first schedule, mainland to Green Island.**

_____ ✗ This is the total number of arrival and departure times shown on the schedule.

_____ ✗ This number is one less than the correct answer.

8.

ANSWER ANALYSIS ▶

_____ ✗ We might assume that James will do this during the business portion of his trip.

_____ ✗ James mentions this as something he will do during the business portion of his trip.

_____ ✗ This is confused with James mentioning that he has visited the island with his family in the past.

_____ ✓ **In the e-mail, James refers to this as a "pleasure trip."**

9.

ANSWER ANALYSIS ▶

_____ ✗ This is the cost of a one-way ticket for a passenger without a car.

_____ ✗ This is the cost of a one-way ticket with a car.

_____ ✓ **James mentions that he will have a car and says he will return the next morning, so he needs a round-trip ticket for a passenger with a car.**

_____ ✗ This is the cost of a roundtrip ticket for a passenger without a car.

10.

ANSWER ANALYSIS ▶

✓ **James wants to take the last ferry of the afternoon. The last ferry for Green Island leaves at 5:00, according to the schedule.**

✗ This is when the second ferry of the day leaves.

✗ This is when the last ferry leaves from the island going to the mainland.

✗ This is when the first ferry of the day leaves.

11.

ANSWER ANALYSIS ▶

_____ ✗ This is what he will do in the morning, not the evening, of February 6.

_____ ✗ This is what he will do on the evening of February 5.

_____ ✓ **James will go to the island on February 5. The next day, February 6, he will return to Seattle and get a 9:30 p.m. flight home.**

_____ ✗ This is what he will probably do before his visit to the island.

PROGRESSIVE PRACTICE: Go for the TOEIC® Test

Directions: In this part, you will read different types of texts. The texts are followed by questions. Choose the best answers to the questions, and mark (A), (B), (C), or (D).

Questions 1–3 refer to the following article.

Lamp Sales Up

Wilson Manufacturers announced that sales of lamps, the company's major product, increased dramatically during the final quarter of the year. Sales were up 15 percent from the preceding quarter and were 25 percent higher than during the same period of the preceding year. "Of course we normally expect higher sales during the holiday season," said company spokesperson Amanda Randall. "But that doesn't explain such a dramatic increase, especially when you compare the figures to last year's holiday sales. This year's sales are significantly higher." Ms. Randall attributes the success to her company's new approach to marketing. "We've put advertisements everywhere, and everyone is talking about them," she said. The rise in popularity of the lamps has inspired other companies to jump on the bandwagon and manufacture a similar line of products. "We aren't afraid of competitors," said Ms. Randall. "We know we have a quality product. It's the best in the market. Even though we may have higher pricing, people still know a genuine Wilson lamp when they see one."

---

1. When did lamp sales go up?

(A) Sometime in the first six months of the year

(B) During the last three months of the year

(C) At the beginning of last year

(D) In the middle of last year

2. According to Ms. Randall, what caused sales to go up?

(A) The holiday season

(B) An advertising campaign

(C) Lack of competitors

(D) Improved manufacturing

3. What does Ms. Randall say about her company's product?

(A) It is superior to other companies' products.

(B) It costs less than other companies' products.

(C) It has been selling well for several years.

(D) Its popularity will continue to increase.

Questions 4–6 refer to the following instructions.

TX 9000 Owner's Manual
Using Your New TX 9000

- To ensure proper functioning, make sure the battery is fully charged before use. Attach the accompanying power cord and connect it to an electrical outlet for at least ten hours.

- To make a call, press the power button and wait until you hear a dial tone. Then dial the number.

- Frequently used numbers may be stored. Press *1 and follow the instructions on the screen to store a number.

- To retrieve your voicemail, press *9 and follow the recorded instructions.

Maintenance
- Harsh detergents and coarse materials such as steel wool may scratch the surface of the TX 9000. Complete immersion in water may damage it permanently. Wipe gently with a damp cloth. A small amount of mild soap may be applied. Dry with a clean cloth or paper towel.

- If the TX 9000 should cease to function, do not attempt to repair it yourself. Call a qualified technician.

---

4. What are these instructions for?

(A) A CD player

(B) A telephone

(C) A battery charger

(D) A dishwasher

5. The word "retrieve" in line 12 is closest in meaning to

(A) get

(B) send

(C) share

(D) record

6. How should the TX 9000 be cleaned?

(A) By scrubbing it with steel wool

(B) By rubbing it softly with a cloth

(C) By pouring detergent into it

(D) By dipping it in water

Questions 7–9 refer to the following article.

Cotton is heading for a big slump as this year's harvest swells supplies. Shortages that drove costs higher than ever before over the past five years are now easing up. As a result, by the end of September, prices had plunged 25 percent for the year and will probably drop even more before the end of December, according to figures reported by the National Cotton Producers Association. In the meantime, supplies have expanded, boosting inventories to higher levels than have been seen in at least five years.

Cotton production is expanding and is expected to continue to do so. Last year's price rise encouraged farmers to plant more, and successful methods of combating common diseases and pests have increased crop yields. The continuing spell of favorable weather has also been encouraging to cotton producers, many of whom were almost wiped out by the droughts of the past decade. The National Cotton Producers Association will release the final figures for this year's harvest in its annual report, due out in January.

7. What does the article say about this year's cotton prices?

(A) They have gone up.

(B) They have gone down.

(C) They will stay the same.

(D) They are expected to go up soon.

8. What has affected this year's cotton supply?

(A) Increased production

(B) Poor weather conditions

(C) Decreased demand

(D) Devastation by disease

9. When will the yearly report on cotton production be available?

(A) At the beginning of the year

(B) At the end of the year

(C) In September

(D) Before December

Questions 10–14 refer to the following two letters.

November 16, 20—

Edmund Marcus
Marketing Director
Findlay Manufacturing Company
P.O. Box 99
Outback, IL 79930

Dear Mr. Marcus:

I am interested in applying for a position in the Marketing Department of the Findlay Manufacturing Company. I recently graduated from the university with a degree in sales and marketing. My job experience includes working as an assistant at a local import-export firm. I worked at this job for three summers in a row while I was completing my university degree. Although I don't have any direct experience working in marketing, I took several university courses in this area, and I got high grades in all my classes. I am enclosing my résumé and can provide you with letters of recommendation from my professors as well as from my supervisor at the import-export firm. I am particularly interested in market research. However, I would be happy to consider any available positions you may have in your department. I look forward to hearing from you.

Sincerely,

Myra Collins

November 30, 20—

Myra Collins
156 Robin Lane
Outback, IL 79932

Dear Ms. Collins:

Thank you very much for your letter inquiring about positions at our company. Your academic record is impressive, as is your enthusiasm for your future career. I appreciate your interest in working for Findlay Manufacturing. Unfortunately, we don't have any openings in our department for someone with your limited work history. The research work in which you expressed an interest requires a minimum of three years, experience in the field. Other positions in our department would require something similar. I suggest that you spend some time gaining some practice in your chosen field. One way to do this would be to get a position as an intern. While you would not be paid for this type of position, it would help you get the experience you need. My colleague Ms. Richardson is currently looking for interns to help out in the Marketing Department at her company. With your permission, I would like to forward the information you sent me to her office. Then she would be in touch with you about an internship with her company. Please let me know if this would work for you. Again, thank you for your interest in Findlay, and I wish you all the best of luck.

Sincerely,

Edmund P. Marcus

10. Why did Ms. Collins write the letter?

(A) To ask for employment

(B) To ask for a recommendation

(C) To ask for information about the company

(D) To ask for Ms. Richardson's contact information

11. What field of work is Ms. Collins interested in?

(A) Importing and exporting

(B) Teaching college

(C) Manufacturing

(D) Marketing

12. What does Mr. Marcus say about Ms. Collins?

(A) She is highly skilled in her field.

(B) She lacks interest in her career.

(C) She was a bad student.

(D) She has insufficient experience.

13. What does Mr. Marcus recommend to Ms. Collins?

(A) Taking university courses

(B) Getting more work experience

(C) Looking for a job with higher pay

(D) Applying for a position as a researcher

14. What does Mr. Marcus want to send to Ms. Richardson?

(A) A résumé

(B) Academic records

(C) A university diploma

(D) Letters of recommendation

Questions 15–19 refer to the following schedule and e-mail.

Association of Financial Consultants
Annual Conference

Ryegate Convention Center

May 10–12, 20—

Friday,	May 10	
	5:00–7:00 p.m.	Social Hour
	7:30 p.m.	Dinner
		Keynote Address by Dr. Andrew Brown
Saturday,	May 11	
	8:30 a.m.–12:00 P.M.	Morning Workshop Sessions
	12:30–1:30 P.M.	Lunch
	2:00–5:00 P.M.	Afternoon Workshop Sessions
	8:00 P.M.	Awards Banquet
Sunday,	May 12	
	8:30–9:30 P.M.	Breakfast
	10:00 P.M.	City Sightseeing by Bus

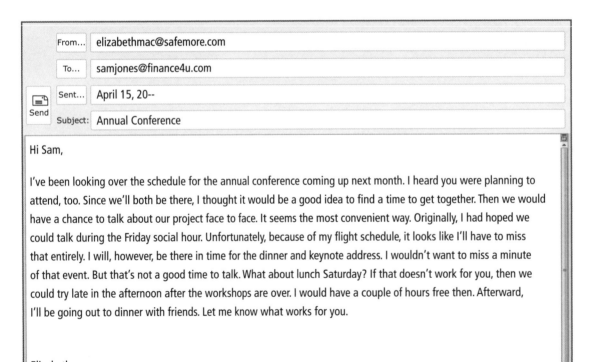

From... elizabethmac@safemore.com

To... samjones@finance4u.com

Sent... April 15, 20--

Subject: Annual Conference

Hi Sam,

I've been looking over the schedule for the annual conference coming up next month. I heard you were planning to attend, too. Since we'll both be there, I thought it would be a good idea to find a time to get together. Then we would have a chance to talk about our project face to face. It seems the most convenient way. Originally, I had hoped we could talk during the Friday social hour. Unfortunately, because of my flight schedule, it looks like I'll have to miss that entirely. I will, however, be there in time for the dinner and keynote address. I wouldn't want to miss a minute of that event. But that's not a good time to talk. What about lunch Saturday? If that doesn't work for you, then we could try late in the afternoon after the workshops are over. I would have a couple of hours free then. Afterward, I'll be going out to dinner with friends. Let me know what works for you.

Elizabeth

15. What is probably Elizabeth's job?

(A) Administrative assistant

(B) Financial consultant

(C) Conference planner

(D) Tour guide

16. Why did Elizabeth write the e-mail?

(A) To schedule a meeting with Sam

(B) To ask for workshop information

(C) To invite Sam to attend the conference

(D) To propose a new project

17. What time will Elizabeth arrive on Friday?

(A) At 5:00

(B) Before 7:00

(C) By 7:30

(D) After 7:30

18. What will Elizabeth do on Saturday evening?

(A) Attend the banquet

(B) Meet Sam

(C) Talk with colleagues

(D) Eat with friends

19. What event will happen on Sunday?

(A) A lunch

(B) A tour

(C) A workshop

(D) A banquet

Practice TOEIC® Test: Reading

TAKING THE PRACTICE TEST

The following Reading Practice Test will help you evaluate the TOEIC test-taking skills that you have learned for the Reading Section of the test. The Reading Practice Test is divided into three parts, just as on the actual test. The level of difficulty of the written material is like that of the TOEIC test. The timing should also be set like the test, so try to complete the Reading Test in 75 minutes or less.

We advise you to simulate the actual test when you take the Reading Practice Test. Take the test in a quiet setting. Be sure to follow the directions exactly as instructed.

Use the answer sheet on page 187 to mark your answers as you will on the actual test. You may remove the answer sheet from the book or make a photocopy for reuse if you want to try the test again. Use a #2 pencil. Mark your answers by filling in the letters of your answer choices on the answer sheet.

For example, the test taker below has chosen "B."

Be sure you mark only one answer per item on your answer sheet. If you want to change an answer, be sure to erase it completely. Do NOT cross it out! On the actual test, this will be scored as two answers and the item will be marked as incorrect.

SCORING THE TEST

After you complete the Reading Practice Test, check your answers in the answer key that starts on page 212. Scores on the actual test are determined by the number of correct answers. This raw score is then converted to a scaled score. Only the scaled score is released to the test taker. While your score on this practice test is not a sure guarantee of your TOEIC® test score, you can calculate a comparable scaled score by referring to the scoring chart on page 246.

Reading Comprehension Practice Test Answer Sheet

101. Ⓐ Ⓑ Ⓒ Ⓓ   126. Ⓐ Ⓑ Ⓒ Ⓓ   151. Ⓐ Ⓑ Ⓒ Ⓓ   176. Ⓐ Ⓑ Ⓒ Ⓓ
102. Ⓐ Ⓑ Ⓒ Ⓓ   127. Ⓐ Ⓑ Ⓒ Ⓓ   152. Ⓐ Ⓑ Ⓒ Ⓓ   177. Ⓐ Ⓑ Ⓒ Ⓓ
103. Ⓐ Ⓑ Ⓒ Ⓓ   128. Ⓐ Ⓑ Ⓒ Ⓓ   153. Ⓐ Ⓑ Ⓒ Ⓓ   178. Ⓐ Ⓑ Ⓒ Ⓓ
104. Ⓐ Ⓑ Ⓒ Ⓓ   129. Ⓐ Ⓑ Ⓒ Ⓓ   154. Ⓐ Ⓑ Ⓒ Ⓓ   179. Ⓐ Ⓑ Ⓒ Ⓓ
105. Ⓐ Ⓑ Ⓒ Ⓓ   130. Ⓐ Ⓑ Ⓒ Ⓓ   155. Ⓐ Ⓑ Ⓒ Ⓓ   180. Ⓐ Ⓑ Ⓒ Ⓓ

106. Ⓐ Ⓑ Ⓒ Ⓓ   131. Ⓐ Ⓑ Ⓒ Ⓓ   156. Ⓐ Ⓑ Ⓒ Ⓓ   181. Ⓐ Ⓑ Ⓒ Ⓓ
107. Ⓐ Ⓑ Ⓒ Ⓓ   132. Ⓐ Ⓑ Ⓒ Ⓓ   157. Ⓐ Ⓑ Ⓒ Ⓓ   182. Ⓐ Ⓑ Ⓒ Ⓓ
108. Ⓐ Ⓑ Ⓒ Ⓓ   133. Ⓐ Ⓑ Ⓒ Ⓓ   158. Ⓐ Ⓑ Ⓒ Ⓓ   183. Ⓐ Ⓑ Ⓒ Ⓓ
109. Ⓐ Ⓑ Ⓒ Ⓓ   134. Ⓐ Ⓑ Ⓒ Ⓓ   159. Ⓐ Ⓑ Ⓒ Ⓓ   184. Ⓐ Ⓑ Ⓒ Ⓓ
110. Ⓐ Ⓑ Ⓒ Ⓓ   135. Ⓐ Ⓑ Ⓒ Ⓓ   160. Ⓐ Ⓑ Ⓒ Ⓓ   185. Ⓐ Ⓑ Ⓒ Ⓓ

111. Ⓐ Ⓑ Ⓒ Ⓓ   136. Ⓐ Ⓑ Ⓒ Ⓓ   161. Ⓐ Ⓑ Ⓒ Ⓓ   186. Ⓐ Ⓑ Ⓒ Ⓓ
112. Ⓐ Ⓑ Ⓒ Ⓓ   137. Ⓐ Ⓑ Ⓒ Ⓓ   162. Ⓐ Ⓑ Ⓒ Ⓓ   187. Ⓐ Ⓑ Ⓒ Ⓓ
113. Ⓐ Ⓑ Ⓒ Ⓓ   138. Ⓐ Ⓑ Ⓒ Ⓓ   163. Ⓐ Ⓑ Ⓒ Ⓓ   188. Ⓐ Ⓑ Ⓒ Ⓓ
114. Ⓐ Ⓑ Ⓒ Ⓓ   139. Ⓐ Ⓑ Ⓒ Ⓓ   164. Ⓐ Ⓑ Ⓒ Ⓓ   189. Ⓐ Ⓑ Ⓒ Ⓓ
115. Ⓐ Ⓑ Ⓒ Ⓓ   140. Ⓐ Ⓑ Ⓒ Ⓓ   165. Ⓐ Ⓑ Ⓒ Ⓓ   190. Ⓐ Ⓑ Ⓒ Ⓓ

116. Ⓐ Ⓑ Ⓒ Ⓓ   141. Ⓐ Ⓑ Ⓒ Ⓓ   166. Ⓐ Ⓑ Ⓒ Ⓓ   191. Ⓐ Ⓑ Ⓒ Ⓓ
117. Ⓐ Ⓑ Ⓒ Ⓓ   142. Ⓐ Ⓑ Ⓒ Ⓓ   167. Ⓐ Ⓑ Ⓒ Ⓓ   192. Ⓐ Ⓑ Ⓒ Ⓓ
118. Ⓐ Ⓑ Ⓒ Ⓓ   143. Ⓐ Ⓑ Ⓒ Ⓓ   168. Ⓐ Ⓑ Ⓒ Ⓓ   193. Ⓐ Ⓑ Ⓒ Ⓓ
119. Ⓐ Ⓑ Ⓒ Ⓓ   144. Ⓐ Ⓑ Ⓒ Ⓓ   169. Ⓐ Ⓑ Ⓒ Ⓓ   194. Ⓐ Ⓑ Ⓒ Ⓓ
120. Ⓐ Ⓑ Ⓒ Ⓓ   145. Ⓐ Ⓑ Ⓒ Ⓓ   170. Ⓐ Ⓑ Ⓒ Ⓓ   195. Ⓐ Ⓑ Ⓒ Ⓓ

121. Ⓐ Ⓑ Ⓒ Ⓓ   146. Ⓐ Ⓑ Ⓒ Ⓓ   171. Ⓐ Ⓑ Ⓒ Ⓓ   196. Ⓐ Ⓑ Ⓒ Ⓓ
122. Ⓐ Ⓑ Ⓒ Ⓓ   147. Ⓐ Ⓑ Ⓒ Ⓓ   172. Ⓐ Ⓑ Ⓒ Ⓓ   197. Ⓐ Ⓑ Ⓒ Ⓓ
123. Ⓐ Ⓑ Ⓒ Ⓓ   148. Ⓐ Ⓑ Ⓒ Ⓓ   173. Ⓐ Ⓑ Ⓒ Ⓓ   198. Ⓐ Ⓑ Ⓒ Ⓓ
124. Ⓐ Ⓑ Ⓒ Ⓓ   149. Ⓐ Ⓑ Ⓒ Ⓓ   174. Ⓐ Ⓑ Ⓒ Ⓓ   199. Ⓐ Ⓑ Ⓒ Ⓓ
125. Ⓐ Ⓑ Ⓒ Ⓓ   150. Ⓐ Ⓑ Ⓒ Ⓓ   175. Ⓐ Ⓑ Ⓒ Ⓓ   200. Ⓐ Ⓑ Ⓒ Ⓓ

Reading Practice Test

PART 5: INCOMPLETE SENTENCES

Directions: Each sentence is missing a word or phrase. Four possible answer options are shown. Choose the best answer option and mark the corresponding letter on your answer sheet.

101. We are relying on the _____ of everyone in the department to meet the deadline on this project.

(A) collaborate

(B) collaborator

(C) collaboration

(D) collaboratively

102. As soon as Ms. Lark _____ the documents, I will put them in an envelope and mail them.

(A) is signing

(B) will sign

(C) signed

(D) signs

103. Since so few people were able to attend, we decided to put _____ the meeting until next week.

(A) off

(B) on

(C) up

(D) in

104. The amount they paid the consultant is quite low and not fair _____ for the high quality of work he did.

(A) expenditure

(B) disbursement

(C) compensation

(D) indebtedness

105. _____ the office is located in a prime downtown location, the rent is actually not very high.

(A) Because

(B) Although

(C) Even

(D) Therefore

106. If you place your desk _____ those two windows, you will be able to take advantage of the natural sunlight.

(A) through

(B) between

(C) inside of

(D) from

107. Several members of the audience left the auditorium before the speaker _____ his speech.

(A) finishing

(B) have finished

(C) had finished

(D) had been finished

108. _____ we expected work on this project to be finished by June, but now it looks as though we will need a few more weeks.

(A) Initial

(B) Initiate

(C) Initiative

(D) Initially

109. We hope to see a substantial _____ in sales by the end of the quarter.

(A) rise

(B) raise

(C) up

(D) elevate

110. Mr. Kim expects _____ with several clients during his trip to the coast.

(A) meet

(B) meeting

(C) to meet

(D) meets

111. Anyone who remains _____ in finding out more about this opportunity should contact the program director.

(A) interest

(B) interested

(C) interesting

(D) interests

112. Because of our large backlog, we won't be able to review your request _____ Friday.

(A) to

(B) soon

(C) until

(D) as

113. Unless you have a minimum of five years' experience in this field, you won't _____ for the job.

(A) qualify

(B) quantify

(C) quantity

(D) qualification

114. Dr. Chantal _____ in Europe this week, but she will be back in the office next Monday.

(A) travel

(B) have traveled

(C) did travel

(D) is traveling

115. It really is a very informative article if you _____ a few minor factual errors.

(A) overhead

(B) overload

(C) overstay

(D) overlook

116. If you leave the office early this afternoon, you _____ the holiday party we have planned.

(A) miss

(B) will miss

(C) have missed

(D) are missing

117. _____ with your supervisor directly about this problem is probably the best way to handle it.

(A) Speak

(B) Speaks

(C) Speaking

(D) Will speak

118. Any employee who has worked here a minimum of two years _____ eligible for a raise.

(A) is

(B) are

(C) be

(D) have

119. We probably should put some money aside in a special _____ to ensure that we can meet these extra expenses.

(A) account

(B) accountant

(C) accounting

(D) accountable

120. It will be difficult to go back and change the details of the contract _____ it has been signed.

(A) by

(B) once

(C) during

(D) following

Go to the next page. ➔

121. Roger decided not to accept the job
_____ the salary he was offered was a
good deal less than he had hoped for.

(A) unless

(B) since

(C) though

(D) despite

122. Miranda gained a lot of _____ into
French culture while living and working in
Paris all those years.

(A) inspire

(B) inside

(C) insight

(D) inspect

123. We _____ have job openings in this office,
so I suggest you submit your application to
another department of the company.

(A) seldom

(B) always

(C) usually

(D) often

124. We cannot do anything to correct the
problem if no one is willing to take
_____ for the mistakes that were made.

(A) response

(B) responsible

(C) responsibly

(D) responsibility

125. If the weather hadn't been so bad, more
people _____ up for the meeting.

(A) showed

(B) shown

(C) had shown

(D) would have shown

126. Mr. Smithers is not in the office right now,
but you could _____ him on his cell
phone.

(A) call

(B) to call

(C) calling

(D) will call

127. I considered _____ for a job with that
company, but I finally decided to stay where
I am.

(A) apply

(B) to apply

(C) applying

(D) applied

128. In order to _____ expenses on our trip,
we have decided to stay at a less luxurious
hotel.

(A) minimal

(B) minimize

(C) minimum

(D) miniature

129. Everybody _____ that the new city
theater is a great improvement over the old
one.

(A) agree

(B) agrees

(C) have agreed

(D) agreements

130. After the conference in Honolulu, I plan to
catch a plane _____ Tokyo.

(A) to

(B) by

(C) at

(D) on

131. Neither the bus _____ the train will get
you to the meeting on time.

(A) either

(B) and

(C) nor

(D) or

132. The play last night wasn't bad, but I thought
the one we saw last week was _____.

(A) entertained

(B) entertainment

(C) most entertaining

(D) more entertaining

133. After you have reviewed those documents, _____ them on my desk.

(A) leave

(B) to leave

(C) leaving

(D) have left

134. I never eat in the cafeteria because I don't like the _____ of food they offer.

(A) select

(B) selective

(C) selection

(D) selectively

135. We have been _____ this space for the past seven years and would like to stay for at least another seven.

(A) rent

(B) rents

(C) rented

(D) renting

136. Of all the reports I have read about the situation, this one is certainly the _____.

(A) more comprehensive

(B) most comprehensive

(C) comprehensive

(D) comprehension

137. We plan on _____ at least a week at the beach next month.

(A) spend

(B) to spend

(C) spending

(D) may spend

138. I have asked the new assistant _____ me put the mailing together.

(A) helped

(B) can help

(C) helping

(D) to help

139. We decided to have the entire office _____ before the conference next month.

(A) painted

(B) painter

(C) painting

(D) paint

140. I _____ in an apartment ever since I sold my house last summer.

(A) live

(B) lived

(C) am living

(D) have been living

This is the end of Part 5.

Go to the next page to start Part 6. →

PART 6: TEXT COMPLETION

Directions: Read the passages. Four answer options are given below each of the incomplete sentences. Choose the best answers to complete the sentences. Mark (A), (B), (C), or (D).

Questions 141–143 refer to the following e-mail.

From: marina@company.com

To: larry@larryinc.com

Subject: Car

Hi Larry,

I hope everything is going well with your business. I'm writing to ask if you would do me a tremendous favor. A client will be visiting from out of town tomorrow. We have meetings and appointments planned at several different locations around the city, and I was expecting to use my car to get to them. Unfortunately, it broke down yesterday and is now at the garage. The _____ says he can't have it repaired and ready for me until sometime next week.

141. (A) mechanic

(B) mechanical

(C) mechanism

(D) mechanistic

So I was wondering if I could _____ your car tomorrow. I would pick it up at your house in the

142. (A) lend

(B) give

(C) loan

(D) borrow

morning and bring it back to you by early evening. I would even drop you off at the subway station so you could get to work. Please _____ me know if you can help me out. I would greatly

143. (A) to let

(B) lets

(C) let

(D) letting

appreciate it.

Thanks,

Marina

Questions 144–146 refer to the following instructions.

Store Return Policy

You may return your purchase to the store for a complete refund at any time and for any reason _____ 60 days of the purchase date. You must return your purchase in

144. (A) without

(B) within

(C) during

(D) while

_____ original packaging, and you must include all parts. Returns must be accompanied

145. (A) it

(B) its

(C) their

(D) yours

by the receipt as proof of place and date of purchase. Any item that is obviously used or mishandled or that is missing parts is not returnable. You may choose to receive your refund in the form of _____ cash or store credit. Please direct any questions about this policy

146. (A) either

(B) both

(C) also

(D) nor

to the store manager.

Go to the next page. ➜

Questions 147–149 refer to the following article.

The City Council voted yesterday to _____ ten million dollars in additional funds

147. (A) disprove

(B) reprove

(C) approve

(D) improve

to expand parking in the downtown commercial district. Shoppers and merchants _____

148. (A) agree

(B) equal

(C) same

(D) alike

have long been complaining about the lack of adequate parking downtown. "It simply drives customers away," said Charlene Pembroke, spokesperson for the Downtown Merchants Association. "It hurts our bottom line." A recent poll sponsored by the association showed that more and more shoppers are choosing to spend their time and dollars in suburban malls rather than fight for parking spaces downtown. Pembroke expressed _____ with the decision

149. (A) satisfaction

(B) satisfactorily

(C) satisfactory

(D) satisfy

of the City Council. "On behalf of the members of the Downtown Merchants Association, I thank the City Council for finally showing some sense," she said in an interview yesterday.

Questions 150–152 refer to the following memo.

InterOffice Memo

To: All staff

From: P. Jenkins, Office Manager

Subject: Out of the office

I will be out of the office for all of next week. In my absence, any questions regarding office procedures should _____ to my assistant, Mary Stevens. She will also have the key to the supply closet

150. (A) direct

(B) directed

(C) be directed

(D) are directing

and can _____ you with any office supplies you may need during this time. If you have been

151. (A) instruct

(B) provide

(C) require

(D) arrange

contemplating any large purchase orders, I ask you _____ until my return on August 10. I will be

152. (A) wait

(B) waiting

(C) to wait

(D) may wait

happy to assist with ordering at that time.

Thank you.

This is the end of Part 6.

Go to the next page to start Part 7. ➜

PART 7: READING COMPREHENSION

Directions: In this part you will read different types of texts. The texts are followed by questions. Choose the best answers to the questions, and mark (A), (B), (C), or (D).

Questions 153–154 refer to the following advertisement.

Come on down to **Herbert's** for the annual

end-of-the-year sale.

Only three days left to get unbelievable prices on selected items.

Men's and Ladies' Sweaters----------$20–$30

All Footwear in Store----------------30% off

Children's Winter Jackets-----------$10, $15, or $20 off

Men's Shirts and Pants--------------up to 20% off

Coupon

Herbert's

$20 off coupon

Good for any purchase exclusive of sale items

One coupon per customer per visit

Good through December 21

---

153. What is on sale at a 30 percent discount?

(A) Jackets

(B) Sweaters

(C) Shoes and boots

(D) Shirts and pants

154. What can the coupon be used for?

(A) All items

(B) All sale items

(C) All children's items

(D) All regularly priced items

Questions 155–158 refer to the following notice.

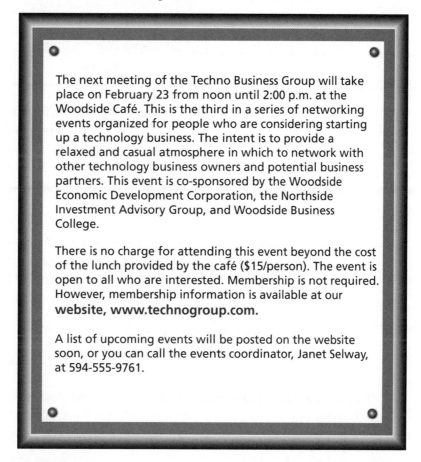

The next meeting of the Techno Business Group will take place on February 23 from noon until 2:00 p.m. at the Woodside Café. This is the third in a series of networking events organized for people who are considering starting up a technology business. The intent is to provide a relaxed and casual atmosphere in which to network with other technology business owners and potential business partners. This event is co-sponsored by the Woodside Economic Development Corporation, the Northside Investment Advisory Group, and Woodside Business College.

There is no charge for attending this event beyond the cost of the lunch provided by the café ($15/person). The event is open to all who are interested. Membership is not required. However, membership information is available at our **website, www.technogroup.com.**

A list of upcoming events will be posted on the website soon, or you can call the events coordinator, Janet Selway, at 594-555-9761.

155. Who is the meeting for?

(A) Business entrepreneurs

(B) Business professors

(C) Investment advisors

(D) Development organizations

156. How many meetings have already taken place?

(A) One

(B) Two

(C) Three

(D) Four

157. What is the purpose of the meeting?

(A) To have lunch

(B) To meet others with similar interests

(C) To learn about making investments

(D) To recruit members

158. What information does Janet Selway offer?

(A) A schedule of future events

(B) Reports on past events

(C) Membership applications

(D) Café lunch menus

Go to the next page. →

Questions 159–160 refer to the following document.

Steadman Brothers Company

Estimate

Date:	May 14
Job description:	To paint the premises at 346 Cornwall Avenue, Suite 34. Walls and ceilings. Includes prep work: spackling, sanding, minor repairs, and cleanup after job. Start date May 21, with completion by May 30.
Colors:	Ceilings: flat white Walls: satin light blue
Estimate:	$4,000. We require a 25% deposit. Please remit a check for $1,000 made out to Steadman Brothers Company. Balance of $3,000 due upon completion of the job.

Thank you for your business!

---

159. When will the painting work begin?

(A) May 14

(B) May 12

(C) May 21

(D) May 30

160. How much has to be paid before the work begins?

(A) $1,000

(B) $2,500

(C) $3,000

(D) $4,000

Questions 161–162 refer to the following advertisement.

For Rent First floor of Main Street building suitable for retail. Large display windows facing street, storage area, manager's office, total of 5,000 square feet. Customer parking in rear. In mixed residential/ commercial neighborhood convenient to public transportation. Call landlord for further information: 867-555-4825. Open house next Sunday, 2–5 p.m. 436 South Main Street. Looking for something a little different? We have other commercial properties available. Visit our website to see what's available.

161. What is for rent?

(A) A house

(B) Office space

(C) Store space

(D) An apartment building

162. How can you see the space?

(A) Call the owner for an appointment

(B) Speak with the property manager

(C) Visit it next Sunday

(D) Look at a website

Questions 163–165 refer to the following brochure.

Sunshine, Inc.
Winter Packages

Has winter got you down? Try a little Sunshine!

We'll whisk you away to a tropical paradise where you can luxuriate in the warm sand and gentle ocean breezes. You'll stay at a luxury beachside hotel with all the amenities. You can spend your days relaxing poolside or take advantage of any of our optional side excursions. If a more active vacation suits your fancy, we also have a variety of hiking, fishing, sailing, and horseback riding trips. See inside to find out more.

Beach Resort Vacations

Seven days, breakfast and dinner included.........$1500/person (double occupancy)*
Ten days, breakfast and dinner included...........$2000/person (double occupancy)*
Two weeks, breakfast included.........................$2700/person (double occupancy)*

* subtract $50 a day for single occupancy
All prices exclusive of airfare. Call our office for current prices on airline tickets at **800-555-4300.**

163. What kind of business is Sunshine, Inc.?

(A) A hotel resort

(B) A travel company

(C) A cruise ship company

(D) A package delivery service

164. The word "amenities" in line 6 is closest in meaning to

(A) services

(B) rooms

(C) meals

(D) guests

165. What is NOT found in the brochure?

(A) The office phone number

(B) Information about trips

(C) Airline ticket prices

(D) A list of vacation types

Go to the next page. ➜

Questions 166–169 refer to the following article.

Disaster Loans Available

Disaster relief programs that arose after the Green River overflowed its banks last spring are still in operation, providing assistance to homeowners and businesses alike. Government and private charitable organizations have been making funds available in the form of both loans and grants to people who lost property as a result of the flood. These are monies offered to help families rebuild homes that were washed away and to assist businesses with replacing inventory that was submerged in the flood waters.

In addition, a number of local banks have set up programs for people who need smaller amounts of money to repair lesser damages caused by the disaster. Stateside Bank is one of several banks that have set up a special loan program to make it possible for local residents to complete small jobs, such as repairing flooded basements and replacing waterlogged furnaces. Stateside is offering loans in amounts up to $15,000 per family. The low rate of four percent with a maximum term of ten years makes it possible for working families to take on these loans without undue financial burden. So far, the bank has lent out over $500,000 in these loans, and strong interest in the loans continues. As a result of the continuing interest, the bank has decided to extend the program for three more months. Qualifying families have until December 31 to apply. The bank has earmarked one million dollars for these special disaster-relief loans. Property insurance typically covers fires, storms, and earthquakes but not flood damage unless special flood insurance has been purchased, so this type of loan assistance is crucial to the recovery of the region.

166. What was the disaster?

(A) A flood

(B) A fire

(C) A storm

(D) An earthquake

167. Who qualifies for the Stateside Bank loans?

(A) Families who lost their homes

(B) Business owners who lost their inventory

(C) People who want to buy homes

(D) Families whose houses had minor damage

168. When do the Stateside Bank loans have to be repaid?

(A) Before December 31

(B) Before next spring

(C) Within three months

(D) Within ten years

169. What is the total amount Stateside Bank plans to lend in disaster loans?

(A) $15,000

(B) $150,000

(C) $500,000

(D) $1,000,000

Questions 170–172 refer to the following notice.

NOTICE

The next meeting of the Oakmont Condo Association will take place on Saturday, September 12 at 1:00 p.m. in the first floor lounge. This is the regular general monthly meeting and is open to all building residents. Items on the agenda will include:
- Fixing the roof: costs, schedule, bid procedure
- Improving visitor parking: whether we need more spaces, possible locations
- Building maintenance crew: whether we need additional workers
- Painting interior halls: we need to vote on a color

In addition, the Social Committee will present their ideas for the annual holiday party and also ask for ideas from the association members. We plan to adjourn at 2:30 p.m., at which time refreshments will be served. All who wish to may stay to enjoy a social hour. The room has been reserved by another group at 5:00 p.m. Please be considerate and leave the room clean.

170. Who is the meeting for?

(A) Occupants of the building

(B) Visitors to the building

(C) Building staff

(D) Committee heads

171. Which of the following will NOT be discussed?

(A) Building repairs

(B) Hiring staff

(C) Social events

(D) Condo fees

172. The word "adjourn" in line 14 means

(A) begin

(B) enjoy

(C) end

(D) stay

Go to the next page. →

Questions 173–176 refer to the following article.

Is Breakfast Part of Your Day?

Do you often find yourself feeling sluggish midmorning? Do you reach for coffee, a sugary soda, or a candy bar in order to keep going? Unfortunately, this scenario is all too common. Walk into any office around 11:00 in the morning and you are likely to see desks littered with candy bar wrappers and empty cups. Contrary to what you may think, this is not due to heavy morning workloads. The problem starts earlier in the day, at the breakfast table. There is nothing truer than that old adage, "Breakfast is the most important meal of the day." Some people skip breakfast because they are in a hurry. Others are watching their weight and want to avoid the calories. However, starting the day without breakfast actually ends up causing more problems later in the day. A nutritious breakfast provides you with the energy you need to stay alert and productive throughout the morning. Without it, you end up reaching for that caffeine or candy bar. This gives you a short burst of energy but then leaves you feeling even more tired. And, as everyone knows, candy and soda provide you with only empty calories and no nutritional value. So make breakfast part of your day. It doesn't have to be a huge meal but should be nutritionally balanced. Make sure it includes fruit, protein, and a grain. You'll arrive at the office with the energy you need to tackle whatever is waiting for you at your desk.

173. Who is this information for?

(A) Office workers

(B) Nutritionists

(C) Dieters

(D) Cooks

174. What commonly happens around midmorning?

(A) People start to feel tired.

(B) The workload gets heavier.

(C) People clean up their desks.

(D) There is a scheduled coffee break.

175. The word "skip" in line 10 is closest in meaning to

(A) share

(B) omit

(C) dislike

(D) prefer

176. What does the writer recommend?

(A) Drink coffee

(B) Eat at your desk

(C) Eat low-calorie food

(D) Have breakfast

Questions 177–180 refer to the following letter.

July 10, 20—
Roberta Palmer
Marketing Director
The Waldo Company
P.O. Box 295040
Outerbridge, WY 73901

Dear Ms. Palmer,

I very much enjoyed meeting with you yesterday and discussing career opportunities at Waldo. The tour of the Waldo facilities was very informative. The spirit of cooperation among the Waldo staff is quite evident, and the friendly yet professional atmosphere made it seem like such a pleasant place to work. I was especially interested to see the work of the overseas section of the Marketing Department, as international marketing is a particular interest of mine. As I mentioned to you yesterday, I would love to have the opportunity to gain experience in this area.

I am still very much interested in pursuing a possible position at Waldo. You already have my résumé and letters of reference, and I would be glad to provide you with any further information you may need. I am enclosing a copy of my review of current innovations in marketing, which I mentioned to you yesterday. It appeared in the March issue of *Modern Marketing* journal and explains in some detail my thoughts on several of the approaches we discussed yesterday.

Again, thank you for taking the time to meet with me yesterday. I look forward to hearing from you.

Sincerely,
Carlos Lopez

177. Why did Carlos write this letter?

(A) To provide an evaluation of the Waldo company

(B) To inquire about job openings at Waldo

(C) To follow up on a job interview

(D) To offer Ms. Palmer a job

178. The word "evident" in paragraph 1, line 3 is closest in meaning to

(A) nice

(B) clear

(C) unusual

(D) needed

179. What does Carlos say about international marketing?

(A) He spent a year overseas in college.

(B) He is an international expert in this area.

(C) He would like to expand his experience.

(D) He thinks the company should be more involved.

180. What did Carlos send with the letter?

(A) A copy of an article

(B) A journal he wrote

(C) A résumé

(D) A reference letter

Go to the next page. ➔

SKILLS FOR THE TOEIC® TEST: LISTENING AND READING

Questions 181–185 refer to the following brochure and form.

Professional Development Opportunities

The Human Resources Department is pleased to present a series of professional development opportunities. These workshops are available to all company employees at no charge. The one exception to this is Word Processing training, which is provided by an outside company. See below for further information.

If you are interested in attending any of these workshops, please fill out the attached form and submit it to the Human Resources Department at least two weeks prior to the date of the workshop. Please don't forget to have your supervisor sign to indicate approval. Please address any questions about workshop content or registration procedures to Mr. Clark in the Human Resources Department.

WORKSHOPS

Writing
Business Writing   May 10, 8:00 a.m.–3:00 p.m.
Proposal Writing   May 14, 10:00 a.m.–4:00 p.m.
Technical Writing   May 14, 8:00 a.m.–3:00 p.m.
                      May 21, 8:00 a.m.–3:00 p.m.
Writing for the Web   May 18, 10:00 a.m.–2:00 p.m.
Instructors: To be determined

Computer Skills
Databases   May 10, 1:00 p.m.–4:00 p.m.
Web Design   May 11, 8:00 a.m.–3:00 p.m.
Word Processing* May 12, 8:00 a.m.–4:00 p.m.
Instructors: To be determined

The writing workshops will take place in Conference Room A. The computer skills workshops will take place in the training room.

*The cost of this workshop is $250 for the entire day, or $150 for the morning only. If you have any concerns about your ability to pay, speak with Mr. Clark in Human Resources.

Workshop Registration Form

Date: April 12, 20--

Name: Louise Flynn
Department: Public Relations
Title: Public Relations Assistant

I wish to register for the following workshop(s):

TITLE	DATE
Databases	May 10
Web Design	May 11

Approved by *Ellen Jones*
Please submit to Mr. Clark in the Human Resources Department.

181. Which workshop is offered twice?

(A) Business Writing

(B) Proposal Writing

(C) Technical Writing

(D) Writing for the Web

182. Which workshop is offered in the afternoon only?

(A) Writing for the Web

(B) Databases

(C) Web Design

(D) Word Processing

183. Where will Louise go to take her workshops?

(A) Human Resources Department

(B) Public Relations Office

(C) Conference Room A

(D) Training room

184. How much will Louise pay for her workshops?

(A) $0

(B) $150

(C) $250

(D) $500

185. Who had to sign Louise's form?

(A) Her co-worker

(B) Human Resources

(C) The instructor

(D) Her supervisor

Go to the next page. →

Questions 186–190 refer to the following advertisement and letter.

Wanted: Experienced office manager for small downtown business firm. Organize office procedures, monitor supplies, maintain appointments calendar, organize meetings/events, answer phones, greet clients. Must have minimum three years' experience in a similar position and basic knowledge of office software. Benefits include health, dental, and vision insurance, paid sick leave and vacation days, retirement. Send résumé detailing relevant experience and names of three references to: Sylvia Burns, HR Director, P.O. Box 17, Scarborough, ME 04070.

June 14, 20—

Sylvia Burns
HR Director
P.O. Box 17
Scarborough, ME 04070

Dear Ms. Burns:

I am responding to the employment ad you ran in yesterday's *Scarborough Times*. I believe I am the perfect candidate for the position you advertised. You ask for three years' experience in a similar position, and I have a total of six years' office experience. Until a month ago, I was employed as an administrative assistant at a local engineering firm and was in that position for four years. Before that, while I was still in school, I worked in the school office for two years. I graduated from Scarborough Business College five years ago, and my school records show that I was at the top of my class. In addition, I have taken computer training classes at the Computer Institute and received certificates of expertise in several types of office software.

Aside from my school and work experience, I believe I have the qualities needed to perform well at the job. I am efficient, reliable, adaptable, and friendly. I am good at organizing things and enjoy interacting with clients.

I am enclosing the information you asked for in the ad, including the names and contact information of three people who have agreed to write letters of recommendation for me. Thank you very much. I look forward to meeting you.

Sincerely,

David McHugh

186. When did the ad appear in the newspaper?

(A) June 13

(B) June 14

(C) June 15

(D) June 16

187. Which of the following types of insurance is NOT mentioned as a job benefit?

(A) Life

(B) Health

(C) Dental

(D) Vision

188. What position is David applying for?

(A) Human resources director

(B) Administrative assistant

(C) Office manager

(D) Engineer

189. How many years did David work at his most recent job?

(A) Two

(B) Three

(C) Four

(D) Six

190. What did David enclose with his letter?

(A) Letters of recommendation

(B) A training certificate

(C) His school records

(D) A résumé

Go to the next page. ➔

Questions 191–195 refer to the following meeting agenda and e-mail.

Clemson, Inc.
Monthly Staff Meeting
January 10, 20—
Conference Room 3

9:00–9:30	Report from the London office	Nigel Brinkley
9:30–10:00	Quarterly sales report	Maria Bridgewater
10:00–10:30	Marketing plan	Peter O'Hare / Jon Greene
10:30–10:45	Break	
10:45–11:30	Budget report	Marta Guzman
11:30–12:00	Personnel issues	Rita Garibaldi

Following the meeting, lunch will be served in Conference Room 1.

To: Maria Bridgewater

From: Jon Greene

Date: January 11, 20--

Hello Maria,

You asked me to let you know about yesterday's staff meeting since you were unable to be there. I'm happy to say that it went quite well. I gave your presentation for you; thank you for the files you sent me for that. The graphs and charts were very helpful. Peter took over the marketing plan report and gave that entire presentation himself. He did a good job and ended up going 15 minutes over his scheduled time, but we all agreed it was worth it. Since Marta needed less time than she anticipated, we were able to end exactly on time. I thought you would want the figures for the budget report, so I'm attaching a copy. You'll want them when you meet with the New York office next week. I'm sorry you had to miss the meeting, but of course if a client needs your help, that must take priority. I hope everything went well with that. Let me know if you need any further information.

Jon

191. Who gave the quarterly sales report?

    (A) Jon Greene

    (B) Maria Bridgewater

    (C) Peter O'Hare

    (D) Marta Guzman

192. What time did the meeting end?

    (A) 11:30

    (B) 11:45

    (C) 12:00

    (D) 12:15

193. Why did Jon send the e-mail to Maria?

    (A) To ask her for some files

    (B) To report on the meeting

    (C) To tell her about a client who needs help

    (D) To find out why she was absent from the meeting

194. What did Jon attach to the e-mail he sent Maria?

    (A) Charts and graphs

    (B) A meeting agenda

    (C) The lunch menu

    (D) The budget report

195. Where was Maria yesterday?

    (A) Sick at home

    (B) With a client

    (C) At the New York office

    (D) At the staff meeting

Go to the next page. ➔

Questions 196–200 refer to the following ad and e-mail.

Executive Transportation Services

Does this describe your situation? You want to give your out-of-town clients the luxury treatment, but your company doesn't want the hassle and expense of maintaining its own fleet of cars.

Executive Transportation Services is here to help. We provide transportation in comfortable, luxurious cars driven by certified professional drivers.

FEES

Vehicle Type	Per Hour (in the city)	Per Hour (outside of the city)	Per Day
Luxury Sedan (seats 4-6)	$50	$65	$350
Small Limousine (seats 8)	$100	$125	$700
Large Limousine (seats 12)	$125	$135	$850
Van (seats 20)	$150	$165	$1,000

Ask about our Airport Special. We will take you from the airport to any downtown location for $55 per passenger. See our website for limitations and restrictions on this offer.

From: Marcella Hynes

Date: Monday, October 10, 20—

To: Executive Transportation Services

Subject: Hiring your service

Hi,

I saw your ad in the newspaper recently and am interested in hiring your service. Our company will be hosting four clients from Tokyo next week. They'll be arriving on Sunday and will stay at the Flint Hotel downtown, so I'd like to arrange for a car to meet them at the airport and take them to their hotel. We'll be taking them to visit various sites around the city on Tuesday, so I'd like to hire a car for that entire day. In addition to the clients, two or three of our staff members will be with them, so we'll need a car large enough to accommodate everyone. Then on Wednesday, we plan to take them to visit our factory in Farmingham. A larger group will be going along on that trip, so I'd like to hire a van. Although that is an out of town trip, it's nearby, so I think we'll just need the car for a few hours. Finally, our visitors have an early flight back to Tokyo on Friday morning and will need transportation to the airport. Please let me know if you can accommodate all these needs. Also, let me know how much you require for a deposit, and I'll send a messenger with a check for you right away.

Thank you for your help.

Marcella Hynes

196. How much does it cost to rent a luxury sedan for one day?

(A) $50

(B) $65

(C) $350

(D) $700

197. How much does a trip to the airport cost?

(A) $55 for each person

(B) $55 for each hour

(C) $55 for each car

(D) $55 for the entire day

198. What size car should Ms. Hynes hire on Tuesday?

(A) Luxury sedan

(B) Small limousine

(C) Large limousine

(D) Van

199. How much will Ms. Hynes pay per hour for transportation on Wednesday?

(A) $125

(B) $135

(C) $150

(D) $165

200. When will the clients return home?

(A) Sunday

(B) Monday

(C) Wednesday

(D) Friday

This is the end of the Reading Test. If you finish before the time ends, you may go back to Parts 5, 6, and 7 and check your work.

Answer Key and Listening Scripts

ANSWER KEY

Listening Part 1

WALK THROUGH: Photos pg 7
B

GET IT RIGHT: Statements About Activities
TIP TASK pgs 8–9
1. talking **2.** pulling **3.** pushing **4.** climbing

GET IT RIGHT: Statements About Condition
TIP TASK pgs 10–11
1. Circled Words: clipboard, glasses, boxes
  Correct Statement: A
2. Circled Words: tables, tablecloths, chairs, trees
  Correct Statement: B
3. Circled Words: vase, clock, chair, drawers
  Correct Statement: B

GET IT RIGHT: Statements About Location
TIP TASK pgs 12–13
1. between
2. over / above
3. on
4. in front of
5. next to / beside
6. in
7. next to / beside
8. on

GET IT RIGHT: Incorrect Information
TIP TASK pg 14
1. man
2. woman
3. open
4. reading (or looking at)
5. next to (or beside)
6. light
7. on his head
8. chefs (or cooks)
9. kitchen
10. bottle
11. cooking (or preparing)
12. empty

Try a TOEIC Test Question pg 14
Incorrect Information: (B) wrong condition, (C) wrong person, (D) wrong activity **Correct Answer:** A

GET IT RIGHT: Similar-Sounding Words
TIP TASK 1 pg 15
Words That Sound Similar: stomachache, steak, cake, lake
Correct Answer: D

TIP TASK 2 pg 16
1. drinking **3.** train **5.** meeting **7.** coughing
2. aisle **4.** warming **6.** package **8.** coat

Try a TOEIC Test Question pg 16
Incorrect Similar-Sounding Words: smile, aisle, pile
Correct Answer: C

GET IT RIGHT: Similar-Sounding Words with Incorrect Meanings
TIP TASK pgs 17–18
1. B **2.** A **3.** B **4.** A

Try a TOEIC Test Question pg 19
Items in Photo: plane, watch, man, jacket
Correct Answer: B
Incorrect Similar-Sounding Words: watching, handing, plain

Progressive Practice: Get Ready (See *Answer Analysis* boxes for explanations.) pgs 20–21
1. C **2.** A **3.** B **4.** D

Progressive Practice: Get Set pgs 22–23
1. Correct Answer: C **Answer Analysis:** A, C, B, D
2. Correct Answer: B **Answer Analysis:** D, C, A, B
3. Correct Answer: A **Answer Analysis:** D, B, A, C
4. Correct Answer: D **Answer Analysis:** D, A, C, B
5. Correct Answer: A **Answer Analysis:** C, A, D, B
6. Correct Answer: C **Answer Analysis:** B, D, A, C

Progressive Practice: Go for the TOEIC Test pgs 25–27
1. B. Some people with umbrellas are crossing a city street.
2. A. Two ferry boats are tied up at a dock.
3. D. Two customers are at the checkout line of a grocery store.
4. C. A full pitcher sits on the corner of the table.
5. D. A businessman is standing behind a podium talking to an audience.
6. A. A conference table is ready for a meeting. There are bottles and drinking glasses on it.
7. C. Workers are loading packages onto a plane.
8. B. A young woman is writing on a computer.
9. B. People are sitting at tables that are lined up in rows.
10. C. A woman in a white coat is standing in a pharmacy and talking on the phone.

Listening Part 2

WALK THROUGH: Question-Response pg 29
1. B   **2.** A

GET IT RIGHT: Information Questions
TIP 1 TASK pg 30

1. When	**3.** How often	**5.** Who
2. Whose	**4.** Where	

TIP 2 TASK pg 30

1. f	**3.** d	**5.** a
2. b	**4.** g	

Try a TOEIC Test Question pg 31
Question Word: What; a time
Correct Answer: C

GET IT RIGHT: *Yes-No* Questions
TIP 1 TASK pg 32

1. embedded question	**4.** polite request
2. simple *yes-no* question	**5.** embedded question
3. simple *yes-no* question	

TIP 2 TASK pg 33

1. g	**3.** b	**5.** c
2. d	**4.** e	

Try a TOEIC Test Question pg 33
Key Word: Will; needs a *yes-no* response
Correct Answer: A

GET IT RIGHT: Statements
TIP 1 TASK pg 34

1. statement	**3.** *or* question	**5.** statement
2. tag question	**4.** tag question	

TIP 2 TASK pg 34

1. f	**3.** a	**5.** b
2. d	**4.** e	

Try a TOEIC Test Question pg 34
Correct Answer: C

GET IT RIGHT: Similar-Sounding Words
TIP 1 TASK pg 36

1. Similar-Sounding Words / Homonyms: hear, here, near
   Correct Answer: B

2. Similar-Sounding Words / Homonyms: order, order, border
   Correct Answer: A

3. Similar-Sounding Words / Homonyms: department, apartment, compartment
   Correct Answer: C

4. Similar-Sounding Words / Homonyms: weather, wetter, whether
   Correct Answer: A

5. Similar-Sounding Words / Homonyms: choose, chews, refuse
   Correct Answer: C

6. Similar-Sounding Words / Homonyms: blue, red, read, blew
   Correct Answer: C

GET IT RIGHT: Other Distracter Types
TIP TASK pg 37

1. A. correct answer
   B. a-repeated word (restaurant)
   C. b-related word (waiter)

2. A. c-*yes-no* answer to information question
   B. b-related word (beach)
   C. correct answer

3. A. d-wrong verb tense (sat)
   B. correct answer
   C. b-repeated word (desk)

4. A. c-*yes-no* answer to information question
   B. correct answer
   C. b-related word (room)

5. A. correct answer
   B. b-related word (stamps)
   C. b-related word (envelope)

Try a TOEIC Test Question pg 37
Key Word: Is
Distracters: fine, meeting
Correct Answer: B

Progressive Practice: Get Set (See *Answer Analysis* boxes for explanations.) pgs 40-41

1. Correct Answer: C **Answer Analysis:** A, C, B
2. Correct Answer: A **Answer Analysis:** C, B, A
3. Correct Answer: A **Answer Analysis:** A, C, B
4. Correct Answer: B **Answer Analysis:** B, C, A
5. Correct Answer: C **Answer Analysis:** B, C, A
6. Correct Answer: B **Answer Analysis:** C, A, B
7. Correct Answer: B **Answer Analysis:** B, A, C
8. Correct Answer: A **Answer Analysis:** C, A, B
9. Correct Answer: A **Answer Analysis:** A, C, B
10. Correct Answer: C **Answer Analysis:** A, C, B

Progressive Practice: Go for the TOEIC Test pg 42

1. B. The suggestion to take an umbrella is a logical response to the tag question about rain.
2. A. "This afternoon" answers the question "When?"
3. A. "They're waiting for the director" is the reason "why" the meeting hasn't started.
4. A. "By subway" answers the "or" question: "by bus or by subway?"
5. C. "Five dollars" answers the question "How much?"
6. B. "I can't" is a logical response to the suggestion to play tennis.
7. C. "I like it, too" expresses agreement with the opinion about the restaurant.

8. C. "He retired last year" explains why John doesn't work here anymore.

9. B. "In that closet" answers the question "Where?"

10. B. "At 2:30" answers the question "What time?"

11. A. "Some friends" answers the question "Who?"

12. C. The possessive "Sarah's" answers the question "Whose?"

13. C. The suggestion to call a repairperson is a logical response to the complaint about the machine not working.

14. A. "Certainly" is a polite response to a request.

15. B. "Mr. Brown" answers the question "Who?"

16. B. "I'm sorry" is a polite response to a request.

17. A. "Fifty" answers the question "How many?"

18. C. "A post office on the corner" answers the question "Where?"

19. B. "At a store downtown" answers the question "Where?"

20. C. "3:20" answers the question "What time?"

Listening Part 3

WALK THROUGH: Conversations pg 44

1. C   **2.** C   **3.** D

GET IT RIGHT: Topic / Main Idea Questions

TIP 1 TASK pg 45

1. B   **2.** A   **3.** C

TIP 2 TASK pg 46

1. Vocabulary Clues: total, paying, cash, credit, debit card **Correct Answer:** a.

2. Vocabulary Clues: Broadwater Inn, check in, concierge **Correct Answer:** b.

3. Vocabulary Clues: front desk, Room 114, room service **Correct Answer:** b.

Try a TOEIC Test Question pg 46

Vocabulary Clues: got a delivery, leave it with me, sign for it, dropped off, box

Correct Answer: D

GET IT RIGHT: Detail Questions About Plans, Problems, Requests, or Suggestions

TIP 1 TASK pg 48

1. a   **2.** a   **3.** b

TIP 2 TASK pg 48

1. bank = woman; downtown train station = man; new to area = man; time to station = woman

2. old accounts = man; file cabinet = woman; files on desk = woman; orders = man

Try a TOEIC Test Question pg 48

Wrong Speaker: She needs a ticket.

Correct Answer: C

GET IT RIGHT: Detail Questions About Causes and Effects

TIP 1 TASK pg 49

1. to visit   **3.** to complete

2. to cut   **4.** to withdraw

TIP 2 TASK pg 49

1. Expression for Effects: haven't been able **Expression for Cause:** since **Answer:** The printer is broken.

2. Expression for Effects: been asked to **Expression for Cause:** because **Answer:** The electricity bill was too high.

Try a TOEIC Test Question pg 50

Infinitives in Answer Options: To visit, To place, To make, To pick up

Signal Words: have to go, because **Correct Answer:** A

GET IT RIGHT: Detail Questions About Duration, Frequency, or Quantity

TIP 1 TASK pg 51

1. A   **2.** A   **3.** A

TIP 2 TASK pg 51

1. c   **3.** d   **5.** e

2. b   **4.** a

Try a TOEIC Test Question pg 51

Transition Word: Unfortunately **Correct Answer:** B **Paraphrased Part of Script:** because it's a weeklong trip

GET IT RIGHT: Detail Questions About Time

TIP 1 TASK pg 52

1. Event: meet **Distracters:** 6:00, 6:30, 5:00
Correct Answer: A

2. Event: meet **Distracters:** today, tomorrow, this Friday, on Monday
Correct Answer: C

TIP 2 TASK pg 53

1. e   **3.** a   **5.** b

2. d   **4.** c

Try a TOEIC Test Question pg 53

Distracters: this afternoon, this morning, by Friday **Correct Answer:** C

GET IT RIGHT: Detail Questions About Identifying People or Places

TIP 2 TASK 1 pg 54

1. Action: contact   **3. Action:** increase
Correct Answer: a   **Correct Answer:** c

2. Action: speak
Correct Answer: b

TIP 2 TASK 1 pg 54

1. B

TIP 2 TASK 2 pg 54

1. Distracters: Mr. Jackson
Correct Answers: a. The woman, b. The man

2. Distracters: The printer, Ms. Anderson
Correct Answers: a. Robert, b. The man

TIP 3 TASK pg 55

1. Person: the man **Correct Answer:** a

2. Thing: the package **Correct Answer:** a

TIP 4 TASK 1 pg 55

1. D

TIP 4 TASK 2 pg 55

☐ New York: b

☑ Boston: c

☐ Chicago: d

☐ Los Angeles: a

Try a TOEIC Test Question pg 56

Distracters: office of Harold Crane, warehouse, State Hospital

Correct Answer: C

GET IT RIGHT: Inference Questions

TIP 1 TASK pgs 56–57

1. Key Words/Expressions: ready to order, menu, something to drink, glass of water

Correct Answer: In a restaurant

2. Key Words/Expressions: room key, staying in Room 117, pool, vending machines, Room service

Correct Answer: In a hotel

TIP 2 TASK pg 57

post office = mail, package; hospital = doctor, patient; office = copy machine, secretary; airport = flight, ticket

Try a TOEIC Test Question pg 57

Key Words: Principal Henderson, chemistry teacher position

Correct Answer: A

Progressive Practice: Get Set

(See *Answer Analysis* boxes for explanations.)

Practice Set 1 pg 61

1. Correct Answer: B **Answer Analysis:** C, D, B, A

2. Correct Answer: A **Answer Analysis:** A, D, B, C

3. Correct Answer: D **Answer Analysis:** C, A, B, D

Practice Set 2 pg 62

1. Correct Answer: C **Answer Analysis:** D, B, C, A

2. Correct Answer: B **Answer Analysis:** B, C, D, A

3. Correct Answer: A **Answer Analysis:** B, D, C, A

Practice Set 3 pg 63

1. Correct Answer: A **Answer Analysis:** A, D, B, C

2. Correct Answer: B **Answer Analysis:** D, A, C, B

3. Correct Answer: A **Answer Analysis:** B, A, D, C

Progressive Practice: Go for the TOEIC Test pgs 64–65

1. Correct Answer: C **Answer Analysis:** The man talks about a boarding pass, checking in, a plane, and going to Chicago.

2. Correct Answer: B **Answer Analysis:** The man says he lost his boarding pass.

3. Correct Answer: D **Answer Analysis:** The woman says she needs to see his identification before printing a new pass.

4. Correct Answer: C **Answer Analysis:** The woman asks the man to take over Mary's paperwork. From the context of the conversation, we can assume that Mary is a co-worker.

5. Correct Answer: B **Answer Analysis:** The woman says she can help out if the man needs a hand.

6. Correct Answer: B **Answer Analysis:** The man says he'll be in a meeting all day on Wednesday.

7. Correct Answer: B **Answer Analysis:** The woman wants to meet with Jim Carter to talk about selling her home.

8. Correct Answer: B **Answer Analysis:** The man says Mr. Carter is meeting with another client until a quarter after ten, which is equal to 10:15.

9. Correct Answer: A **Answer Analysis:** The woman says to tell Mr. Carter that she will be late.

10. Correct Answer: A **Answer Analysis:** The woman says that the Accounting Department just released next year's budget, and the speakers discuss how to use it.

11. Correct Answer: D **Answer Analysis:** The woman says that adding new clients caused the increase in funding.

12. Correct Answer: D **Answer Analysis:** The man says he will check prices at a few retailers.

13. Correct Answer: B **Answer Analysis:** The man mentions a ten percent price increase, and the speakers discuss how to react to it.

14. Correct Answer: A **Answer Analysis:** The man says it's time to take their business to another company.

15. Correct Answer: B **Answer Analysis:** The woman says that she is meeting with her sales team in a few minutes.

16. Correct Answer: C **Answer Analysis:** The man asks how the woman's stay was, and the woman mentions checking out.

17. Correct Answer: B **Answer Analysis:** The woman says she needs advice because she doesn't know if the convention center has parking. She wants to know how the man would get there.

18. Correct Answer: A **Answer Analysis:** The man says the convention center is close enough to walk to, and the woman states that she doesn't want to drive or pay cab fare.

Listening Part 4

WALK THROUGH: Talks pg 67

1. B   **2.** B   **3.** D

GET IT RIGHT: Topic / Main Idea Questions

TIP 1 TASK pg 68

1. D   **2.** A   **3.** B

TIP 2 TASK pg 69

(Answers may vary.)

1. concert;   **4.** boss, manager;   **7.** clothing, outfit;

2. illness;   **5.** buy, purchase;   **8.** leave, go

3. trip, vacation;   **6.** store, shop;

TIP 3 TASK pgs 69–70

1. **Synonyms:** retailer, store
   Correct Answer: a
2. **Synonyms:** café, restaurant
   Correct Answer: b
3. **Synonyms:** excursion, vacation
   Correct Answer: a

Try a TOEIC Test Question pg 70

The annual City Festival of Music will take place next weekend at the National Theater. The doors open on Sunday morning at 9:00 a.m., and there will be musical performances by local and national orchestras and bands all day until eight in the evening. This one-day-only event is a unique opportunity to hear performances by some of the country's top musicians. Don't miss it. Tickets are on sale at the National Theater box office. Order your ticket today.

Correct Answer: D

GET IT RIGHT: Detail Questions About Suggestions, Advice, Instructions, or Requests

TIP TASK pg 71

1. **Woman**: We will allow first-class passengers to board first. Show your ticket to the gate agent when boarding the train. [instructions]
2. **Man**: The icy weather has made road conditions very dangerous, and several accidents have already been reported. If you witness an accident, you should report it immediately to the local police. [request]
3. **Woman**: It's a good idea to buy your ticket before the end of the month because the company will give you a ten percent discount. [advice]
4. **Man**: Please have your money ready for the cashier before you reach the head of the line. This will help the line move faster. [request]
5. **Woman**: Visitors are asked to register with the receptionist before going upstairs. A visitor's pass will be issued at that time. [suggestion]

Try a TOEIC Test Question pg 71

Request: Stop by Norby's department store's annual jewelry sale.
Correct Answer: C

GET IT RIGHT: Detail Questions About Duration, Frequency, Quantity, or Time

TIP TASK pg 72

1. (B) Monday
2. (B) 60
3. (A) Two days
4. (B) 30
5. (A) Fifth

Try a TOEIC Test Question pg 72

For all passengers traveling on the 10:14 train to Cambridge, the train has been delayed 15 minutes due to engine problems. Repeat, the 10:14 train to Cambridge has been delayed 15 minutes and will now be departing at 10:29 a.m. Please adjust your travel plans accordingly.

1. How late is the train?
   (A) 10 minutes
   (B) 14 minutes
   (C) 15 minutes
   (D) 50 minutes

Correct Answer: C

GET IT RIGHT: Inference Questions

TIP TASK pg 73

Correct Answer: a

2. **Correct Answer:** C

Try a TOEIC Test Question pg 74

Hi, this is Jennifer Leska speaking. I'm calling to let you know that I'm very upset with the service I received at your store last week. I wanted to exchange a birthday gift I had gotten from a friend, but the salesperson who helped me was terrible. He had no idea what to do! It took about an hour, and in the end I still didn't get my gift because he couldn't find the right color and size. I'm extremely dissatisfied, so I'd like to speak with a manager. Please call me at . . .

Correct Answer: B

GET IT RIGHT: Types of Talks

TIP TASK pg 75

Announcements: 3	Reports: 7
Speeches: 5	Introductions: 1
Tours: 2	Voicemail: 4
Advertisements: 8	Instructions / Lectures: 6

Progressive Practice: Get Set (See *Answer Analysis* boxes for explanations.)

Practice Set 1 pg 79

1. **Correct Answer:** C **Answer Analysis:** C, A, B, D
2. **Correct Answer:** B **Answer Analysis:** D, B, A, C
3. **Correct Answer:** D **Answer Analysis:** B, A, C, D

Practice Set 2 pg 80

1. **Correct Answer:** C **Answer Analysis:** A, C, D, B
2. **Correct Answer:** D **Answer Analysis:** D, A, B, C
3. **Correct Answer:** A **Answer Analysis:** D, B or C, C or B, A

Practice Set 3 pg 81

1. **Correct Answer:** A **Answer Analysis:** B, C, A, D
2. **Correct Answer:** A **Answer Analysis:** D, B, C, A
3. **Correct Answer:** D **Answer Analysis:** C, D, B, A

Progressive Practice: Go for the TOEIC Test pgs 82–83

1. D. The bank closes at noon on Saturday.
2. A. You can check the balance in your accounts by pressing "1."
3. B. You can get information about loans by pressing "2."
4. A. The speaker mentions Mr. Peterson's beautiful nature photographs.
5. D. He will talk about his travels in Asia.
6. D. Listeners will be able to call in and ask Mr. Peterson questions.
7. B. The speaker recommends different ways to get exercise.
8. B. The speaker recommends eating fruit and unsweetened cereal and avoiding meat and pastries.
9. A. The speaker says, "don't take the elevator."

10. C. The report is about a collision, or crash, between two cars and a truck.

11. C. The speaker says the collision occurred at approximately 8:00 a.m.

12. A. A doctor in the emergency room was interviewed by a reporter.

13. B. The speaker says that snow is being cleared from the train tracks.

14. D. The speaker says that he is unable to give an exact time.

15. B. Passengers are invited to have a complimentary, or free, breakfast in the station café.

16. A. The instructions are for using an automated system for paying for purchases.

17. D. The first instruction given is to insert a credit card.

18. D. The customer can use the red call light to ask for assistance.

Listening Practice Test pgs 86–97

Part 1: Photos

1. B	4. C	7. B	10. D
2. A	5. A	8. D	
3. D	6. C	9. C	

Part 2: Question-Response

11. C	19. B	27. C	35. C
12. A	20. A	28. B	36. A
13. A	21. B	29. A	37. B
14. B	22. C	30. C	38. B
15. B	23. C	31. C	39. A
16. C	24. A	32. A	40. C
17. A	25. A	33. B	
18. C	26. B	34. A	

Part 3: Conversations

41. B	49. A	57. B	65. A
42. C	50. C	58. D	66. B
43. D	51. D	59. B	67. C
44. A	52. D	60. D	68. B
45. C	53. A	61. C	69. B
46. C	54. B	62. D	70. C
47. B	55. C	63. A	
48. D	56. B	64. D	

Part 4: Talks

71. C	80. B	89. C	98. A
72. A	81. A	90. B	99. B
73. C	82. D	91. B	100. C
74. A	83. C	92. C	
75. B	84. C	93. A	
76. D	85. B	94. D	
77. D	86. D	95. C	
78. C	87. A	96. A	
79. B	88. B	97. B	

Reading Part 5

WALK THROUGH: Incomplete Sentences, pg 105

1. C	2. C	3. A

GET IT RIGHT: Vocabulary Completions
TIP 1 TASK 1 pg 107

1. relayed - delayed
2. eraser - erasable
3. undo - redo

TIP 1 TASK 2 pg 109

1. admit	2. recipe	3. subscription

TIP 1 TASK 3 pg 110

1. break	3. due	5. allowed
2. bored	4. their	

TIP 2 TASK pg 111

1. let	2. tell	3. lie

TIP 3 TASK pg 112

1. any	2. many	3. a little

Try a TOEIC Test Question pg 112

1. C

GET IT RIGHT: Word-Form Completions
TIP 1 TASK pg 114

1. a	2. b	3. b

TIP 2 TASK pg 115

1. -able; adjective	4. -ize (or -ized); verb
2. -ate (or -ated); verb	5. -ive; adjective
3. -ship; noun	

TIP 3 TASK pg 115

1. printing	2. to ask	3. to review

TIP 4 TASK pg 116

1. her	2. Our	3. theirs

TIP 5 TASK pg 116

1. hard	2. good	3. fast

Try a TOEIC Test Question pg 116

1. B

GET IT RIGHT: Combination Completions
Try a TOEIC Test Question pg 117

1. A

GET IT RIGHT: Grammar Completions
Missing Subject
TIP 1 TASK pg 118

1. Training; gerund
2. To finish the project; to infinitive
3. Ms. Tazi; noun

TIP 2 TASK pg 119

1. She   **2.** We   **3.** He

TIP 3 TASK pg 119

1. are - is   **2.** are - is   **3.** Buy - Buying

TIP 4 TASK pg 119

1. ✓ To walk   **3.** ✓ To start the project
2. I   immediately

TIP 5 TASK pg 120

1. training   **2.** jogging   **3.** concerned

GET IT RIGHT: Grammar Completions
Missing Verb
TIP 1 TASK pg 121

1. are   **3.** is
2. are   **4.** are

TIP 2 TASK pg 122

1. Asks - Ask
2. trains - train *or* training
3. takes - take

GET IT RIGHT: Grammar Completions
Missing Object
TIP 1 TASK pg 122

1. product; noun   **4.** to complain; infinitive
2. biography; noun   **5.** quitting; gerund
3. us; pronoun

TIP 2 TASK pg 123

1. myself   **2.** her   **3.** him

TIP 3 TASK pg 123

1. Mr. Perez found it hard to believe that none of the meeting rooms were available.
2. Roberta thinks it unlikely that the company will hire new employees soon.
3. Kayla's positive attitude makes it easy to see why people love to work with her.

GET IT RIGHT: Grammar Completions
Missing Complement
TIP 1 TASK pg 124

1. a   **2.** b   **3.** b

GET IT RIGHT: Grammar Completions
Missing Adjective or Preposition
TIP 1 TASK pg 125

1. of   **2.** to   **3.** for   **4.** with

TIP 2 TASK pg 125

1. shorter   **3.** largest   **5.** happier
2. best   **4.** most amazing

Try a TOEIC Test Question pg 125

1. C

Progressive Practice: Get Set pgs 129–133

1. Correct Answer: C **Answer Analysis:** B, C, A (or D), D (or A)
2. Correct Answer: A **Answer Analysis:** B, C, D, A
3. Correct Answer: D **Answer Analysis:** C, B, D, A
4. Correct Answer: C **Answer Analysis:** C, A, D, B
5. Correct Answer: B **Answer Analysis:** D, C, A, B
6. Correct Answer: A **Answer Analysis:** D, A, B, C
7. Correct Answer: A **Answer Analysis:** A, D, B, C
8. Correct Answer: C **Answer Analysis:** B, C, D, A
9. Correct Answer: B **Answer Analysis:** A, C, D, B
10. Correct Answer: D **Answer Analysis:** D, A, C, B
11. Correct Answer: D **Answer Analysis:** C, D, A, B
12. Correct Answer: B **Answer Analysis:** C, A, D, B
13. Correct Answer: C **Answer Analysis:** C, A, B, D
14. Correct Answer: D **Answer Analysis:** B, D, C, A
15. Correct Answer: A **Answer Analysis:** D, B, A, C

Progressive Practice: Go for the TOEIC Test pgs 134–135

1. B. "Expand" means "to increase or make bigger."
2. C. The third person singular verb "enjoys" agrees with the third person singular subject "everybody."
3. D. This is a time clause with "as soon as," so it requires a present tense verb.
4. A. This is an imperative sentence. The correct negative form for the negative imperative is "don't" plus the verb.
5. C. This is an adjective following the linking verb "be."
6. A. "Show up" means "to appear" or "to arrive."
7. B. "Before" introduces a time clause that describes the action that will follow the action in the main clause.
8. D. This is an object pronoun—the indirect object of the verb "send."
9. D. This is the only verb choice that agrees with the plural subject "employees."
10. A. "From" correctly completes the phrase "across the street from." There is no other way to complete this phrase.
11. B. "Import" means "to bring in things from other countries."
12. C. "Enough" means "adequate in number" or "sufficient."
13. A. "Should" is a modal, so it is followed by a base form verb.
14. A. "Are going to interview" is the correct form to refer to a future action.
15. D. "Extension" is the noun form, and a noun is needed following the article "an."
16. C. "Although" introduces a clause that has an unexpected or contradictory result.
17. C. "As well" is a comparative adverb of equality.
18. B. The main verb "consider" is followed by a gerund.
19. D. "Reliable" means "dependable."
20. A. A future real conditional uses present tense in the "if" clause.

Reading Part 6

WALK THROUGH: Text Completion, pg 137
1. D **2.** A **3.** C

GET IT RIGHT: Passage Types
TIP 1 TASK 1 pg 138
1. a business letter
2. months; days of the week
3. yes
4. yes
5. no

TIP 1 TASK 2 pg 139
1. a **3.** b **5.** a
2. b **4.** a

Try a TOEIC Test Question pg 139
1. B

GET IT RIGHT: Grammar-Based Questions
TIP 1 TASK pg 140
1. close on **3.** finish up
2. applied for

TIP 2 TASK pg 141
1. Tara knew Mr. Finely would write her a glowing recommendation.
2. Due to her brief absence, Amparo was not aware of the changes in the office.
3. Terrance Industries outearned its leading competitor last year.

TIP 3 TASK pg 141
Due to; Consequently; Regardless

Try a TOEIC Test Question pg 142
1. C **2.** C **3.** A

GET IT RIGHT: Contextual Questions
TIP 1 TASK pg 142
Banking: loan, withdraw, checkbook
Employment: hiring manager, recruit, résumé
Marketing: billboard, ad campaign, target customer
Accounting: expense, receipt, balance sheet

TIP 2 TASK pg 143
1. ✗ **4.** ✓ **7.** ✓
2. ✓ **5.** ✗ **8.** ✓
3. ✗ **6.** ✓ **9.** ✗

Try a TOEIC Test Question pg 143
1. C **2.** A **3.** D

Progressive Practice: Get Ready
Questions 1–3, Part A pg 144
1 - a past tense verb; 2 - a singular pronoun; 3 - a gerund form of a verb

Progressive Practice: Get Set pgs 146–148
1. Word Type: Part of a passive verb
Correct Answer: C
Answer Analysis: D, C, B, A
2. Word Type: A singular noun
Correct Answer: A
Answer Analysis: D, C, B, A
3. Word Type: An adjective
Correct Answer: C
Answer Analysis: C, B, A, D
4. Word Type: A future tense verb
Correct Answer: B
Answer Analysis: A, D, C, B
5. Word Type: A base form of a verb
Correct Answer: A
Answer Analysis: D, B, A, C
6. Word Type: A plural form of a noun
Correct Answer: A
Answer Analysis: A, C, D, B

Progressive Practice: Go for the TOEIC Test pg 149–151
1. C. "Operation" is a noun following a preposition.
2. B. The verb "avoid" is followed by a gerund.
3. D. "Inconvenience" means "difficulty" or "discomfort."
4. B. "Advice" is a noun that's the object of the preposition "for" and modified by the adjective "financial."
5. C. "Experienced" means "knowledgeable."
6. B. "Yours" is a second person possessive pronoun. It refers to the person to whom the letter is addressed.
7. A. "Mandatory" means "required."
8. D. The writer of the memo wants to hear about the reasons "ahead of time," which is the meaning of "before."
9. A. "Should" is a modal, so it is followed by a base form verb.
10. A. "Comforts" is a plural noun.
11. D. "Access" means "get to or reach something."
12. B. "It" is the singular pronoun that refers to the phrase about reserving a room at the hotel.

Reading Part 7

WALK THROUGH: Reading Comprehension, pg 153
1. B **2.** A **3.** D

GET IT RIGHT: Passage Types
TASK pgs 155–156
a. Graphical text **e.** Notice
b. Article **f.** Instructions
c. General correspondence **g.** Advertisement
d. Form

GET IT RIGHT: Double Passages
TIP 1 TASK pg 157
1. B

TIP 2 TASK pg 158
Correct Answer: a. The correction says the advertisement should say "a free tent light with any purchase over $50." Only the tent is over $50.

TIP 3 TASK pg 159
1. c **2.** b **3.** a

GET IT RIGHT: Main Idea Questions

TIP 1 TASK pg 160

1. c **2.** a **3.** b

TIP 2 TASK pg 160

1. b **2.** a **3.** b

TIP 3 TASK pg 161

☑ A new study shows that performance-based payment may not be as effective as experts once believed. ☒ In a recent survey, researchers asked employees at companies that offer performance-based payment for feedback. ☒ Out of one hundred employees surveyed, only ten reported being "very happy" with the system. ☒ The majority of employees (nearly seventy percent) reported being "unhappy" or "very unhappy" with the system.

TIP 4 TASK pg 161

1. shoe store; **2.** pharmacy; **3.** grocery store

TIP 5 TASK pg 162

I am writing to inquire about the assistant position advertised in the classified section of last Sunday's edition of *The Harrington Tribune*.
1. b

Try a TOEIC Test Question pg 162
1. B

GET IT RIGHT: Detail Questions

TIP 1 TASK pg 164

1. When, conference; **Correct Answer:** a; **2.** Why, Ms. Bybee, airport; **Correct Answer:** b; **3.** How much, Mr. Tan, jacket; **Correct Answer:** b; **4.** NOT true, Bloomfield Industries; **Correct Answer:** a; **5.** Where, company's headquarters; **Correct Answer:** b

TIP 2 TASK pg 164

List 1: 1. ✓ 2. ✓ 4. ✓ 5. ✓ **List 2:** 1. ✓ 3. ✓

TIP 3 TASK pg 165

1. d **2.** b

Try a TOEIC Test Question pg 165
1. B **2.** A

GET IT RIGHT: Inference Questions

TIP 1 TASK pg 166

Times / Dates: Ten nights; March 4; March 23; April 5
Locations: Fort Lauderdale, Florida; Mexico; Belize; Cayman Islands

TIP 2 TASK pg 166

1. ☑ Ten nights **3.** ☑ Ports of call in Mexico, Belize, and the Cayman Islands

Try a TOEIC Test Question pg 167
1. B **2.** A

GET IT RIGHT: Vocabulary Questions

TIP 1 TASK pg 168

1. considerably **2.** frigid **3.** financial

TIP 2 TASK pg 168

1. renewals - renovations **2.** limited - suspicious
3. terminals - candidates

Try a TOEIC Test Question pg 169
1. D **2.** A

Progressive Practice: Get Set pgs 173–178
1. **Correct Answer:** B **Answer Analysis:** D, B, C, A
2. **Correct Answer:** C **Answer Analysis:** C, D, A, B
3. **Correct Answer:** D **Answer Analysis:** A, B, D, C
4. **Correct Answer:** A **Answer Analysis:** B, A, D, C
5. **Correct Answer:** B **Answer Analysis:** B, C, A, D
6. **Correct Answer:** B **Answer Analysis:** C, D, B, A
7. **Correct Answer:** B **Answer Analysis:** C, B, D, A
8. **Correct Answer:** A **Answer Analysis:** D, C, B, A
9. **Correct Answer:** D **Answer Analysis:** A, C, D, B
10. **Correct Answer:** C **Answer Analysis:** C, B, D, A
11. **Correct Answer:** B **Answer Analysis:** C, A, B, D

Progressive Practice: Go for the TOEIC Test pgs 179–185
1. B. One quarter of a year is equivalent to three months. According to the article, sales went up during the last quarter of the year.
2. B. The article states, "Ms. Randall attributes the success to her company's new approach to marketing," and she mentions advertising, so (B) is an appropriate inference.
3. A. The article quotes Ms. Randall as saying about her product, "It's the best in the market." This means it is superior to other companies' products.
4. B. You can use the TX 9000 to make a call, dial a number, and hear voicemail, so it must be a telephone. Option (B) is an appropriate inference.
5. A. "Retrieve" means "get" or "pick up."
6. B. The instructions say, "Wipe gently with a damp cloth." Option (B) is a correct paraphrase.
7. B. According to the article, prices have "plunged." This means the same as (B).
8. A. According to the article, "Cotton production is expanding" This means farmers have planted more, so (A) is an appropriate inference.
9. A. The annual report is "due out in January." This is the beginning of the year.
10. A. Ms. Collins writes that she is "interested in applying for a position" This means she is asking for employment.
11. D. Ms. Collins states at the beginning of her letter that she is interested in a position in the Marketing Department, and she later says she is particularly interested in market research.
12. D. Mr. Marcus mentions, her "limited work history." This means she has "insufficient experience."
13. B. Mr. Marcus writes, "I suggest that you spend some time gaining some practice in your chosen field."

14. A. Ms. Collins enclosed a résumé with her letter, and Mr. Marcus wants to send the information she gave him to Ms. Richardson. The "information" refers to the résumé.

15. B. She is planning to attend a conference for financial consultants.

16. A. She wants to find a time to get together and talk with Sam during the conference.

17. C. She says she will miss the entire social hour (5:00–7:00) but will arrive in time for the dinner, which starts at 7:30. So she will arrive sometime between 7:00 and 7:30.

18. D. She tells Sam that she will have dinner with friends on Saturday.

19. B. The schedule lists "City Sightseeing by Bus" on Sunday morning.

Reading Practice Test pgs 188–211

Part 5

101. C	111. B	121. B	131. C
102. D	112. C	122. C	132. D
103. A	113. A	123. A	133. A
104. C	114. D	124. D	134. C
105. B	115. D	125. D	135. D
106. B	116. B	126. A	136. B
107. C	117. C	127. C	137. C
108. D	118. A	128. B	138. D
109. A	119. A	129. B	139. A
110. C	120. B	130. A	140. D

Part 6

141. A	144. B	147. C	150. C
142. D	145. B	148. D	151. B
143. C	146. A	149. A	152. C

Part 7

153. C	165. C	177. C	189. C
154. D	166. A	178. B	190. D
155. A	167. D	179. C	191. A
156. B	168. D	180. A	192. C
157. B	169. D	181. C	193. B
158. A	170. A	182. B	194. D
159. C	171. D	183. D	195. B
160. A	172. C	184. A	196. C
161. B	173. A	185. D	197. A
162. C	174. A	186. A	198. B
163. B	175. B	187. A	199. D
164. A	176. D	188. C	200. D

Audio Scripts for Listening

Part 1

Track 1-01 pg 7

Narrator: LISTENING Part 1: Photos
WALK THROUGH: Photos
What You'll Hear

Look at the photo marked number 1 in your test book.

(A) They're looking for seating.

(B) They're having a meeting.

(C) They're reading newspapers.

(D) They're eating a meal.

Track 1-02 pgs 10–11

Narrator: GET IT RIGHT: Statement Types
Statements About Condition
TIP TASK

Narrator: Number 1. A.

Woman: The woman has a clipboard.

Narrator: B.

Woman: The man's glasses are in his hand.

Narrator: Number 2. A.

Man: The tables have umbrellas.

Narrator: B.

Man: The tables are outside.

Narrator: Number 3. A.

Woman: The vase is empty.

Narrator: B.

Woman: There's a clock on the desk.

Track 1-03 pg 14

Narrator: GET IT RIGHT: Common Distracter Types
Incorrect Information
Try a TOEIC Test Question
A.

Man: He's pointing at the screen.

Narrator: B.

Man: The computer is closed.

Narrator: C.

Man: She's looking at the screen.

Narrator: D.

Man: He's buying a computer.

Track 1-04 pg 16

Narrator: GET IT RIGHT: Common Distracter Types
Similar-Sounding Words
TASK 2
Number 1.

Woman: The man is drinking tea at his desk.

Narrator: Number 2.

Man: She's standing in the aisle.

Narrator: Number 3.

Woman: The train is ready to leave.

Narrator: Number 4.

Man: He's warming food on the stove.

Narrator: Number 5.

Woman: They're ready for the meeting.

Narrator: Number 6.

Man: The package is on the floor.

Narrator: Number 7.

Woman: The patient is coughing.

Narrator: Number 8.

Man: There's a coat on the desk.

Track 1-05 pg 16
Narrator: GET IT RIGHT: Common Distracter Types
        Similar-Sounding Words
        Try a TOEIC Test Question
        A.

Man: She has a big smile.

Narrator: B.

Man: The aisle drawer is empty.

Narrator: C.

Man: She's looking at the files.

Narrator: D.

Man: The pile is very high.

Track 1-06 pgs 17–18
Narrator: GET IT RIGHT: Common Distracter Types
        Similar-Sounding Words with Incorrect
        Meanings
        TIP TASK
        Number 1. A.

Woman: The seats are set up in rows.

Narrator: B.

Woman: The rose is on the table.

Narrator: Number 2. A.

Man: The closet is full of clothes.

Narrator: B.

Man: The closet door is closed.

Narrator: Number 3. A.

Woman: The man is wearing eyeglasses.

Narrator: B.

Woman: There are glasses on the table.

Narrator: Number 4. A.

Man: The raft is on top of a wave.

Narrator: B.

Man: The boaters are waving good-bye.

Track 1-07 pg 19
Narrator: GET IT RIGHT: Common Distracter Types
        Similar-Sounding Words with Incorrect Meanings
        Try a TOEIC Test Question
        A.

Man: He's watching the plane.

Narrator: B.

Man: He's looking at his watch.

Narrator: C.

Man: He's handing the man his bag.

Narrator: D.

Man: He's wearing a plain jacket.

Track 1-08 pgs 20–21
Narrator: Progressive Practice: Get Ready
        Part A
        Number 1. A.

Woman: The lamps are over the bed.

Narrator: B.

Woman: The curtain is open.

Narrator: C.

Woman: The phone is next to the lamp.

Narrator: D.

Woman: The pillows are on the floor.

Narrator: Number 2. A.

Man: They're looking at a book.

Narrator: B.

Man: They're trying to cook.

Narrator: C.

Man: They're reading a newspaper.

Narrator: D.

Man: They're greeting each other.

Narrator: Number 3. A.

Woman: There's a clock on the wall.

Narrator: B.

Woman: The book is open.

Narrator: C.

Woman: There are words on the monitor.

Narrator: D.

Woman: Someone is sitting in the chair.

Narrator: Number 4. A.

Man: The men are taking cans.

Narrator: B.

Man: The men are waving at each other.

Narrator: C.

Man: The men are wearing glasses.

Narrator: D.

Man: The men are shaking hands.

Track 1-09 pgs 22–23

Narrator: Progressive Practice: Get Set

      Part A

      Number 1. A.

Woman: The plate is on the tray.

Narrator: B.

Woman: There's a cup on the table.

Narrator: C.

Woman: The waiter is serving dessert.

Narrator: D.

Woman: The customer is drinking water.

Narrator: Number 2. A.

Man: There's no room to sit on the bench.

Narrator: B.

Man: The bench is in the park.

Narrator: C.

Man: The night is very dark.

Narrator: D.

Man: They're walking through the park.

Narrator: Number 3. A.

Woman: The train is in the station.

Narrator: B.

Woman: The rain is coming down fast.

Narrator: C.

Woman: The passengers are sitting on the train.

Narrator: D.

Woman: The plane is ready to leave.

Narrator: Number 4. A.

Man: They both look quite cross.

Narrator: B.

Man: Their bags are in the car.

Narrator: C.

Man: The path is quite steep.

Narrator: D.

Man: They're in the crosswalk.

Narrator: Number 5. A.

Woman: He's fixing the car.

Narrator: B.

Woman: He's opening the hood.

Narrator: C.

Woman: He's working on a farm.

Narrator: D.

Woman: He's mixing something good.

Narrator: Number 6. A.

Man: The lamps are on the wall.

Narrator: B.

Man: The rug is under the door.

Narrator: C.

Man: The picture is over the sofa.

Narrator: D.

Man: The stairs are in front of the sofa.

Track 1-10 pgs 25–27

Narrator: Progressive Practice: Go for the TOEIC Test

      Part 1: Photos

      Directions: Look at each photo. You will hear four statements about the photo. The statements are not in your book. Mark the letter of the statement that best describes the photo. You will hear each statement only once.

      Number 1. A.

Woman: They're trying to sleep.

Narrator: B.

Woman: They're crossing the street.

Narrator: C.

Woman: They're buying umbrellas.

Narrator: D.

Woman: They're talking on the train.

Narrator: Number 2. A.

Man: The boats are at the dock.

Narrator: B.

Man: The waiters are very calm.

Narrator: C.

Man: The boots are wet and muddy.

Narrator: D.

Man: The ships are out at sea.

Narrator: Number 3. A.

Woman: They're checking out of a hotel.

Narrator: B.

Woman: They're hopping down the line.

Narrator: C.

Woman: They're trying on shoes.

Narrator: D.

Woman: They're at the checkout line.

Narrator: Number 4. A.

Man: A picture is hanging on the wall.

Narrator: B.

Man: The basket is empty.

Narrator: C.

Man: There's a pitcher on the table.

Narrator: D.

Man: The bread is on the plate.

Narrator: Number 5. A.

Woman: He's walking toward the audience.

Narrator: B.

Woman: He's wearing his glasses.

Narrator: C.

Woman: He's pointing at the chart.

Narrator: D.

Woman: He's standing behind the podium.

Narrator: Number 6. A.

Man: There are bottles on the table.

Narrator: B.

Man: The computer is closed.

Narrator: C.

Man: There are three pictures on the wall.

Narrator: D.

Man: The clock is on the table.

Narrator: Number 7. A.

Woman: The passengers are getting on the plane.

Narrator: B.

Woman: The plane is ready to leave.

Narrator: C.

Woman: They're loading the plane.

Narrator: D.

Woman: They're working in the rain.

Narrator: Number 8. A.

Man: The pens are to the right of the computer.

Narrator: B.

Man: She's writing on her computer.

Narrator: C.

Man: The scissors are in her hand.

Narrator: D.

Man: She's talking on the phone.

Narrator: Number 9. A.

Woman: The rose is quite large.

Narrator: B.

Woman: The tables are in rows.

Narrator: C.

Woman: They're facing the screen.

Narrator: D.

Woman: The tables are empty.

Narrator: Number 10. A.

Man: The farmer is working hard.

Narrator: B.

Man: The doctor is walking home.

Narrator: C.

Man: The pharmacist is talking on the phone.

Narrator: D.

Man: The patient is looking for help.

Part 2

Track 2-01 pg 29

Narrator: LISTENING Part 2: Question-Response
     WALK THROUGH: Question-Response
     What You'll Hear
     Number 1.

Man: Where should I put this package?

Narrator: A.

Woman: It's from the Tokyo office.

Narrator: B.

Woman: On that table over there.

Narrator: C.

Woman: Ms. Jones sent it.

Narrator: Number 2.

Woman: Who made these photocopies?

Narrator: A.

Man: Peter made them.

Narrator: B.

Man: He made ten copies.

Narrator: C.

Man: The copies are on your desk.

Track 2-02 pg 30

Narrator: GET IT RIGHT: Question and Statement Types
     Information Questions
     TIP 1 TASK
     Number 1.

Woman: When do you take your vacation?

Narrator: Number 2.

Man: Whose coat is that on the chair?

Narrator: Number 3.

Woman: How often is there a staff meeting?

Narrator: Number 4.

Man: Where can we have lunch?

Narrator: Number 5.

Woman: Who helped you write the report?

Track 2-03 pg 31

Narrator: GET IT RIGHT: Question and Statement Types
     Information Questions
     Try a TOEIC Test Question

Man: What time does the train leave?

Narrator: A.

Woman: The rain has stopped.

Narrator: B.

Woman: Buy your ticket here.

Narrator: C.

Woman: At ten o'clock.

Track 2-04 pg 32
Narrator: GET IT RIGHT: *Yes-No* Questions
      TIP 1 TASK
        Number 1.

Man: Do you know where Mr. Kim is?

Narrator: Number 2.

Woman: Has the bus left yet?

Narrator: Number 3.

Man: Is there a nice restaurant nearby?

Narrator: Number 4.

Woman: Could you carry these boxes inside for me?

Narrator: Number 5.

Man: Can you tell me when the movie starts?

Track 2-05 pg 33
Narrator: GET IT RIGHT: *Yes-No* Questions
      Try a TOEIC Test Question
Man: Will you be working this weekend?
Narrator: A.
Woman: I'm not sure.
Narrator: B.
Woman: I'll get it.
Narrator: C.
Woman: Yes, it is.

Track 2-06 pg 34
Narrator: GET IT RIGHT: Other Question Types
      TIP 1 TASK
        Number 1.
Woman: It's very cold in here.

Narrator: Number 2.

Man: You've been to Paris before, haven't you?

Narrator: Number 3.

Woman: Do you drive to work or take the bus?

Narrator: Number 4.

Man: You like chicken, don't you?

Narrator: Number 5.

Woman: The door is locked.

Track 2-07 pg 34
Narrator: GET IT RIGHT: Other Question Types
      Try a TOEIC Test Question
Woman: These books are so heavy.
Narrator: A.
Man: I like to read books.
Narrator: B.
Man: I can book a hotel room.
Narrator: C.
Man: I'll carry them for you.

Track 2-08 pg 36
Narrator: GET IT RIGHT: Common Distracter Types
      TIP 1 TASK
        Number 1.

Man: Did you hear the news?

Narrator: A.

Woman: Yes, he's here.

Narrator: B.

Woman: Yes. It's very exciting.

Narrator: C.

Woman: Yes, they're quite near.

Narrator: Number 2.

Woman: It's time to order more paper.

Narrator: A.

Man: Yes, and we need some pens, too.

Narrator: B.

Man: Everything is in order.

Narrator: C.

Man: The border is closed.

Narrator: Number 3.

Man: Who's in charge of this department?

Narrator: A.

Woman: They live in a large apartment.

Narrator: B.

Woman: There's one in that compartment.

Narrator: C.

Woman: Ms. Brown is the supervisor.

Narrator: Number 4.

Woman: The weather is lovely today.

Narrator: A.

Man: It is. We should walk in the park.

Narrator: B.

Man: Everything is getting wetter.

Narrator: C.

Man: I don't know whether she's here.

Narrator: Number 5.

Man: Choose anything you like from the menu.

Narrator: A.

Woman: He always chews so loudly.

Narrator: B.

Woman: It was an offer impossible to refuse.

Narrator: C.

Woman: Thanks. I'll have the baked fish.

Narrator: Number 6.

Woman: Do you prefer blue or red?

Narrator: A.

Man: I read that article, too.

Narrator: B.

Man: The wind blew very hard.

Narrator: C.

Man: I always think blue is nicer.

Track 2-09 pg 37

Narrator: GET IT RIGHT: Common Distracter Types

TIP 2 TASK

Number 1.

Man: Is the food at this restaurant good?

Narrator: A.

Woman: Yes, it's delicious.

Narrator: B.

Woman: I enjoy eating at restaurants.

Narrator: C.

Woman: No, I haven't seen the waiter.

Narrator: Number 2.

Woman: When will you take your vacation?

Narrator: A.

Man: No, it wasn't much fun.

Narrator: B.

Man: I usually go to the beach.

Narrator: C.

Man: At the end of August.

Narrator: Number 3.

Man: Who uses this desk?

Narrator: A.

Woman: He sat there yesterday.

Narrator: B.

Woman: Mr. Stephens works there.

Narrator: C.

Woman: It's a very tidy desk.

Narrator: Number 4.

Woman: Which hotel did you stay at?

Narrator: A.

Man: Yes, it was a very nice place.

Narrator: B.

Man: The big one near the train station.

Narrator: C.

Man: We had a room with a view.

Narrator: Number 5.

Man: Has the mail been delivered yet?

Narrator: A.

Woman: Yes, I put it on your desk.

Narrator: B.

Woman: You can buy stamps downstairs.

Narrator: C.

Woman: No, that envelope is too small.

Track 2-10 pg 37

Narrator: GET IT RIGHT: Common Distracter Types

Try a TOEIC Test Question

Woman: Is the meeting tomorrow at nine?

Narrator: A.

Man: That's fine.

Narrator: B.

Man: Yes, it is.

Narrator: C.

Man: There's a meeting.

Track 2-11 pg 38

Narrator: Progressive Practice: Get Ready

Part A

Number 1.

Woman: Whose purse is this?

Narrator: A.

Man: She's a nurse.

Narrator: B.

Man: This is a purse.

Narrator: C.

Man: It's Mary's.

Narrator: Number 2.

Man: Where can I park my car?

Narrator: A.

Woman: In the garage.

Narrator: B.

Woman: Let's walk in the park.

Narrator: C.

Woman: It's not very far.

Narrator: Number 3.

Woman: It's a very cold day.

Narrator: A.

Man: Yes, he sold it.

Narrator: B.

Man: I'll wear a coat.

Narrator: C.

Man: The meeting's today.

Narrator: Number 4.

Man: When is the party?

Narrator: A.

Woman: At Peter's house.

Narrator: B.

Woman: Tomorrow at five.

Narrator: C.

Woman: I like a good party.

Narrator: Number 5.

Woman: Who took this phone message?

Narrator: A.

Man: I took it.

Narrator: B.

Man: The phone is ringing.

Narrator: C.

Man: It's in the book.

Track 2-12 pg 40

Narrator: Progressive Practice: Get Set

Part A

Number 1.

Woman: I'm very hungry.

Narrator: A.

Man: Please hurry.

Narrator: B.

Man: No, I'm not angry.

Narrator: C.

Man: Let's have lunch now.

Narrator: Number 2.

Man: How was the hotel?

Narrator: A.

Woman: Very comfortable.

Narrator: B.

Woman: Tell me the time.

Narrator: C.

Woman: I'm ready to check out.

Narrator: Number 3.

Woman: What's in that closet?

Narrator: A.

Man: Just some office supplies.

Narrator: B.

Man: Yes, it's a closet.

Narrator: C.

Man: I already closed it.

Narrator: Number 4.

Man: Did you like the museum?

Narrator: A.

Woman: Yes, I went to a museum.

Narrator: B.

Woman: Yes, it was very interesting.

Narrator: C.

Woman: Yes, it looked like him.

Narrator: Number 5.

Woman: Who's that man over there?

Narrator: A.

Man: There's one in here.

Narrator: B.

Man: It's John's chair.

Narrator: C.

Man: He's my boss.

Narrator: Number 6.

Man: How much did the tickets cost?

Narrator: A.

Woman: I don't think they're lost.

Narrator: B.

Woman: Ten dollars each.

Narrator: C.

Woman: Yes, I got them.

Narrator: Number 7.

Woman: Would you bring me a cup of coffee?

Narrator: A.

Man: Please stop coughing.

Narrator: B.

Man: Of course. With or without sugar?

Narrator: C.

Man: My cup is on the table.

Narrator: Number 8.

Man: Aren't you going to New York soon?

Narrator: A.

Woman: Yes, I'm leaving tomorrow.

Narrator: B.

Woman: No, it's before noon.

Narrator: C.

Woman: New York is a big city.

Narrator: Number 9.

Woman: Will you see Susan tonight?

Narrator: A.

Man: Yes, I'll see her at the dinner.

Narrator: B.

Man: Yes, I saw her at lunch.

Narrator: C.

Man: Yes, her name is Susan.

Narrator: Number 10.

Man: Can I pay by check?

Narrator: A.

Woman: No, it's not on the deck.

Narrator: B.

Woman: I can check your answers for you.

Narrator: C.

Woman: Yes, and we also accept credit cards.

Track 2-13 pg 42

Narrator: Progressive Practice: Go for the TOEIC Test

Part 2: Question-Response

Directions: Listen to the question or statement and three possible responses. You will hear them only one time, and they are not in your book. Choose the best response, and mark the corresponding letter on your answer sheet.

Number 1.

Woman: It's raining, isn't it?

Narrator: A.

Man: Yes. He's running very fast.

Narrator: B.

Man: Yes. You should take an umbrella.

Narrator: C.

Man: Yes. They're training in the gym.

Narrator: Number 2.

Man: When will Mr. Kim return?

Narrator: A.

Woman: He should be back this afternoon.

Narrator: B.

Woman: Yes, turn left here.

Narrator: C.

Woman: Return your books to the library.

Narrator: Number 3.

Woman: Why hasn't the meeting started?

Narrator: A.

Man: They're waiting for the director to get here.

Narrator: B.

Man: I enjoyed meeting them, too.

Narrator: C.

Man: Thanks, but I never eat meat.

Narrator: Number 4.

Man: Do you come by bus or by subway?

Narrator: A.

Woman: By subway. It's much faster.

Narrator: B.

Woman: The waiter will bus the table.

Narrator: C.

Woman: Yes, I like the bus.

Narrator: Number 5.

Woman: How much does it cost to park here?

Narrator: A.

Man: My car needs new tires.

Narrator: B.

Man: It's too dark in here.

Narrator: C.

Man: Only five dollars a day.

Narrator: Number 6.

Man: Do you want to play tennis this weekend?

Narrator: A.

Woman: Yes, there are ten of us.

Narrator: B.

Woman: I can't. I have to work.

Narrator: C.

Woman: No, I didn't.

Narrator: Number 7.

Woman: This is a great restaurant.

Narrator: A.

Man: I'm ready to take a rest now.

Narrator: B.

Man: The waiter is bringing the menus.

Narrator: C.

Man: I like it, too. We should eat here more often.

Narrator: Number 8.

Man: John doesn't work here anymore, does he?

Narrator: A.

Woman: No, thanks. I don't want any more.

Narrator: B.

Woman: No, I haven't heard about any new work.

Narrator: C.

Woman: No, he retired last year.

Narrator: Number 9.

Woman: Where do you keep printer paper?

Narrator: A.

Man: You can sleep in this room.

Narrator: B.

Man: In that closet over there.

Narrator: C.

Man: I'm printing it out now.

Narrator: Number 10.

Man: What time is your dentist appointment?

Narrator: A.

Woman: I have a bad toothache.

Narrator: B.

Woman: At 2:30.

Narrator: C.

Woman: It was a real disappointment.

Narrator: Number 11.

Woman: Who did you have dinner with last night?

Narrator: A.

Man: Some friends from work.

Narrator: B.

Man: He's a lot thinner.

Narrator: C.

Man: It was a delicious meal.

Narrator: Number 12.

Man: Whose computer is that on the desk?

Narrator: A.

Woman: I have a computer.

Narrator: B.

Woman: Yes, it's his.

Narrator: C.

Woman: It's Sarah's.

Narrator: Number 13.

Woman: The photocopy machine isn't working.

Narrator: A.

Man: The photocopy machine is in here.

Narrator: B.

Man: I've been working here for quite a while.

Narrator: C.

Man: We'll have to call a repairperson.

Narrator: Number 14.

Man: Would you call Dr. Smith's office and cancel my appointment?

Narrator: A.

Woman: Certainly. I'll call right away.

Narrator: B.

Woman: Yes, I can sell those for you.

Narrator: C.

Woman: No, this isn't a doctor's office.

Narrator: Number 15.

Woman: Who's responsible for ordering new supplies?

Narrator: A.

Man: Paper, pens, and envelopes, usually.

Narrator: B.

Man: Mr. Brown does that.

Narrator: C.

Man: It was a big surprise.

Narrator: Number 16.

Man: Could you cash this check for me?

Narrator: A.

Woman: That was a rash decision.

Narrator: B.

Woman: I'm sorry. I don't have any money.

Narrator: C.

Woman: I'll check it for mistakes.

Narrator: Number 17.

Woman: How many notebooks should I get?

Narrator: A.

Man: We'll need about fifty.

Narrator: B.

Man: I know it's a good book.

Narrator: C.

Man: Don't get them wet.

Narrator: Number 18.

Man: Where can I buy some stamps?

Narrator: A.

Woman: Stamps are very expensive.

Narrator: B.

Woman: You should mail those letters today.

Narrator: C.

Woman: There's a post office on the corner.

Narrator: Number 19.

Woman: Where did you buy that suit?

Narrator: A.

Man: The pants are too long.

Narrator: B.

Man: At a store downtown.

Narrator: C.

Man: It's not an expensive suit.

Narrator: Number 20.

Man: Do you know what time the flight leaves?

Narrator: A.

Woman: Yes, I do.

Narrator: B.

Woman: The train leaves at 1:00.

Narrator: C.

Woman: At 3:20 from Gate 11.

Part 3

Track 3-01 pg 44

Narrator: LISTENING: Part 3: Conversations

WALK THROUGH: Conversations
What You'll Hear
Questions 1 through 3 are based on the following conversation.

Man: Has the copier at the reception desk been fixed yet?

Woman: No. I called the technician, but he can't make it out here until next Monday at the earliest.

Man: We have a meeting on Friday, though. We can't do our presentation unless everyone has copies of our work.

Woman: We'll have to get them done by a professional. I'll run to the copy shop tomorrow. It'll cost a little extra money, but we won't have to delay our presentation.

Narrator: Question 1. What problem are the speakers discussing?

Narrator: Question 2. When is the speakers' meeting?

Narrator: Question 3. What will the speakers probably do next?

Track 3-02 pg 45

Narrator: GET IT RIGHT: Question Types

Topic / Main Idea Questions
TIP 1 TASK
Number 1.

Man: Excuse me. I'm in Room 217, but I seem to have lost my room key.

Woman: That's no problem, sir. I'll just need some ID before I can issue the new one.

Narrator: Number 2.

Man: Anne, please tell me if I'm getting this right. I insert the paper face down. And then I just press "start"?

Woman: Not quite. You have to choose how many copies you want to make.

Narrator: Number 3.

Woman: Mr. Anderson, the driver from the limousine service just called. Your ride to the airport is going to be late.

Man: I see. Then we'd better get a taxi here right away. I can't afford to miss this flight.

Track 3-03 pg 46
Narrator: GET IT RIGHT: Question Types
      Topic / Main Idea Questions
      TIP 2 TASK
      Number 1.

Man: Your total comes to ten fifty. Will you be paying with cash or credit?

Woman: Actually, I'd like to pay with a debit card, if I can.

Narrator: Number 2.

Woman: Hello, sir. Welcome to the Broadwater Inn. Are you ready to check in?

Man: Uh, yes, but first I need to speak with the concierge about getting some tickets for tonight.

Narrator: Number 3.

Man: You've reached the front desk. This is Paul speaking.

Woman: Yes, this is Ms. Aimes in Room 114. I need a menu for room service.

Track 3-04 pg 46
Narrator: GET IT RIGHT: Question Types
      Topic / Main Idea Questions
      Try a TOEIC Test Question

Man: Good afternoon. I've got a delivery for Shannon Meyers.

Woman: Oh, this is Ms. Meyers's office, but she's out on a business lunch with a client. Can you leave it with me?

Man: That's no problem. I'll need you to sign for it, just so we have proof that someone was here when it was dropped off.

Woman: Of course. If you'll put the box by that office, I'll get a pen.

Track 3-05 pg 48
Narrator: GET IT RIGHT: Question Types
      Detail Questions About Plans, Problems, Requests, or Suggestions
      TIP 2 TASK
      Number 1.

Man: Excuse me. I'm new here. I need to get to the downtown train station. Can you tell me where it is?

Woman: Of course. Just keep walking straight down this street. When you pass the bank, turn right. It's just a few minutes from here.

Man: Great, thanks for your help.

Narrator: Number 2.

Woman: Mr. Hanson, I pulled those files you requested. Should I leave them on your desk?

Man: No. I'll need you to reorganize them. Some of those are old accounts that aren't active anymore, and I want to put them in a different location.

Woman: I'll put them in the new file cabinet. But which ones should I put there?

Man: Check the orders. Move any account that hasn't placed an order in the last year.

Track 3-06 pg 48
Narrator: GET IT RIGHT: Question Types
      Detail Questions About Plans, Problems, Requests, or Suggestions
      Try a TOEIC Test Question

Woman: Hi, I just saw a movie here. But when I got to my car, I realized I didn't have my keys.

Man: I'm sorry. Do you think they fell out during the movie?

Woman: Maybe. But I also bought candy. So they could have fallen out when I pulled my wallet out of my purse.

Man: OK. If you still have your ticket, I can let you in to search the theater. I'll check at the refreshment stand.

Track 3-07 pg 49
Narrator: GET IT RIGHT: Question Types
      Detail Questions About Causes and Effects
      TIP 1 TASK
      Number 1.

Man: Why weren't you at the conference last weekend?

Woman: I'm really sorry. I had to visit my mother. She wasn't feeling very well, so I drove up to be sure she was OK.

Narrator: Number 2.

Woman: I just saw that my purchase request was denied.

Man: I know. Since business has slowed down, we've been forced to reduce the budget.

Narrator: Number 3.

Man: Sarah, what are you doing in the office on a Saturday?

Woman: I came in because I have a project I need to finish.

Narrator: Number 4.

Woman: Hi, I was reviewing my credit card bill, and I saw a ten dollar service charge.

Man: Yes. We applied that fee since you used your card to get money from an ATM.

Track 3-08 pg 49
Narrator: GET IT RIGHT: Question Types

Detail Questions About Causes and Effects
TIP 2 TASK
Number 1.

Man: Carol, why aren't the June sales figures on my desk? I asked for them yesterday.

Woman: I'm sorry, Mr. James. I still haven't been able to print them, since the printer is broken.

Narrator: Number 2.

Woman: It's hot in here. Why don't we turn on the air conditioning?

Man: We've been asked to open windows instead because the electricity bill was too high.

Track 3-09 pg 50
Narrator: GET IT RIGHT: Question Types

Detail Questions About Causes and Effects
Try a TOEIC Test Question

Woman: Mr. Anderson, is it OK if I get out of the office a little earlier than usual?

Man: Well, I'm expecting a few important phone calls. And the documents for the Howard presentation aren't prepared. Is it an emergency?

Woman: No, it's not like that. I just have to go to my optometrist because my glasses need to be adjusted.

Man: I see. I guess it's all right. But make sure those documents are prepared tomorrow morning. I don't want us making copies just before Mr. Howard arrives.

Track 3-10 pg 51
Narrator: GET IT RIGHT: Question Types

Detail Questions About Duration, Frequency, or Quantity
TIP 1 TASK
Number 1.

Man: So do all employees get a discount on store purchases?

Woman: Yes, we offer a ten percent discount. However, new employees get only a five percent discount until they've been here for six months.

Narrator: Number 2.

Woman: Frank, you must be excited about your trip to Brazil! How long are you staying?

Man: I was going to stay for two weeks. But the hotel increased its prices, so I'm going for only seven days.

Narrator: Number 3.

Man: Ms. Jackson, here's your pain medication.

Woman: Oh, thank you. How often should I take it?

Man: Normally, I'd say take it once every six hours. But your injury is pretty severe, so for that reason, I recommend taking it once every four hours.

Track 3-11 pg 51
Narrator: GET IT RIGHT: Question Types

Detail Questions About Duration, Frequency, or Quantity
Try a TOEIC Test Question

Woman: Michael, are you going to Carl's retirement party? It's on Friday the tenth, two weeks from now.

Man: I wish I could. But I'm meeting new clients in Mexico the day after. I'll be getting ready for that trip.

Woman: Oh, too bad. It would be great if you could come. Even if you stayed only for an hour or two.

Man: I wanted to do that. Unfortunately, because it's a weeklong trip, I'll need time to pack. I've been working on this account for a month, and I want everything to go perfectly.

Track 3-12 pg 52
Narrator: GET IT RIGHT: Question Types

Detail Questions About Time
TIP 1 TASK
Number 1.

Man: So is the meeting for 6:00 still on?

Woman: No. Mary has dinner plans at 6:30. And Tim has an appointment with his doctor at 5:00.

Man: OK. Can everyone make it if we have it earlier?

Woman: Yes. We moved it to 4:00.

Narrator: Number 2.

Woman: Michael, I'm so sorry, but I'll have to cancel our meeting today.

Man: Oh, that's no problem. Should we reschedule for tomorrow?

Woman: Actually, I think next Wednesday is best. We just had a major deadline moved up to this Friday.

Man: I understand. I'll call you on Monday to set up a time.

Track 3-13 pg 53
Narrator: GET IT RIGHT: Question Types

Detail Questions About Time
Try a TOEIC Test Question

Man: Grace, has that shipment of lab equipment arrived? It was supposed to arrive this afternoon.

Woman: No, I'm sorry. The manufacturer called this morning and said there was a delay. Didn't you get my e-mail about it?

Man: I must have missed it. So when will it arrive? I need those tests completed by Friday.

Woman: The clerk I spoke with said it was coming tomorrow.

Track 3-14 pg 54
Narrator: GET IT RIGHT: Question Types

Detail Questions About Identifying People or Places
TIP 2 TASK 2
Number 1.

Woman: I have a meeting with my realtor at noon, so I don't think I'll be able to make that conference call with Mr. Jackson at 12:30. I need to cancel it.

Man: Yes, Ms. Adams. I'll take care of that for you.

Narrator: Number 2.

Man: The printer just called, and our pamphlets are ready for pickup. Should I go get them?

Woman: I wouldn't do that. Just send Robert. I need you to work on the presentation for Ms. Anderson.

Track 3-15 pg 55
Narrator: GET IT RIGHT: Question Types
Detail Questions About Identifying People or Places
TIP 3 TASK
Number 1.

Woman: Hi, John, it's Carol Murphy. Can we set up a meeting for later today?

Man: Actually, I'm on my way to the bank right now. Can I call you back?

Narrator: Number 2.

Man: Excuse me. I have a delivery for Martin Allen. Do you know where his office is?

Woman: Oh, he's the manager. It's upstairs, but I forget the number. Just ask Mary at the receptionist's desk, and she'll let you know.

Track 3-16 pg 55
Narrator: GET IT RIGHT: Question Types
Detail Questions About Identifying People or Places
TIP 4 TASK 2

Man: So you're headed to Chicago?

Woman: I was supposed to be. But then the client changed the location. Now we're meeting in New York.

Man: I see. And then you're coming back here?

Woman: No. I think I'll visit some family in Boston first. And then I'll be back here in Los Angeles by the end of the month.

Track 3-17 pg 56
Narrator: GET IT RIGHT: Question Types
Detail Questions About Identifying People or Places
Try a TOEIC Test Question

Woman: You've reached the office of Harold Crane. How can I help you?

Man: Hi, Joe Hewett speaking. I'm down in the warehouse, and I have to check with Mr. Crane on an order.

Woman: He's actually on his way to corporate headquarters downtown. Can I take a message?

Man: Sure. We've got a delivery for State Hospital. But it doesn't say which department to send it to.

Track 3-18 pg 56
Narrator: GET IT RIGHT: Question Types
Inference Questions
TIP 1 TASK
Number 1.

Man: Are you ready to order, ma'am?

Woman: I'll need another few minutes with the menu, thanks.

Man: Of course. Can I get you something to drink in the meantime?

Woman: Yes, a glass of water, please.

Narrator: Number 2.

Woman: OK, here's your room key. You'll be staying in Room 117. It's just past the pool and vending machines.

Man: Great, thanks. Is the kitchen still open? I'm starving.

Woman: It is. Room service is available until 10:00. You can charge it to your room or pay with a credit card.

Man: I'll just put it on the bill for the room, thanks.

Track 3-19 pg 57
Narrator: GET IT RIGHT: Question Types
Inference Questions
Try a TOEIC Test Question

Woman: Hello, I'm here to see Principal Henderson.

Man: Do you have an appointment?

Woman: Yes, I'm Amy Reynolds. I'm her 3:00 interview for the chemistry teacher position.

Man: OK. Please take a seat. Ms. Henderson is meeting with the library staff. She'll be out shortly.

Track 3-20 pg 58
Narrator: Progressive Practice: Get Ready
Practice Set 1
Questions 1 through 3 refer to the following conversation.

Woman: Healthcare Associates, Claire speaking. How can I help you?

Man: Hi, this is Carl Waterson. I have an appointment this morning with Dr. Garcia. But I'm not going to be able to make it in.

Woman: I see. There will be a cancellation fee since you didn't call twenty-four hours in advance. Did you still want to cancel?

Man: Yes, go ahead, please. I have an important meeting with new clients at 12:00 that I can't miss. I'll call back later this week to see if I can reschedule.

Narrator: Question 1. What are the speakers talking about?

Narrator: Question 2. Who most likely is the woman?

Narrator: Question 3. When is the man's meeting with the clients?

Track 3-21 pg 59
Narrator: Progressive Practice: Get Ready
Practice Set 2
Questions 1 through 3 refer to the following conversation.

Woman: Mr. Robertson, it's good to see you again. Let's see, according to your chart, it's been two years. Why so long?

Man: It's nice to see you, too, Dr. Grant. And to be honest, my old glasses prescription was just fine for day-to-day reading. So I didn't feel like I needed to come in.

Woman: Well, you know you should get your eyes checked annually anyway. But you're having problems with your vision now?

Man: Just a bit. About a month ago, I was typing up a report at home. I noticed that small print on my computer screen was getting hard to read.

Narrator: Question 1. Where most likely are the speakers?

Narrator: Question 2. How often should the man come in?

Narrator: Question 3. What did the man have trouble with?

Track 3-22 pg 61

Narrator: Progressive Practice: Get Set

Practice Set 1
Questions 1 through 3 refer to the following conversation.

Woman: Hi, my friend lives overseas, and it's her birthday next week. I'd like to get this gift to her before then. Do you think that's possible?

Man: Well, that depends. All overseas mail goes by air. But if you pay for express delivery, it will get there in two days. Priority delivery would take three days. And standard shipping can take longer than a week.

Woman: I see. It's important that it arrive on time, so I'll take express delivery. How much will that cost?

Man: That depends on the weight. If you hand me the box, I'll weigh it and tell you the cost of postage.

Narrator: Question 1. Where most likely are the speakers?

Narrator: Question 2. How long will it take for the gift to arrive by express delivery?

Narrator: Question 3. Why does the man ask for the box?

Track 3-23 pg 62

Narrator: Progressive Practice: Get Set

Practice Set 2
Questions 1 through 3 refer to the following conversation.

Man: OK, Ms. Miller. I've looked up your file, and it looks like you're not scheduled to refill this prescription for a few more days.

Woman: I know. But I'm going on a trip with my kids next week, and I won't be able to refill it then. The secretary at my doctor's office said I could just explain that at the pharmacy.

Man: I see. Sorry, but she was wrong about that. A pharmacist can't alter your prescription. I'll have to call your primary physician.

Woman: That's fine. I'll just make a few business calls while I wait, if that's OK with you.

Narrator: Question 1. What is the woman concerned about?

Narrator: Question 2. Where is the woman going next week?

Narrator: Question 3. Who will the man talk to?

Track 3-24 pg 63

Narrator: Progressive Practice: Get Set

Practice Set 3
Questions 1 through 3 refer to the following conversation.

Woman: Carl, I just got an e-mail from Mr. Jenson. Why didn't you get the budget proposal to him this morning?

Man: This morning? The deadline isn't until the end of Thursday.

Woman: That was the original due date. But it was bumped up because Mr. Jenson is meeting with the CEO on Wednesday. I left a message on your voicemail.

Man: Oh, that explains it. I lost my cell phone over the weekend.

Narrator: Question 1. What are the speakers discussing?

Narrator: Question 2. How did the woman deliver her message?

Narrator: Question 3. Who was supposed to complete the report?

Track 3-25 pgs 64–65

Narrator: Progressive Practice: Go for the TOEIC Test

Part 3: Conversations

Directions: Listen to a conversation between two speakers. Then choose the correct answers to the three questions about that conversation. Fill in the letter A, B, C, or D. You will hear each conversation only once. Questions 1 through 3 refer to the following conversation.

Man: Excuse me, I seem to have lost my boarding pass. I ate lunch at the food court just after I checked in. I must've thrown it away with the trash.

Woman: I see. Fortunately, I can print out another one for you. What's your name, sir?

Man: It's Frank Dobbs, D-O-B-B-S. I'm on the flight from here to Chicago that leaves around 3:00.

Woman: All right. I'll just need to see some identification before I can print your new boarding pass.

Narrator: Question 1. Where does the conversation take place?

Narrator: Question 2. What does the man want?

Narrator: Question 3. What will the man likely do next?

Narrator: Questions 4 through 6 refer to the following conversation.

Woman: Alan, I just heard that Mary will be out sick until next Monday. Do you think you can take over her paperwork starting tomorrow?

Man: I can, but there's just one problem. I'll be in a meeting all day Wednesday.

Woman: In that case, I'll cover for her that day. And I can help out the rest of the week, too, if you need a break.

Man: Thanks. I'll let you know if I need a hand.

Narrator: Question 4. What are the speakers discussing?

Narrator: Question 5. What does the woman offer to do?

Narrator: Question 6. When is the man's meeting?

Narrator: Questions 7 through 9 refer to the following conversation.

Man: Hello, you've reached Jim Carter's office. How may I help you?

Woman: Hi, this is Ann Walters. I'm trying to reach Mr. Carter. We have an appointment at 10:30 to talk about selling my home.

Man: I'm sorry, Ms. Walters. Mr. Carter is meeting with another client until quarter after ten. Can he call you back in five minutes?

Woman: That won't be necessary. My doctor's appointment took longer than expected. Please just tell him that I'll be a half hour late.

Narrator: Question 7. Who most likely is Jim Carter?

Narrator: Question 8. When does Mr. Carter's meeting end?

Narrator: Question 9. What does the woman ask the man to do?

Narrator: Questions 10 through 12 refer to the following conversation.

Woman: The Accounting Department just released next year's budget. With all the new clients we've attracted, we got a five percent increase in funding.

Man: That's great. We can finally bring in some new people.

Woman: Well, maybe. We need to update the computers around here first.

Man: That's true. I'll check computer prices at a few retailers. Hopefully, we can afford to hire someone after buying the new equipment.

Narrator: Question 10. What are the speakers talking about?

Narrator: Question 11. Why did the funding change?

Narrator: Question 12. What will the man likely do next?

Narrator: Questions 13 through 15 refer to the following conversation.

Man: Office Works just increased their general prices by ten percent. I think it's time we consider taking our business to another company. What do you think?

Woman: I'd have to agree. It's the third increase this year. So how should we start?

Man: Let's compare the rates of other suppliers first. Then we can see if anyone out there offers better rates. Can you look into that for me today?

Woman: Sure. I have a meeting with my sales team in a few minutes. But I'll call a few other suppliers about rates right after that.

Narrator: Question 13. What problem do the speakers discuss?

Narrator: Question 14. What does the man want to do?

Narrator: Question 15. What will the woman probably do next?

Narrator: Questions 16 through 18 refer to the following conversation.

Man: Good morning, ma'am. How was your stay?

Woman: Great, thanks. Before I check out, let me ask your advice. Would you drive to the convention center or take a cab? I don't know if there's any parking there.

Man: Actually, it's close enough to walk. If you turn right at the corner next to the restaurant and then go two blocks, you'll be there. It's just past the train station.

Woman: Wonderful. I'd rather not drive around looking for parking or pay cab fare.

Narrator: Question 16. Where are the speakers?

Narrator: Question 17. Why does the woman ask for advice?

Narrator: Question 18. How will the woman get to the convention center?

Part 4

Track 4-01 pg 67

Narrator: LISTENING: Part 4: Talks

WALK THROUGH: Talks

What You'll Hear

Listen to a talk. Then choose the correct answers to the three questions about that talk. Fill in the letter (A), (B), (C), or (D). You will hear each talk only once. Questions 1 through 3 are based on the following talk.

Man: Good morning and welcome to Flight 83 to Los Angeles. Our trip today should take just under four hours, and we'll be arriving at Los Angeles International Airport at eleven o'clock local time. We have clear skies today and should be able to have a good view of the Rocky Mountains. I'll point them out, as well as other sights of interest, as we approach them. For your entertainment, we'll be showing an in-flight movie in about an hour. In a minute, the flight attendants will begin the beverage service, so sit back, relax, and enjoy your trip.

Narrator: Question 1. Where is the speaker?

Narrator: Question 2. How long will the trip take?

Narrator: Question 3. What will happen next?

Track 4-02 pg 68

Narrator: GET IT RIGHT: Question Types

Topic / Main Idea Questions

TIP 1 TASK

Number 1.

Woman: You have reached the Electron Computer Company telephone help line. Our technicians are standing by ready to help you.

Narrator: Number 2.

Man: Welcome. Our tour today will begin here in the West Gallery with our exhibit of modern European paintings.

Narrator: Number 3.

Woman: Many of our listeners are out of work these days, so on today's show we're going to address several issues of importance to employment seekers. Plus, we'll have tips that will help you find the job of your dreams.

Track 4-03 pg 69
Narrator: GET IT RIGHT: Question Types

> **Topic / Main Idea Questions**
> **TIP 3 TASK**
> Number 1.

Man: Welcome to Park Place, the city's largest retailer, where we treat our customers like royalty.

Narrator: Number 2.

Woman: If you're looking for an inexpensive place for a delicious post-theater dinner, the Riverview Café might well suit your needs.

Narrator: Number 3.

Man: Do you need an escape from the stresses of work? Sign up for one of our weeklong excursions to the beaches of Mexico.

Track 4-04 pg 70
Narrator: GET IT RIGHT: Question Types

> **Topic / Main Idea Questions**
> **Try a TOEIC Test Question**

Woman: The annual City Festival of Music will take place next weekend at the National Theater. The doors open on Sunday morning at 9:00 a.m., and there will be musical performances by local and national orchestras and bands all day until eight in the evening. This one-day-only event is a unique opportunity to hear performances by some of the country's top musicians. Don't miss it. Tickets are on sale at the National Theater box office. Order your ticket today.

Track 4-05 pg 71
Narrator: GET IT RIGHT: Question Types

> **Detail Questions About Suggestions, Advice, Instructions, or Requests**
> **Try a TOEIC Test Question**

Woman: Don't know what to get your loved one for Valentine's Day? Then we have the answer for you! Stop by Norby's department store's annual jewelry sale! Today we're featuring any number of deals on necklaces, earrings, and even diamond rings. They make great gifts that let your loved one know just how you feel. Norby's department store—gift solutions for people who really care.

Track 4-06 pg 72
Narrator: GET IT RIGHT: Question Types

> **Detail Questions About Duration, Frequency, Quantity, or Time**
> **TIP TASK**
> Number 1.

Man: We'll have rainy weather all weekend, but the sky should start to clear up by Monday morning.

Narrator: Number 2.

Woman: Tickets go on sale this week and cost just sixty dollars apiece.

Narrator: Number 3.

Man: The doctor will be out of the office for two days and will return next Wednesday.

Narrator: Number 4.

Woman: Last night only thirty people attended the meeting at City Hall about a tax increase.

Narrator: Number 5.

Man: Our office is on the fifth floor of the Woodbridge Building.

Track 4-07 pg 72
Narrator: GET IT RIGHT: Question Types

> **Detail Questions About Duration, Frequency, Quantity, or Time**
> **Try a TOEIC Test Question**

Man: For all passengers traveling on the 10:14 train to Cambridge, the train has been delayed 15 minutes due to engine problems. Repeat, the 10:14 train to Cambridge has been delayed 15 minutes and will now be departing at 10:29 a.m. Please adjust your travel plans accordingly.

Track 4-08 pg 73
Narrator: GET IT RIGHT: Question Types

> **Inference Questions**
> **TIP TASK**
> Number 1.

Woman: Northeast 1782 to Wichita is now ready to board at Gate 17. Remember, only two carry-ons per passenger are permitted. Please have your boarding pass out and ready to present to . . .

Narrator: Number 2.

Man: Thank you very much for joining us today on *Where to Get Great Deals!* I'm Herb Niedermayer, and I'm here to teach you how to buy what you want for less. One great trick is to always offer cash. By offering cash, many stores will give you a discount—sometimes up to 25 percent! You can also save money by shopping during sales. Be sure to read your local newspapers to find out which stores are having sales right now. Another thing that can help is to . . .

Track 4-09 pg 74
Narrator: GET IT RIGHT: Question Types

> **Inference Questions**
> **Try a TOEIC Test Question**

Woman: Hi, this is Jennifer Leska speaking. I'm calling to let you know that I'm very upset with the service I received at your store last week. I wanted to exchange a birthday gift I had gotten from a friend, but the salesperson who helped me was terrible. He had no idea what to do! It took about an hour, and in the end I still didn't get my gift because he couldn't find the right color and size. I'm extremely dissatisfied, so I'd like to speak with a manager. Please call me at . . .

Track 4-10 pg 75

Narrator: GET IT RIGHT: Types of Talks

TIP TASK

Number 1.

Man: I'm very pleased to welcome to our show tonight Dr. Melissa Jones, author of the book *How to Achieve Financial Success*. Dr. Jones is a world-renowned expert on personal finances and lectures widely on the subject, both in this country and abroad.

Narrator: Number 2.

Woman: Welcome, everyone. We'll begin our tour today in the first-floor galleries, where we will enjoy an exhibit of modern European paintings.

Narrator: Number 3.

Man: Attention all passengers for Chicago. The train will begin boarding in five minutes. Please proceed to Track 1 and have your ticket ready to give to the agent.

Narrator: Number 4.

Woman: Yes, this is Samantha Wilson calling. I'm going to have to cancel my four o'clock appointment today with Dr. Overton because of an emergency at the office. I'll call back later to reschedule.

Narrator: Number 5.

Man: It is my great pleasure to be able to address this meeting of the National Association of Economists. We are gathered here in this conference hall to discuss some of the major economic issues facing the world today. We have a great task ahead of us.

Narrator: Number 6.

Woman: If you travel frequently for business, you know how important it is to keep your business attire looking clean and fresh. If you follow these few simple steps when packing your suitcase, your business clothes will remain fresh-looking and wrinkle-free throughout your trip. First, turn your jackets inside out.

Narrator: Number 7.

Man: According to statistics released by the mayor's office yesterday, crime in the city has decreased over twenty percent in the last year. "Our streets are safer than ever," Mayor Smith said during a press conference at City Hall. The mayor will be running for reelection next year.

Narrator: Number 8.

Woman: Office Outfitters is the store for all your office supplies. Do you need paper? Ink? Printers? Computers? Desks and tables? We have it all at prices you can afford.

Track 4-11 pg 76

Narrator: Progressive Practice: Get Ready

Practice Set 1.

Questions 1 through 3 refer to the following weather report.

Man: Good morning. We're starting the day with beautiful sunny skies, and there's not a cloud to be seen. High temperatures today will reach a relatively warm 40 degrees. Enjoy this pleasant weather while you can because rain will be moving in by midafternoon. It will continue overnight and into tomorrow morning. Looking ahead, a cold front will move in over the weekend, and we may even see some snow late in the weekend. Stay tuned for the next weather update at nine o'clock.

Narrator: Question 1. What is the weather like now?

Narrator: Question 2. What will the high temperature be today?

Narrator: Question 3. When might it snow?

Track 4-12 pg 77

Narrator: Progressive Practice: Get Ready

Practice Set 2.

Questions 1 through 3 refer to the following announcement.

Woman: Welcome aboard. We're enjoying pleasant weather and should have a smooth trip. Our flight today will take three hours. We're a bit ahead of schedule and expect to be landing at our destination about fifteen minutes before our scheduled arrival time. In just a few minutes, flight attendants will begin beverage service, so we ask you to remain seated during this time. When the beverage service is complete, you may get up and move around the cabin. We have magazines and newspapers available for your enjoyment. You may request them from any of the attendants.

Narrator: Question 1. Who is this announcement for?

Narrator: Question 2. How long will the trip last?

Narrator: Question 3. What does the speaker ask listeners to do?

Track 4-13 pg 79

Narrator: Progressive Practice: Get Set

Practice Set 1.

Questions 1 through 3 refer to the following voicemail message.

Woman: Yes. Good morning. This is Chris Brown, and it's seven thirty on Wednesday morning. I'm calling about my two o'clock appointment this afternoon with Dr. Kim. I'm sorry, but I won't be able to make it, as I've been called out of town on an emergency trip. I know this is last minute, but there's nothing I can do about it. I'll be back on Saturday, so I'll call again next week to speak with someone about rescheduling. I'm very sorry for any inconvenience I've caused. Thanks.

Narrator: Question 1. What time did the speaker call the doctor's office?

Narrator: Question 2. Why did the speaker call?

Narrator: Question 3. When will the speaker call back?

Track 4-14 pg 80

Narrator: Progressive Practice: Get Set

Practice Set 2.

Questions 1 through 3 refer to the following advertisement.

Man: You wear your best business suits to the office, so why arrive there in an old car? Now you can afford to drive to work in style because this week Eastford Motors is offering special prices on our complete line of luxury automobiles. That's right. Our dealership is offering all these beautiful vehicles at greatly reduced prices. How much of a discount would you expect from a local dealership? Ten percent? Fifteen percent? How about twenty percent? Guess again! At Eastford, we are offering twenty-five percent off every single one of our luxury vehicles. We also have specials on car parts and supplies as well as repairs. But don't wait. These deals are good only through Sunday. So come on down today, and drive home in the car of your dreams.

Narrator: Question 1. What is being advertised?

Narrator: Question 2. How much is the discount?

Narrator: Question 3. When is the sale over?

Track 4-15 pg 81

Narrator: Progressive Practice: Get Set

Practice Set 3.

Questions 1 through 3 refer to the following talk.

Woman: Our tour will begin in just a few minutes. If you haven't gotten your ticket yet, please do so now. Tickets are free, but you must have one. We'll begin here on the ground floor in our main exhibit showing the history of industry in our city, with artifacts from some of the city's original factories. We'll also see a special exhibit showing the development of the city harbor, including a replica of a fishing boat. From there, we'll move to the second floor to view some temporary exhibits. Let me remind you that food and drinks are not permitted inside the museum, nor is photographing the exhibits. Please visit our gift shop to purchase pictures and other souvenirs.

Narrator: Question 1. How much do tickets cost?

Narrator: Question 2. Where does the tour take place?

Narrator: Question 3. What does the guide suggest?

Track 4-16 pgs 82–83

Narrator: Progressive Practice: Go for the TOEIC Test

Part 4: Talks

Directions. Listen to a talk. Then choose the correct answers to the three questions about that talk. Fill in the letter (A), (B), (C), or (D). You will hear each talk only once.

Questions 1 through 3 refer to the following voicemail message.

Man: Thank you for calling Webster's Bank. We value your call. We're open Monday through Friday from nine a.m. to five p.m., and Saturday from eight a.m. until noon. Please listen carefully to the following menu. To check the balance in your savings account or checking account, press "1." For information about loans, press "2." For investment advice, press "3." To find out about our special services for small business owners, press "4." To speak with a customer service representative, please stay on the line, or call back during our regular hours of operation.

Narrator: Question 1. What time does the bank close on Saturday?

Narrator: Question 2. How can you find out how much money is in your bank account?

Narrator: Question 3. Who should press "2"?

Narrator: Questions 4 through 6 refer to the following introduction.

Woman: I'm very happy to introduce our guest on this evening's radio program, Mr. Mark Peterson. Mr. Peterson's beautiful nature photographs have appeared in several major travel magazines, and a book of his photography, *Wild Life*, was published last year. His work, which has received numerous awards, is all the more remarkable since he is completely self-trained, with no formal education in his field. Mr. Peterson will talk with us tonight about his recent travels in Asia. During the second half of the show, we'll invite listeners to call in with their questions for our guest. We'll begin our conversation with Mr. Peterson right after this news report. Stay tuned.

Narrator: Question 4. Who is Mr. Peterson?

Narrator: Question 5. What will Mr. Peterson talk about?

Narrator: Question 6. What will happen in the second half of the show?

Narrator: Questions 7 through 9 refer to the following talk.

Man: As a busy office worker, you may think that you don't have time for regular exercise. Well, think again. Exercise simply means moving your body, and it's easy to do. First, for energy, start the day with a healthy breakfast of fruit and unsweetened cereal. Avoid heavy foods, such as meat and pastries. Then walk, don't ride. If you live close enough to your office, walk there instead of driving or taking the bus. If you must drive, park some distance from your office and walk the rest of the way. At your building, don't take the elevator. Use the stairs instead. The more you move, the better you'll feel. And you might lose some weight, too.

Narrator: Question 7. What is this talk about?

Narrator: Question 8. According to the speaker, what should you eat for breakfast?

Narrator: Question 9. What does the speaker advise?

Narrator: Questions 10 through 12 refer to the following news report.

Woman: Good evening, and welcome to the six o'clock news. A three-vehicle collision during this morning's rush hour resulted in the closure of several downtown streets. A car traveling east on Main Street at approximately eight a.m. collided with a car traveling south on Oak Street. A pickup truck was also involved. The exact cause of the crash is still unknown. Firefighters rushed to the scene, and the drivers were taken to Memorial Hospital. An emergency room doctor who was interviewed by our reporter said that there were no serious injuries and all three drivers have been released from the hospital. Despite the street closure, there were no major disruptions to traffic, and streets were reopened by ten o'clock.

Narrator: Question 10. What event is this report about?

Narrator: Question 11. What time did it happen?

Narrator: Question 12. Who talked with a reporter?

Narrator: Questions 13 through 15 refer to the following announcement.

Man: May I have your attention, please? Work crews are still clearing the tracks of snow and ice left by last night's snowstorm. Due to this situation, the eight-thirty train to Seattle will be delayed. We regret the inconvenience. However, our top priority is the safety of our passengers and crew, and the train will not travel until the tracks are one hundred percent safe. At this time, we are unable to give an exact time for the train's departure, but we hope that it will be before noon. In the meantime, please enjoy a complimentary breakfast in the station café. Just show your ticket and you will receive a complete meal service at no cost to you.

Narrator: Question 13. What has caused the train delay?

Narrator: Question 14. When will the train leave?

Narrator: Question 15. What are passengers asked to do?

Narrator: Questions 16 through 18 refer to the following instructions.

Woman: Welcome to the automated checkout system. We make purchasing easy. Please insert your credit card in the slot. Thank you. Now place your first purchase on the counter. When you hear the beep, place your second purchase on the counter. Continue with all your purchases. After your last purchase, please press the star key, then sign your name for credit card validation. If you have a parking ticket, insert it in the slot for validation. If you need assistance, activate the red call light at the end of the counter and an associate will be right with you.

Narrator: Question 16. Where would you hear these instructions?

Narrator: Question 17. What should the customer do first?

Narrator: Question 18. How can the customer ask for help?

Track LPT-01 pgs 86–97
Narrator: Listening Test

Part 1: Photos

Directions. Look at each photo. You will hear four statements about the photo. The statements are not in your book. Mark the letter of the statement that best describes the photo. You will hear each statement only once.

Part 1: Questions 1 to 10.
Number 1. A.

Man: The drawers are open.

Narrator: B.

Man: There's a lamp near the computer.

Narrator: C.

Man: The rug is under the desk.

Narrator: D.

Man: There are two chairs in the room.

Narrator: Number 2. A.

Woman: They're having dinner.

Narrator: B.

Woman: They're pouring the water.

Narrator: C.

Woman: They're talking to the waiter.

Narrator: D.

Woman: They're washing the dishes.

Narrator: Number 3. A.

Man: They're waiting for the train.

Narrator: B.

Man: They're sitting in the rain.

Narrator: C.

Man: They're making a new plan.

Narrator: D.

Man: They're traveling by plane.

Narrator: Number 4. A.

Woman: He has his jacket on.

Narrator: B.

Woman: He's paying for the coffee.

Narrator: C.

Woman: He has a cup in his hand.

Narrator: D.

Woman: He's writing an interesting article.

Narrator: Number 5. A.

Man: The napkin is in the bowl.

Narrator: B.

Man: There's a picture on the wall.

Narrator: C.

Man: The basket is filled with bread.

Narrator: D.

Man: There's food on the plate.

Narrator: Number 6. A.

Woman: She's painting a sign.

Narrator: B.

Woman: She's buying a pen.

Narrator: C.

Woman: She's signing a document.

Narrator: D.

Woman: She's holding an envelope.

Narrator: Number 7. A.

Man: She's playing in the yard.

Narrator: B.

Man: She's paying with a credit card.

Narrator: C.

Man: She's talking with the guard.

Narrator: D.

Man: She's sending a birthday card.

Narrator: Number 8. A.

Woman: The patient is wearing a jacket.

Narrator: B.

Woman: The doctor is waving his hand.

Narrator: C.

Woman: The patient has eyeglasses.

Narrator: D.

Woman: The doctor has a beard.

Narrator: Number 9. A.

Man: He's taking off his apron.

Narrator: B.

Man: He's washing the pans.

Narrator: C.

Man: He's checking the pot.

Narrator: D.

Man: He's cleaning the stove.

Narrator: Number 10. A.

Woman: The basket is on the floor.

Narrator: B.

Woman: He's holding his head.

Narrator: C.

Woman: The shelves are all empty.

Narrator: D.

Woman: He's working in a bakery.

Narrator: This is the end of Part 1.

Narrator: Listening Test

Part 2: Question-Response

Directions. Listen to the question or statement and three possible responses. You will hear them only one time, and they are not in your book. Choose the best response, and mark

the corresponding letter on your answer sheet. Part 2: Questions 11 to 40.

Number 11.

Man: When did the package arrive?

Narrator: A.

Woman: I can drive you there.

Narrator: B.

Woman: The package is for you.

Narrator: C.

Woman: Early this morning.

Narrator: Number 12.

Woman: There's a subway station near here, isn't there?

Narrator: A.

Man: Yes. There's one just down the block.

Narrator: B.

Man: Yes. They weigh several pounds.

Narrator: C.

Man: Yes. I hear their vacation was fun.

Narrator: Number 13.

Man: Who signed the letter?

Narrator: A.

Woman: The director signed it.

Narrator: B.

Woman: That new sign looks much better.

Narrator: C.

Woman: I think it's a nice-looking design.

Narrator: Number 14.

Woman: How long was the plane ride?

Narrator: A.

Man: About ten meters long, I believe.

Narrator: B.

Man: A little over six hours.

Narrator: C.

Man: I long to see my family.

Narrator: Number 15.

Man: Did you enjoy the movie?

Narrator: A.

Woman: No, we didn't move anything.

Narrator: B.

Woman: Yes, it was very entertaining.

Narrator: C.

Woman: The tickets were quite cheap.

Narrator: Number 16.

Woman: Where can I find a pen?

Narrator: A.

Man: It opens at nine.

Narrator: B.

Man: They fined him ten dollars.

Narrator: C.

Man: There's one on my desk.

Narrator: Number 17.

Man: Whose car is this?

Narrator: A.

Woman: It's mine.

Narrator: B.

Woman: In the garage.

Narrator: C.

Woman: Mr. Kim drove it.

Narrator: Number 18.

Woman: What time does the museum close?

Narrator: A.

Man: These clothes are clean.

Narrator: B.

Man: The art museum is close by.

Narrator: C.

Man: At 5:30, I think.

Narrator: Number 19.

Man: The café across the street has great sandwiches.

Narrator: A.

Woman: They enjoy drinking coffee.

Narrator: B.

Woman: Then let's eat lunch there.

Narrator: C.

Woman: I'm not feeling cross at all.

Narrator: Number 20.

Woman: How many stamps should I buy?

Narrator: A.

Man: I think two dozen would be enough.

Narrator: B.

Man: The ramps are by the door.

Narrator: C.

Man: Put them on these envelopes.

Narrator: Number 21.

Man: The sky is very cloudy.

Narrator: A.

Woman: The room isn't very crowded.

Narrator: B.

Woman: It will probably rain soon.

Narrator: C.

Woman: He's quite a shy person.

Narrator: Number 22.

Woman: Could you lend me some money for the bus?

Narrator: A.

Man: There are many bus routes in the city.

Narrator: B.

Man: The bus stops on the corner.

Narrator: C.

Man: Of course. Here are two dollars.

Narrator: Number 23.

Man: Do you know who that man is?

Narrator: A.

Woman: Yes. Two is the right number.

Narrator: B.

Woman: Yes. It belongs to me.

Narrator: C.

Woman: Yes. That's Mr. Green.

Narrator: Number 24.

Woman: Is the party on Friday or Saturday?

Narrator: A.

Man: It's Friday at two o'clock.

Narrator: B.

Man: Yes, I like parties.

Narrator: C.

Man: No, it isn't.

Narrator: Number 25.

Man: When will the conference take place?

Narrator: A.

Woman: Sometime next winter.

Narrator: B.

Woman: At a hotel in New York.

Narrator: C.

Woman: I can give you a reference.

Narrator: Number 26.

Woman: Have you seen John this morning?

Narrator: A.

Man: No, I don't have any.

Narrator: B.

Man: Yes, he's in his office.

Narrator: C.

Man: It happens in the morning.

Narrator: Number 27.

Man: How are you feeling today?

Narrator: A.

Woman: The filing cabinet is over there.

Narrator: B.

Woman: They've stopped stealing things.

Narrator: C.

Woman: I'm much better, thank you.

Narrator: Number 28.

Woman: Why is this room so cold?

Narrator: A.

Man: There's plenty of room inside.

Narrator: B.

Man: The heating system is broken.

Narrator: C.

Man: All of them have been sold.

Narrator: Number 29.

Man: What time will the meeting be over?

Narrator: A.

Woman: Before five o'clock.

Narrator: B.

Woman: In the conference room.

Narrator: C.

Woman: There are several items on the agenda.

Narrator: Number 30.

Woman: Mr. Smith is your boss, isn't he?

Narrator: A.

Man: It's hard to be a good boss.

Narrator: B.

Man: No, I never take the bus.

Narrator: C.

Man: Yes, I've worked for him for several years.

Narrator: Number 31.

Man: I have a terrible headache.

Narrator: A.

Woman: I'm terrible at baking, too.

Narrator: B.

Woman: It's probably repairable.

Narrator: C.

Woman: Lie down and take a rest.

Narrator: Number 32.

Woman: Who's going to give the workshop?

Narrator: A.

Man: John and I are.

Narrator: B.

Man: It's hers.

Narrator: C.

Man: He gave it to me.

Narrator: Number 33.

Man: What did you do last weekend?

Narrator: A.

Woman: My cold has weakened a bit.

Narrator: B.

Woman: I just relaxed at home.

Narrator: C.

Woman: It lasted most of the weekend.

Narrator: Number 34.

Woman: How will you get to the airport?

Narrator: A.

Man: I plan to take a taxi.

Narrator: B.

Man: It only takes 15 minutes.

Narrator: C.

Man: I got my ticket there.

Narrator: Number 35.

Man: Will you be in your office after lunch?

Narrator: A.

Woman: I usually just have a sandwich.

Narrator: B.

Woman: I'll be happy to join you for lunch.

Narrator: C.

Woman: Yes. I'll be there all afternoon.

Narrator: Number 36.

Woman: Why doesn't Ms. Evans answer her phone?

Narrator: A.

Man: She's out of the office today.

Narrator: B.

Man: There's a phone call for Ms. Evans.

Narrator: C.

Man: You can look in the phone directory.

Narrator: Number 37.

Man: What did you buy at the mall?

Narrator: A.

Woman: I love shopping.

Narrator: B.

Woman: Some new shoes to wear to work.

Narrator: C.

Woman: The mall is right by the subway station.

Narrator: Number 38.

Woman: How much did your train ticket cost?

Narrator: A.

Man: I bought it on the Internet.

Narrator: B.

Man: Fifty dollars round-trip.

Narrator: C.

Man: The travel agent made my reservation.

Narrator: Number 39.

Man: When will you meet with the client?

Narrator: A.

Woman: Tomorrow afternoon.

Narrator: B.

Woman: He's really quite defiant.

Narrator: C.

Woman: At his office downtown.

Narrator: Number 40.

Woman: How many guests were at the dinner?

Narrator: A.

Man: I wore my new suit.

Narrator: B.

Man: They're looking much thinner.

Narrator: C.

Man: About ten or twelve.

Narrator: This is the end of Part 2.

Narrator: Listening Test

Part 3: Conversations

Directions. Listen to a conversation between two speakers. Then choose the correct answers to the three questions about that conversation. Fill in the letter (A), (B), (C), or (D). You will hear each conversation only once.

Part 3: Questions 41 to 70.

Questions 41 through 43 refer to the following conversation.

Man: I have a dentist appointment this afternoon. I was planning to walk there, but now it looks like it might rain.

Woman: Is it downtown? Because I'm going to pick up a few things at the mall and I could give you a ride in my car.

Man: Actually, it's in the opposite direction. I'll just take a bus. There's one that goes directly there.

Woman: OK. Maybe I'll see you later this evening, then, at the party.

Narrator: Number 41. Where is the man going?

Narrator: Number 42. When is he going there?

Narrator: Number 43. How will he get there?

Narrator: Questions 44 through 46 refer to the following conversation.

Woman: The coffee machine seems to be out of order. I can't get it to work. I tried making a fresh pot for lunch, but nothing came out.

Man: I know. It hasn't been working all day. I went to the cafeteria across the street at noon and bought coffee there.

Woman: Well, it doesn't look like we can fix this thing. We're going to have to get a new one.

Man: You're right. But we'll have to wait till next Sunday. I'm going to the mall then and can pick one up when I'm there.

Narrator: Number 44. What problem are they discussing?

Narrator: Number 45. What will the man do?

Narrator: Number 46. When will he do it?

Narrator: Questions 47 through 49 refer to the following conversation.

Man: Would you like to order anything else, ma'am?

Woman: No, thank you. Each dish was so delicious, and I send my compliments to the chef, but I couldn't eat another bite. Just bring the check, please.

Man: I have it right here. Your total comes to sixty-five dollars.

Woman: Oh dear, it looks like I left my credit card at home. Just let me check if I have enough cash. Yes, I do. Here you are.

Narrator: Number 47. Who is the man?

Narrator: Number 48. How much does the woman owe?

Narrator: Number 49. How will she pay?

Narrator: Questions 50 through 52 refer to the following conversation.

Woman: Look how late it is. The meeting starts at eleven, and it's already ten forty-five. We'd better make sure everything's ready.

Man: Relax. I got the meeting room all set up. But I was wondering, do you think we have enough chairs? There are twelve in there now.

Woman: That's not enough. The director invited a few clients to attend, so we should have fifteen. Can you get some extra ones?

Man: Of course. I'll have my assistant bring them in right away.

Narrator: Number 50. What time will the meeting start?

Narrator: Number 51. How many chairs will they need?

Narrator: Number 52. Who will bring the extra chairs?

Narrator: Questions 53 through 55 refer to the following conversation.

Man: I'm very sorry to hear that you're unhappy with your room. Is your bed not comfortable?

Woman: No, the bed's fine. It's the view. My room looks right out over the pool, and it's very noisy there, even late at night. Could you move me to another room for tonight?

Man: I'm terribly sorry, but there's nothing I can do about that. All our rooms are occupied. I could give you a discount, though. We do want all our guests to feel happy at our hotel.

Woman: All right. I'll take the discount. I'm leaving tomorrow morning, anyhow.

Narrator: Number 53. What is the problem with the hotel room?

Narrator: Number 54. What will the man do about the problem?

Narrator: Number 55. When will the woman leave the hotel?

Narrator: Questions 56 through 58 refer to the following conversation.

Man: I know I'm late. Again. And I missed the 9:30 staff meeting.

Woman: You did. And your boss noticed, but I told him you were stuck in traffic.

Man: Thanks. You're a real friend. I tried to get up on time, but my clock stopped again. I thought it was six o'clock, but it was really past seven.

Woman: I see. Well, it's almost eleven now, and your assistant has informed me that you have a client waiting for you in your office. He says he has an appointment.

Narrator: Number 56. Why was the man late?

Narrator: Number 57. What time is it now?

Narrator: Number 58. Who wants to see the man now?

Narrator: Questions 59 through 61 refer to the following conversation.

Woman: You're planning to take your vacation next week, right?

Man: I was, but it didn't work out. All the hotels are full then, so I've had to postpone it until later.

Woman: It's really hard to find a place at the beach this time of year, isn't it? It's such a busy time. And it costs more, too.

Man: True, but I'm actually planning to spend my vacation in the mountains. I was finally able to make a reservation for a week in September in a really nice little mountain town.

Narrator: Number 59. Why did the man change the time for his vacation?

Narrator: Number 60. Where will he take his vacation?

Narrator: Number 61. When will he take his vacation?

Narrator: Questions 62 through 64 refer to the following conversation.

Man: I'm so disappointed. I had plans to play tennis with a friend last weekend, but I had to cancel. I had to finish up some work on a project for a client.

Woman: I'm sorry you missed your game. Do you usually play tennis at the club or at the park?

Man: Actually, I found a great deal at a local hotel. You can get a membership that gives you access to the tennis court and swimming pool.

Woman: That sounds nice. Maybe we could play a game there someday. What do you think? I'm free next Saturday.

Narrator: Number 62. What did the man do last weekend?

Narrator: Number 63. Where does the man play tennis?

Narrator: Number 64. When does the woman want to play tennis?

Narrator: Questions 65 through 67 refer to the following conversation.

Man: Is it too late to get tickets for tonight's eight o'clock performance? I don't have reservations, but I really want to see this play.

Woman: You're in luck. We still have seats available. Did you just want one ticket?

Man: I actually wanted three. Is that possible? And I'd rather not sit too close to the front. I'd prefer a center or back row if that's not a problem.

Woman: Not at all. I'll give you three seats in Row 31. That's in the rear, a few seats in.

Narrator: Number 65. Where does this conversation take place?

Narrator: Number 66. How many tickets does the man want?

Narrator: Number 67. Where will the man sit?

Narrator: Questions 68 through 70 refer to the following conversation.

Woman: I'm thinking about renting a new apartment, and I'm going to look at one this afternoon. The landlord gave me the key. Do you want to come along?

Man: What's wrong with the place you live in now? It's so big, and the rent's not high at all.

Woman: It's just not very close to work. I need something closer. I'm planning on going over there around two thirty. You can come with me if you like.

Man: Thanks. I'll come by your office after lunch, and we can drive there in my car.

Narrator: Number 68. What will the woman do this afternoon?

Narrator: Number 69. What time will she do it?

Narrator: Number 70. What does she say about her current apartment?

Narrator: This is the end of Part 3.

Narrator: Listening Test

Part 4: Talks

Directions. Listen to a talk. Then choose the correct answers to the three questions about that talk. Fill in the letter (A), (B), (C), or (D). You will hear each talk only once.

Part 4: Questions 71 to 100.

Questions 71 through 73 refer to the following announcement.

Man: Attention. Flight 92 to Miami will begin boarding in five minutes. All passengers, please approach the waiting area at Gate 16 to be ready for boarding. Please have your ticket ready to show to the gate agent. We will board according to row number, so check the seat and row number on your ticket. As a reminder, passengers are allowed one small carry-on bag each. If you have extra bags, please check them with the gate agent at this time. We will begin boarding with passengers traveling with infants and young children and any others who need special assistance. We will follow this by boarding passengers sitting in the first-class rows.

Narrator: Number 71. What gate will the flight leave from?

Narrator: Number 72. What are passengers asked to do now?

Narrator: Number 73. Who will get on the plane first?

Narrator: Questions 74 through 76 refer to the following message.

Woman: Thank you for calling the City Transportation Office. We're here to serve you. Remember, as of September first, bus and subway fares will increase fifteen percent. For recorded information on bus routes and schedules, press "1." For recorded information on subway routes and schedules, press "2." For recorded information on regular, weekend, and student fares and to find out how to obtain a monthly transit pass, press "3." To hear recorded information about delays and schedule changes due to weather, press "4." For all other information, please stay on the line and an operator will assist you with your questions.

Narrator: Number 74. When will fares go up?

Narrator: Number 75. What happens if you press "one"?

Narrator: Number 76. How can you speak directly with a person?

Narrator: Questions 77 through 79 refer to the following announcement.

Man: The City Museum of Art announces the third annual Young Musicians Concert. Come hear top students from the National School of Music perform pieces by several popular classical composers. This is an outdoor event scheduled to take place on Sunday, April 7 at eight p.m. in the beautiful surroundings of the museum's garden. Following the performance, enjoy sandwiches, pastries, and drinks provided by the famous Chef Pierre Café. Attendance is free, but seats must be reserved in advance. Call the Museum Events Office for more information.

Narrator: Number 77. What event is this announcement about?

Narrator: Number 78. What time does the event begin?

Narrator: Number 79. What will happen after the event?

Narrator: Questions 80 through 82 refer to the following advertisement.

Woman: Dining out should be a special experience. That's why we at the Spring Valley Inn treat all our customers as very important people. At Spring Valley, you enjoy meals prepared by some of the area's top chefs in an elegant and relaxing setting. In addition to our regular menu and daily specials, we also have a special children's menu, so families are welcome at Spring Valley! Are you planning a wedding, party, or other event? Call us to find out about our catering service. Join us on the first Wednesday of every month for a special lunch buffet. Show your business card for a discount. The Spring Valley Inn is open for lunch and dinner Tuesday through Saturday, and for breakfast and lunch on Sunday. Closed Monday.

Narrator: Number 80. What is this advertisement for?

Narrator: Number 81. When is a reduced price available?

Narrator: Number 82. What happens on Sunday?

Narrator: Questions 83 through 85 refer to the following weather report.

Man: Welcome to the early morning weather report. And what a beautiful morning it is! We continue to enjoy the same cloudless blue skies and warm temperatures that we have had all week. These great conditions will continue for the rest of the morning and afternoon, with high temperatures around 55 degrees. Clouds will roll in and winds will start to pick up late in the evening, and temperatures will drop to a low of around 35 overnight. Chilly temperatures and gray skies will continue throughout tomorrow and Sunday and possibly into next week. So enjoy this nice weather while it lasts.

Narrator: Number 83. What's the weather like now?

Narrator: Number 84. How high will the temperature get today?

Narrator: Number 85. When will the weather change?

Narrator: Questions 86 through 88 refer to the following announcement.

Woman: Good morning and welcome to Sunshine City Tours. We're certainly enjoying some fine weather today. Our tour will begin in about ten minutes. The bus will take us first for a ride through City Park, where we'll drive past several monuments of interest. Following that, we'll stop at the City Zoo for about an hour. We'll eat lunch at the Zoo Café and then get back on the bus for a ride to the City Museum of History. We'll end our tour with a drive through some of the city's historic neighborhoods. We'll stop in several places so you can take photos. I'd like to ask you to remain seated while the bus is moving, as it is against city regulations to have standing passengers. Please let me know if you have any questions.

Narrator: Number 86. When will the tour begin?

Narrator: Number 87. What will happen after lunch?

Narrator: Number 88. What is NOT allowed on the bus?

Narrator: Questions 89 through 91 refer to the following introduction.

Man: I am pleased to introduce our speaker for tonight, Ms. Julie Whitaker, president of the local chapter of the Business Owners Association. Ms. Whitaker is a longtime member of the association and the owner of Whitaker's Accounting Services. She will speak to us tonight about ways to finance a new business. Following her talk, we will enjoy some light refreshments, and then John Jones will give a slide show presentation about his trip to the business conference last month. I'd also like to take this opportunity to remind you that next month's meeting will not take place here, but at the Breyerwood Hotel, and will begin at seven thirty instead of the usual eight o'clock. And now, without further ado, here is Julie Whitaker.

Narrator: Number 89. What will Ms. Whitaker talk about?

Narrator: Number 90. What will happen immediately after Ms. Whitaker's talk?

Narrator: Number 91. What time will next month's meeting begin?

Narrator: Questions 92 through 94 refer to the following report.

Woman: Several downtown streets are closed today in preparation for the Independence Day parade, which will take place between noon and two p.m. this afternoon. The weather looks great, so we expect a large turnout for the day's events. People planning to view the parade are advised to travel to the area by bus or subway, as downtown streets are expected to be jammed and parking will be limited. Viewing stands have been constructed along the parade route, so arrive early to ensure getting a good seat. An outdoor festival follows the parade, and there will be fireworks in the evening. Streets will remain closed until tomorrow morning.

Narrator: Number 92. Why are streets closed today?

Narrator: Number 93. What does the speaker suggest that listeners do?

Narrator: Number 94. When will streets reopen?

Narrator: Questions 95 through 97 refer to the following voicemail message.

Man: Hello. I'm calling from the office of Dr. Jones to make sure that you still have on your calendar your appointment for next Monday at four forty-five, for your regular dental checkup and cleaning. If you need to change the time or cancel for any reason, please let us know before the end of the day on Friday. Otherwise, we'll expect to see you next week. Call if you have any questions or concerns. Thank you.

Narrator: Number 95. What is the purpose of the call?

Narrator: Number 96. Who is the appointment with?

Narrator: Number 97. When is the appointment?

Narrator: Questions 98 through 100 refer to the following message.

Woman: Thank you for calling the Natural History Museum. We're open Monday through Friday from nine a.m. until five p.m., and Saturday and Sunday from eleven a.m. until seven p.m. In addition to our permanent exhibits, next Monday, June 11, a temporary show on gemstones will open. That exhibit will be on display until the end of August. Visit us every afternoon at two p.m. for a show about the stars in our planetarium. Special classes for adults and children start next month. Press "1" to request a brochure. To find out more about our programs and exhibits, please stay on the line and someone will be with you shortly.

Narrator: Number 98. When is the museum open?

Narrator: Number 99. What will happen next week?

Narrator: Number 100. How can you get more information about the museum?

Narrator: This is the end of the Listening Test. Turn to Part 5.

Test Score Conversion Chart

This score conversion chart will help you *estimate* your TOEIC test score. Your total score will be *approximate*. It may be higher or lower than the actual TOEIC test score. (If you take the TOEIC test on Monday and then take the TOEIC test again on Tuesday, your score will be different.)

Put the number of your correct answers in the spaces below. Then find the corresponding score on the chart below. Add your Listening and Reading scores. The total will be your *approximate* TOEIC test score.

_____   =   _____

Listening correct answers   Listening score

_____   =   _____

Reading correct answers   Reading score

                                          +

Approximate TOEIC Test Score   _____

#	LC	RC	#	LC	RC	#	LC	RC	#	LC	RC
1	5	5	26	105	60	51	250	215	76	405	365
2	5	5	27	110	65	52	255	225	77	410	370
3	5	5	28	115	75	53	260	230	78	415	380
4	5	5	29	120	85	54	265	235	79	420	385
5	5	5	30	125	90	55	270	240	80	430	390
6	5	5	31	130	95	56	280	245	81	435	395
7	10	5	32	135	100	57	285	255	82	440	400
8	15	5	33	140	105	58	295	260	83	445	405
9	20	5	34	145	115	59	300	265	84	450	410
10	25	10	35	150	125	60	310	270	85	460	415
11	30	10	36	155	130	61	315	275	86	465	420
12	35	15	37	165	135	62	320	285	87	470	425
13	40	15	38	170	140	63	325	290	88	475	430
14	45	20	39	175	145	64	330	295	89	480	435
15	50	20	40	180	150	65	340	300	90	485	445
16	55	25	41	185	155	66	345	305	91	490	450
17	60	25	42	190	160	67	350	310	92	490	460
18	65	30	43	195	170	68	360	320	93	495	470
19	70	30	44	200	175	69	365	325	94	495	480
20	75	30	45	210	180	70	370	335	95	495	485
21	80	35	46	215	190	71	375	340	96	495	490
22	85	35	47	220	195	72	380	345	97	495	495
23	90	40	48	230	200	73	390	350	98	495	495
24	95	45	49	235	205	74	395	355	99	495	495
25	100	50	50	240	210	75	400	360	100	495	495